D1314672

Why My

A Daughter Confronts
Her Family's Past
at the Trial
of Klaus Barbie

SUMMIT BOOKS

Father Died

ANNETTE KAHN

Translated by Anna Cancogni

New York   London   Toronto   Sydney   Tokyo   Singapore

Summit Books
Simon & Schuster Building
Rockefeller Center
1230 Avenue of the Americas
New York, New York 10020

Designed by Caroline Cunningham
Manufactured in the United States of America

1 3 5 7 9 10 8 6 4 2

Library of Congress Cataloging in Publication Data

Kahn, Annette
Why my father died : a daughter confronts her family's
past at the trial of Klaus Barbie / Annette Kahn.
p.   cm.
1. Jews—France—Persecutions.   2. Holocaust, Jewish
(1939-1945)—France.   3. Barbie, Klaus, d1913—
Trials, litigation, etc.   4. War crime trials—France—
Lyon.   5. France—Ethnic relations.   I. Title.
DS135.F83K34 1991
944'.004924—dc20   91-10454
                                                                          CIP

ISBN 0-671-65883-2

CONTENTS

6 CONTENTS

To Emmanuel and Marianne, of course.
To Camille and Clara.
And all their children.

PREFACE

A misty Saturday evening in February 1983: the house is quiet, submerged in winter. My husband, daughter, and I are settled before the fire, where two or three logs are burning down, watching the late news. Suddenly, a startled-looking anchorman announces that Klaus Barbie, "the Butcher of Lyon," has been extradited from Bolivia. He will be tried in France.

I am stunned. Barbie's police escort is passing under a stone arch chiseled with the words "Military Prison"—Fort Montluc, where both my father and my mother were held. My father's murderer, my mother's torturer, will expiate his crimes where he committed them. I can't imagine what kind of political intrigue has brought about Barbie's sudden return; though subconsciously I know that, as a journalist covering the courts for Le Point, I will be reporting on his trial.

As the police van carrying an invisible Barbie passes through the prison gates, I find myself recalling the little I know about my father's death.

August 1944. A few weeks before the liberation of Lyon, the Germans are fleeing. Thousands of French families await the release of friends and relatives—of whom they've had no news for many months—from French and German prisons.

At Fort Montluc in Lyon, prisoners are assembled in the courtyard for a roll call. An SS officer barks fifty names. Fifty men step out of the lines, all Jews. One is Robert Kahn, my father, soon to be thirty-six.

The fifty men are crammed into three trucks and driven to Bron airfield, which has been bombed by the Allies. Since the Allies have just landed on the Côte d'Azur and are advancing quickly through the Rhône Valley, the SS want the airport ready for their escape.

At gunpoint, and under a scorching sun, the fifty men claw and scrape the rocky ground, digging out unexploded bombs with their bare hands. Their fingers are bloodied, their nails ripped; they are exhausted, starving, and dying of thirst. But they know that any day they will be free.

That evening they are gathered along the edge of the craters left by the bombings and are shot. Their bodies fill the shell holes. There are no survivors. On the next day other Jews will join them. After the Liberation, a total of 109 corpses will be pulled out of those pits: adolescents, old people, women. Some are hard to identify, a few will forever remain anonymous.

A small sealed envelope, bearing the number 106 and containing a strip of cloth cut from a jacket and two handkerchiefs, each with an embroidered initial in the corner, will tell us that Robert Kahn, a Jew known as "Renaud" in the Resistance, was among the last victims of Klaus Barbie.

Robert Kahn was in charge of the "Liberation" Resistance network, and then of the Loire section of the Mouvements Unis de Résistance (MUR). His main mission was to recruit opponents of the collaborationist Vichy government's compulsory work service, a civilian draft which sent all French males between eighteen and fifty to slave labor in Germany.

I barely knew my father. The last time I saw him, I was two and a half, too young to remember him. But I do remember that as a child I often hoped that there had been a mistake, that the scraps we had been given as relics were not his, that one night the doorbell would ring and he would suddenly step into the apartment, and that we, his children, who had no real memory of him, would instantly recognize him.

His death always seemed unreal to my brother (just one year my senior) and to me. We never spoke about it, not even when we got older, as if it were a sacred mystery. As I came to understand much later, we each wanted to keep an individual image of our beloved unknown father all to ourselves.

Tonight, frozen to my seat before the late news, I realize for the first time in my life that my father really did die on August 17, 1944. It is as if I have finally grown up, as if I have just buried my father after having missed him for such a long time.

1   Palais de Justice

May 1987

With its wide, graceless steps, stout columns, and sturdy neo-classical air, the Palais de Justice never changes, its stones only grow darker. At its foot, the Saône flows nervously on. Behind it is clustered old Lyon: a maze of cobblestoned streets so narrow that with arms outstretched one can almost reach the tall old houses on both sides. Untouched by the sun, these streets are freezing cold in winter, cool in summer. Old Lyon has become very chic. Its buildings house trendy boutiques and cafés whose tables often spill all the way across the street. But during the war this part of the city was quite deserted and, for that reason, a favorite haunt of both resistants and Jews who sought shelter in its dark doorways and hidden courtyards. Lyon has remained essentially the same since the 1940s; the past has not scarred it physically the way it has scarred it intangibly, in the collective memory of the Lyonnais.

Even the plane trees in front of the Palais de Justice have not changed, but they have grown taller, thicker, more majestic. Their foliage still gives off the same bittersweet scent after a rain. But today people hold their heads high as they stroll, colorfully dressed, along the streets and banks of the river, where a new bow bridge has been built. Forty-four years ago, during Barbie's reign, people did not stroll in Lyon. Then, everyone was afraid in this capital of the Resistance: afraid of others and of themselves, of the Gestapo raids and of Barbie most of all.

Now Barbie no longer frightens anybody, except, of course, the people responsible for keeping him alive, who live in fear of an attempted assassination.

A royal-blue police van delivers Barbie to his trial, its arrival announced by sirens as a motorcade sweeps through the streets of the city. The flashing lights of the police cars are already visible on the other side of the river. The motorcade turns onto the bridge without slowing down, glides by the Palais de Justice, and disappears into a side gate which immediately closes with a loud screech. No one in the crowd has seen the old man yet. I myself have only seen his thin smile and deep-set eyes in a newspaper photo. But soon we will be face to face.

His trial, which has not yet begun, has already cost a fortune: one million francs just to turn the main hall of the Palais de Justice into a temporary courtroom. French law requires that Barbie be tried in the city where the crimes with which he has been charged were committed, and the Lyon courthouse has no other room that can accommodate eight hundred people: journalists from all over the world, lawyers, magistrates, interpreters, representatives from Germany and Israel, plaintiffs and their families, guests, and, of course, the defendant (whose stand, despite objections from the president of the court, will be surrounded by a bulletproof glass screen), and his bodyguards.

Then there are the people of Lyon, who have been waiting behind the police barriers since dawn. Many of them are young: whole classes of high school students accompanied by their teachers, university students eager to fill the gaps in their history books.

French Jews have received little compensation for the suffering they endured in World War II. After the Nazi defeat and the liberation of the concentration camps by the Allies, France turned its entire attention to only one group of victims—those of the Resistance. To chant the praises of the shadow army that had fought for freedom was the easiest way for most French citizens to atone for a record tarnished by fear, cowardice, and collaboration. In the postwar years, the Resistance had far more acolytes and sympathizers than in the thick of battle. But whatever the case, in 1945 France was too busy dressing the wounds of its national ego to worry about the wounds of the Jews.

Military tribunals held one trial after another of French citizens accused of treason. Of the 150,000 people found guilty, 7,000 were sentenced to death and 800 were actually executed: collaborators, spies, and traitors, including an informer named Augier, the man responsible for my mother's deportation. Of the fourteen people he had denounced, only two had survived him. The collaborators tried in court were lucky; there were also many executions without trial, in woods and on street corners.

In such a climate of retribution, the return of Jewish survivors was something of an embarrassment. It was also a practical problem for a country under both moral and economic strain. Though some survivors had families to return to, the vast majority were alone and dispossessed. People knew what they had gone through; a look at those living skeletons was enough to tell their story. But their suffering made their more fortunate countrymen feel guilty. The less they knew, the better they could sleep. After all, it was not their fault that some people were born Jews.

The Klaus Barbie trial is highly symbolic. It will allow the living, the survivors who have never spoken of their experiences before because no one wanted to listen, to speak for the dead, all the dead, including my father. It is supposed to make up for France's earlier indifference.

Barbie has already been tried—in absentia, in 1952 and 1954—for war crimes and convicted of "premeditated, voluntary homicides perpetrated upon numerous French citizens in the regions of Lyon and Grenoble between 1942 and 1944." Then he was given the death penalty. However, under French law no sentence can be executed more than twenty years after it has been pronounced; besides, France abolished the death penalty in 1981.

Barbie is now going to be tried for crimes against humanity, his contribution to Adolf Hitler's "final solution." Though no one can be tried for war crimes more than ten years after they were committed, there is no time limit on the prosecution of crimes against humanity.

War crimes, crimes against humanity—what is the difference? The Charter of the International Military Tribunal, drafted on August 8, 1945, defines them as follows:

> WAR CRIMES: namely, violations of the laws and customs of war. Such violations shall include, but not be limited to, murder, ill-treatment or deportation to slave labor camps or for any other purpose of the civilian population of or in occupied territory, murder or ill-treatment of prisoners of war or persons on the seas, killing of hostages, plunder of public or private property, wanton destruction of cities, towns or villages, or devastation not justified by military necessity.
>
> CRIMES AGAINST HUMANITY: namely, murder, extermination, enslavement, deportation, and other inhumane acts committed against any civilian population, before or during the war; or persecutions on political, racial, or religious grounds in execution of or in connection with any crime within the jurisdiction of the Tribunal, whether or not in violation of the domestic law of the country where perpetrated.

The examining judge during the *instruction*, Christian Riss, presented Barbie with the bill of charges against him in 1983, soon after Barbie was back on French soil. It listed eight specific charges: the raid on the UGIF (Union Générale des Israélites de France) headquarters on February 9, 1943; the raid on the children's home in Izieu, on April 6, 1944; the murder of Commissioner Jules Cros; the massacre of twenty-two hostages in retaliation for an attack against German officers; the arrest, torture, and deportation of numerous resistants; the execution of 109 prisoners at the Bron airfield on August 17 and 18, 1944; the raid on a railway workshop in Oullins; and, finally, the deportation of at least 720 people on the last rail convoy from Lyon, on August 11, 1944.

But Riss—who at thirty-six was born two years after Liberation—was determined to try Barbie for crimes against humanity, and to avoid complicating the issue, eliminated all charges that might fall under the legal definition of war crimes. Thus the Bron massacres, already mistakenly defined as a war crime, could not be tried again. In the end, Riss was left with only three major charges: the two raids, and the last deportation of Jews from Lyon.

Several associations of former resistants immediately challenged Riss's decision. This set off an extremely subtle legal debate between Lyon and Paris which would drag on for four years—four years of procedure during which some people hoped that Barbie would do himself in and save everyone the trouble of an unpleasant trial. At last the Supreme Court redefined the concept of "crimes against humanity" by broadening its application. In 1985, the court decreed that the term "crimes against humanity" could also apply to "certain crimes committed against resistants in the name of a nation that practices a policy of ideological hegemony."

New charges against Barbie began to pour in from both his Jewish and non-Jewish victims. Barbie is now held responsible for all the deportees of August 11, 1944; that is to say, for at least 720 people of varying convictions. While most were Jews, there were also many resistants and other political prisoners, whether communists or STO dodgers, whose religion wasn't an issue. There were also people who had been arrested during a raid simply because they had no papers on them, and those like my mother, guilty only of having married a Jew.

May 1945

I don't know the date, but it doesn't matter; it's a holiday, a feast day. Pruillé, the idyllic village where my brother and I have clan-destinely spent nearly two years, a sweet picture-postcard town bordered on one side by the Mayenne (a river whose banks are hemmed with gorse and draped with delightful little beaches) and on the other by fields and woods, is all decked out for the occasion.

It's the Armistice, celebrating the end of six years of war and the recovered pride of a country humiliated by the Occupation. I am a little more than four years old; Paul-Emile (nicknamed Poumi) is five and a half. We arrived here in September 1943, after our father's arrest in Saint-Etienne. From prison, he had managed to put us in a safe place, with the help of Resistance connections and some loyal friends—comrades we have never been able to thank, because we have never known who they were.

On this particular warm spring evening, a light breeze bears the smells of freshly cut grass and of stables, along with a white mist from the river. The sounds of frogs, crickets, and an occasional hoot owl form a rural concert, soon drowned out by an accordion. On the village square, the fountain cools a heap of *fillettes*, bottles of local light wine miraculously exhumed from caves where they survived the thirst of the Germans. When the dancing starts, people swirl in wild farandoles, girls and boys, grandfathers and grandsons, farmhands and farmowners' wives. What little social stratification existed in Pruillé is gone; now there are only victors.

Paper lanterns and colored streamers—excavated from who knows what attic where they awaited better days—form a Bastille Day sky over our heads. People embrace and slap each other on the back. Everyone loves everyone else tonight. And we, the children, usually long asleep by the time night comes, are as foolish as the adults, though made a little anxious by all this happiness. Born in wartime and accustomed to all its restrictions, we have never known such festivity—feasts, farandoles, music, dancing—or even such bursts of laughter. Aunt Madeleine and Uncle Valentin, Pruillé's solemn primary school teachers, seem to me to have lost their minds. This couple who for two years watched over Poumi and me with the austere and discreet tenderness of country people, this couple so foreign to whim and extroversion, waltz clumsily in a schoolyard that has become the public dance hall.

Then some women lead me into a house near that little school which has been my entire universe for as long as I can remember.

My brother is also there. They undress us in a whirlwind of laughter and fabric and slip a magnificent dress on me—me, who doesn't know anything by way of finery other than the ordinary uniform of Pruillé children, a schoolgirl's jumper during the week and a gingham apron and hair ribbon on Sundays. Tonight I will wear a long striped skirt with a laced black velvet corselet, and my hair is put up in an enormous black satin bow. I hear the women say that I am an Alsatian. It's a little upsetting to be someone else all of a sudden, but the costume seems to me worth such a sacrifice. Rigid with importance, I don't dare move. Out of the side of my eye I can see Poumi, hanging his head like a beaten dog, wearing overalls with a round collar and a big red belt. He is from the Auvergne, the women tell him; and along with another little girl, dressed in white, carrying a big round bouquet of cornflowers, daisies, and poppies, we symbolize France. In a few minutes we will lead the parade.

Hand in hand we travel up and down the village, while all the locals, including inhabitants of the surrounding hamlets, sing and dance behind us. The other children scatter in all directions and send clouds of confetti fluttering over us. But I suddenly want to cry. I clutch my brother's fingers with all my strength.

Ahead of me, borne at the end of a pole by two or three young people, is a strange grimacing fellow they call Hitler. He is a mannequin of straw and bran, crudely fashioned. But how am I to know that? For me, he is a human being; he jumps in step with his porters. His unfinished moonlike face makes him both more terrible and more real. His body is shapeless and chubby, crammed into a dust cover; his limbs are atrophied; on his feet he wears blond wooden clogs. People shout themselves hoarse: "We're going to burn Hitler!" "Hitler to the butcher!"

We are getting ready to throw this man into a bonfire, where he will burn as if in hell. And I know what hell is. Each Sunday Aunt Madeleine takes us to mass, where there is a skinny curate who chats with her in a low voice. He speaks of "their poor parents," and asks if there's any news, if anyone knows "what's become of them in the storm." He says we have been lucky to end up here,

and that we have gone through ordeals too great for children so
young. He also says that we must not hesitate to knock on the door
of the rectory, day or night, if there are problems, because he has
reliable friends.

He has taught us our prayers by rote, and gives us pictures when
we recite them without any mistakes. I have a collection of them.
He also gives eggs to Aunt Madeleine, and sometimes fruit, or
vegetables from his little garden, "for the little ones." He explained
hell to us. They grill you there like chestnuts over the coals, in
atrocious suffering, when you've done evil without repenting.

This man whom they call Hitler must then have committed
terrible crimes, but it doesn't seem to me reason enough to throw
him alive into the fire. (In retrospect, I think it was not his pain
which I feared but my own.)

We have arrived on the banks of the Mayenne, in a large alfalfa
field where I sometimes come to watch the goats with a little curly-
haired boy. I've asked him so many times if he thinks I'm
pretty. . . . The field is favored by lovers on Saturday nights, by
families on Sundays, and by Uncle Valentin, who goes there to
fish for shiners and pike—full of bones!—to improve our bland
diet.

The bonfire burns high and is reflected in the sluggish waters of
the Mayenne. There is a light mist over the river. The dry wood
snaps loudly, the twigs crack like old bones, the sparks make spinning stars in the velvet darkness. Our faces are crimson in the heat,
and with a great shout of joy Hitler is thrown into the flames, which
crackle even more prettily. The body seems to bend over itself,
then shrivels up and moves no more. Soon it is just ashes among
ashes, and seized by panic, I think I've participated in spite of
myself in some ceremony of atonement which I'll have to account
for all my life.

While the flames subside and boys and girls leapfrog over the
coals, I keep my eyes riveted on a wooden clog which got loose
from the mannequin before the sacrifice, fell into the grass, and
was forgotten. It is all that is left of the effigy of a man whom I

would soon learn had gassed, murdered, or burned alive thousands
of children my age.

Several days later, while the cherry trees in the orchards greeted
the first summer without bombings, Bonne-maman arrived in
Pruillé. This in itself was not a surprise. Ever since she had entrusted
us to her brother and sister-in-law, Uncle Valentin and Aunt Madeleine, my mother's mother had come to visit us each month. We
were all she had left of her daughter, of whom she had had no news
for too long. She had already prepared herself for the worst and
was ready to raise us. Today, I only have to look in a mirror to see
my mother's face; mine is a well-crafted copy. But in those days,
when Bonne-maman held me against her, her eyes misted with
tears, and she said, "How much you look like your mother," she
irritated me. I didn't like being compared to someone else, even
my mother, whom I'd already forgotten. And I didn't like it any
better when Bonne-maman in a slip of the tongue—as often happens to grandmothers, I know now from experience—called me
Jeannette instead of Annette.

Bonne-maman's regular visits were tinged with sadness. But no
one was exactly buoyant in those days, and neither Poumi nor I
was disturbed by our grandmother's gravity. She was only in her
fifties, but she seemed to us to be a very old woman. But this time
we saw her disembark radiant from the little grocery truck that
brought her from Angers when it came to Pruillé on its weekly
rounds. She fell, laughing and crying, into the arms of Madeleine.
"Jeanne is alive, she's come back, I spoke to her on the telephone. . . . My God, it was yesterday and I'm still trembling. I'm
going to bring the children back to her."

We stood there, "not particularly moved," Bonne-maman often
recounted later on. But what could we understand of all this, of
war and the lives of adults?

Our universe was Pruillé and its little school, a haven of peace
and security. We didn't know anything else; our memories of an
earlier time had been erased like chalk marks under a wet sponge.

My mother's uncle and his spouse protected us using the simplest of ruses. Since they were teachers, we became their students, Poumi among our great-uncle's boys, me with our great-aunt's girls. This was an era when the word "co-education" was almost an obscenity. At school, as at church, boys sat on one side, girls on the other. These were also the days of single classrooms which held students from nursery school to graduation, the youngest in the front, the eldest in the back rows. (At two and a half, when I entered the school, I sat at the foot of the blackboard.) In the little crowd of students we went unnoticed. In case of a visit from the Gestapo, everything was planned: Poumi and I were duly registered in the school's ledgers as children of a local vintner; some beautiful forged family record books gave proof of our parentage.

Since we barely knew our real identity when we arrived in Pruillé—at least as far as I was concerned—it was hardly difficult for us to adopt a new one from our putative parents. We became unquestioningly Monique and Gérard Thomas. But when Uncle Valentin rang the bell signaling the end of the school day (a task he sometimes assigned to Poumi, who carried it out with a seriousness I have rarely seen in him since), we went not to the vintner's house for our rutabaga soup or vegetable stew, but to a little flat above the classrooms. Through the thin floorboards, dust and the smells of chalk, mildew, and unwashed children drifted up from below. After the war, we were no better nourished than most of our peers, but we knew how to read, write, and do arithmetic at an earlier age; the Occupation guaranteed us an excellent scholastic start.

It's not yet summer vacation, but Poumi and I are getting off early, because in two days we're taking a train to Paris. The prospect of a trip enchants both of us; it's the first time we've ever taken a train. What an adventure! Our little schoolmates are bursting with jealousy. Bonne-maman and Aunt Madeleine quickly assemble our few clothes; my grandmother's bag will be heavy with provisions for my mother. Aunt Madeleine, attentive and thoughtful, also prepares a small flat package: our school notebooks from these past two years. Nothing is missing, from our first clumsy stick drawings to our most recent dictations and multiplications. It seems a matter of professional pride for Aunt Madeleine, but it also seems to say, "You see, Jeanne, we did for them what we would have done for the children we ourselves never had: We prepared them for life."

Two days later, we leave Pruillé, Aunt Madeleine, Uncle Valentin, and the round-headed chestnut trees planted evenly around the schoolyard (which regularly served as examples for interval problems in the older children's classes). We leave in spirited excitement, and in complete indifference to those we are leaving behind.

In the coal-burning train, our fellow travelers—crushed by the heat; faces, necks, and hands already blackened with soot; uncomfortably seated on hard wooden benches—complain about having to get around in such bad conditions. We begin to feel uneasy. What future is ahead of us? Who is this forgotten mother, this stranger waiting for us in Paris? And why hasn't she been near us in the first place, like the mothers of all our friends? Beyond the train windows, pleasant countryside passes by: forests, gardens, red cows on green meadows, and trim little houses. We also pass another kind of scenery: bomb craters, ruins, torn-up fields, blackened woods, empty farmhouses.

Bonne-maman is nervous as well. In what state will she find her daughter?

While each turn of the wheels brings us closer to her, my mother frets on the station platform. She has put on a black suit and a white blouse bought by her mother-in-law the day before at Madame Catherine, a store which sells secondhand clothes "of good quality and good origin for people of good taste," as the sign on the door says. At the time, it's the only way to dress oneself at all properly. She has wrapped a turban around her hair (still a stubbly brush), which gives her a vaguely Turkish, very seductive air.

My mother fears this moment much more than we do. She is sure she won't be able to recognize us and is terrified at the idea that one of us—most likely me, since I'm the younger—or possibly both will recoil or be frightened at seeing her. My poor mother, still a girl at thirty-three, has too brief a history of love to comfort her and too long an experience of grief and pain.

All goes well. She spots us in the crowd filling the platform without a second's hesitation: me the little redhead, Poumi a portrait of her lost husband. He throws himself on her. I am more cautious. Then she takes me in her arms. And there, in the hollow of her neck, I recognize her familiar smell. As if it's only since yesterday that I've missed that scent, I search with my hand for the double-stranded pearl necklace she always wore, and am astonished to find her skin bare. (Some Nazi officer's wife was wearing it, no doubt, I realize now.) But this gesture, which suddenly brings a past of tranquil happiness flooding back, both pierces my mother's heart and gives her courage. We will form again, we three, a family in which my father will always have his place.

2 THIS IS NOT WAR

THE COURT

French criminal justice is quite different from its American counterpart. The *cours d'assises* are the only courts allowed to try murder and assassination cases, but there are as many *cours d'assises* as there are *départements* (geographic divisions like states or counties): that is to say, ninety-five in continental France and five overseas.

Trials take place in the *cour d'assises* of the region where the crimes were committed. The court consists of three magistrates (the president and his two assistant judges); a jury (the *cour d'assises* is the only French law court which employs a popular jury); and the public prosecutor. The three judges sit on a rostrum facing the audience, while the public prosecutor has a desk to the side. Both the president and the public prosecutor wear red gowns trimmed with ermine.

Right across from the judges' bench, facing each other, sit the two sets of lawyers: on one side the defense attorney or attorneys (one may be represented by as many as one wishes), and on the other those for the prosecution. At the Barbie trial, there were thirty-nine attorneys representing 149 plaintiffs (120 individuals and twenty-nine groups).

The president directs the proceedings. In French legalese, he is the "master of his audience." He sets the timetable, decides the order of appearance of witnesses, admonishes the attorneys, calls the courtroom to order, and in extreme cases even orders the court vacated. He also questions the defendant, screens the witnesses, and determines when the public prosecutor and the lawyers may take the floor to intervene. The jurors may also question the defendant and the witnesses by submitting their questions in writing to the president, who will decide whether to ask them or not.

The magistrates participate in the jury's deliberations. It is the president's duty to explain the sentences to the jurors. He has the right to request a particular sentence and to establish its terms, but the magistrates and the jurors are free to decide whether or not to comply. Lastly, it is the president who pronounces the verdict in the courtroom.

As the defender of the public interest, the public prosecutor can intervene whenever he pleases in the course of the proceedings. But the last word is always the defendant's. Before withdrawing to the jury room, the president addresses the defendant with a ritual formula: "Do you have anything to say in your defense?" which allows the defendant to take the floor for as long as he or she pleases—to speak of his childhood, his conjugal problems, his tastes, and the events that have led him to that courtroom.

Any French citizen who is registered to vote, can read and write French, has never been convicted of a crime, and is over twenty-three years of age can be a juror. The names of the final jurors are publicly drawn out of an urn containing thirty-five to forty-five names.

The president can draw six more names to serve as substitute jurors, who are required to follow the proceedings with utmost attention in case they have to replace one or more regular jurors. But not one of the jurors selected for the Barbie trial will miss a day of the proceedings.

The jurors are encouraged to take as many notes as possible in the course of the hearings. Moreover, they are free to read the newspapers, listen to the radio, and watch TV—since they are supposed to be above all influence. On the other hand, they are bound by oath never to speak of the proceedings or of what goes on in the jury room with any outsider. To do so is considered a crime.

The defendant does not have to prove his innocence, but the court must prove his guilt. He has the right to remain silent, to refuse to answer any question. He can reject evidence. If he is tired, he can ask to interrupt the session.

He can also refuse to appear in front of his judges, in which case he puts his defense entirely in the hands of his lawyer.

THE CHARGES

The first of the three main charges brought against Klaus Barbie is his leading role in a Gestapo raid on the Lyon headquarters of the Union Générale des Israélites de France on February 9, 1943. In that raid, eighty-four people were arrested; seventy-eight were deported, of whom only one survived.

The Gestapo did not choose the date randomly. February 9 was one of the days on which subsidies were distributed, along with medical care, baby clothes, coal, money.

The UGIF was not a clandestine organization but was created by order of the Vichy government as part of the Bureau of Jewish Affairs, whose main function was to keep track of the Jewish population, both native and immigrant. Behind this official facade, however, its various branches became real assistance centers for the Jewish population, providing lodgings, work, and various other kinds of help. Many Jews had abandoned their apartments for fear of being reported to the Gestapo by an unfriendly concierge or suspicious neighbors, and they passed from one relative to the next, sleeping in doorways, hiding in cellars. The UGIF also volunteered information on where to get false papers and how to sneak out of France. The Lyon UGIF, for instance, organized the transfer of

Jewish children to Switzerland. When that wasn't possible, it advised parents to hide their children and in case of arrest to tell the Gestapo the children had been taken to Switzerland, they didn't know exactly where. The SS, to avoid antagonizing a neutral country, generally let the matter drop.

In midmorning on February 9, a group of Gestapo agents, militiamen, and SS officers burst into the UGIF headquarters. Everyone inside was pushed into a back office. The secretary alone was left at her desk so that she could keep answering the phone as if nothing were happening. In fact, she was ordered to encourage people to come to the offices as soon as possible. By the end of the afternoon, eighty-six people had been captured and thrown in prison. Two days later, two managed to escape. Seventy-eight of the remaining prisoners suffered brutal reprisals and a few days later were shipped off to Drancy, and from there to Auschwitz.

A detailed account dated February 11, addressed to Helmut Knochen (the head of the SIPO-SD in Paris and signed by Barbie, states:

> At the moment of the operation there were some thirty Jews in the offices, including both employees and visitors. They were all immediately arrested. In the course of the day, several other Jews arrived, bringing the number of arrests to a total of eighty-six. They were all gathered in one office. Most of the Jews destroyed their false ID's before we could search them. Some were about to leave France to seek shelter in Switzerland. [The report concludes]: It has been ascertained that the committee is supported by French Jews with considerable financial means and, in particular, by a Jewish Committee in Geneva.

A brief telegram, also signed by Barbie, with the same date, specifies that "the eighty-six prisoners have been transferred into two rooms of Fort Lamothe, Fort Montluc being too overcrowded to accommodate them." A second telegram from Barbie, dated February 15, states that "only eighty-four Jews have left for Drancy, two having escaped on February 11, unbeknownst to the Gestapo which the

Wehrmacht, in charge of surveillance at Fort Lamothe, did not see fit to inform."

The second charge concerns the raid on a Jewish children's home in Izieu, on April 6, 1944. Forty-four children between four and seventeen years of age and seven adults—their teachers and supervisors—were deported. Only one came back: Lea Feldblum, one of the supervisors.

This colony of Jewish children, one of the few shelters available to them, existed thanks to an extraordinary Jewish couple, Sabina and Miron Zlatin.

Sabina was a nurse in the French Red Cross. A volunteer social worker, she became one of the most active members of the OSE, or Children's Aid Organization, which during the summer of 1941 opened a reception center for Jewish children rescued from the Vichy government's internment camps. Sabina paid twice-weekly visits to the camps at Agde and Rivesaltes, where Gypsy and Jewish families lived in indescribable conditions. Each time, she and her colleagues came back with a sleeping child hidden under their coats. The children rescued by the OSE were sent to Switzerland or, with the help of Quaker groups, to the United States. Very few would be reunited with their parents after the war.

Until 1942, the OSE had only one center, at Palavas in the Hérault department, which, as its address and activities were publicly known, was always very busy. But after the occupation of the free zone in November 1942, the OSE decided to reorganize. It closed Palavas and opened a number of smaller homes in remote villages, where it could carry on its work.

Sabina had an extensive network of friends and accomplices; they found her a big house with a garden which belonged to a religious congregation. The nuns used it only in the summer and were not planning to return for the summer of 1943. Given the political situation, they were glad to rent it out for little money and an indefinite length of time.

Thus, in March 1943, Sabina settled into the villa near Izieu. It was a rustic but charming place, with a courtyard, a well, and, facing south, a long terrace with a wrought-iron balustrade, where it was pleasant to sit on warm evenings, waiting for nightfall. The children liked to use the terrace as a stage for the shows they put on, costumed in clothes they found in the attic. They also liked to spend evenings there, looking for shooting stars and talking about their parents.

The children's new home had another considerable advantage. It was situated at the foot of the mountains near Lelinoz, a small village of three or four farms (dependent on Izieu, a larger town down the road); all it had to offer were fields, cows, and birds. It was not exactly the kind of place that drew visitors.

To supervise the children, whose number rapidly rose from twenty to thirty to forty, Sabina, the headmistress, and Miron, the treasurer, were helped by a devoted staff: Leon Reifman, a medical student who on occasion acted as nurse; his thirty-six-year-old sister, Sarah, a doctor and Sabina's assistant; a few other women who taught and organized recreation; a cook and a maid. The team varied, but all its members took part in one special ritual: a great display of tenderness at bedtime, when the children were most in need of reassurance before they let themselves slip into the unknown.

Officially, the children's home at Izieu was "a colony of refugee children from Hérault," just as other OSE homes were colonies of refugee children from Var or from Vaucluse. All the children who came to these centers knew their "Our Father" and their "Hail Mary" by heart. Also, they were instructed never to reveal their names to people they didn't know. The younger children were supposed to say they didn't know their names; the older ones were assigned aliases.

During the winter of 1943–44, the Lyon Gestapo began to crack down on the Resistance in the Ain region; villages were burnt, peasants murdered. One morning, a Jewish doctor who lived a stone's throw from the villa was arrested. Toward the end of March, an OSE social worker arrived at the home to recommend that the children be dispersed. Sabina and Miron hesitated, but on April 3, Sabina went to Montpellier, where she had numerous contacts among the priesthood, to try to find new lodgings for her "family."

April 6 was Holy Thursday, just one day after the beginning of the Easter holidays. It was a mild, sunny day. The trees were covered with buds, the air filled with the smells of lilac and fresh grass. Just before nine o'clock, two trucks arrived, followed by two cars. No one saw or heard them; no one was on the lookout.

Several Wehrmacht soldiers and three Gestapo officers in civilian clothes burst into the dining room, where everyone was gathered around bowls of hot chocolate and toast with jam. A pall of silence fell over the room which only a few seconds before was full of chatter.

It was common knowledge that the "greens," as Wehrmacht soldiers were called, did not like the work they were ordered to do for the Gestapo. To arrest a five-year-old girl with a red ribbon in her hair, to push a sobbing boy into a military truck, to pull a teddy bear out of the desperate clasp of an eight-year-old child who has nothing else to hold on to: This was not war.

That same evening, Barbie sent a telegram to Knochen, as he did after the UGIF raid a year earlier, describing the morning raid and stating that "the prisoners will be on their way to Drancy by April 7, 1944." This time the Gestapo acted with unusual haste. No other group of prisoners was obliterated quite as quickly. Perhaps Barbie was concerned that some of his superiors might find this particular operation a little obvious, gratuitous, even embarrassing.

Neither the French nor the Germans interfered with the children's departure on April 7. They arrived at Auschwitz on April 15 and, holding hands, walked down the ramp to their deaths.

The third charge involves the last convoy of deportees from Lyon, which left on August 11, 1944, on train number 14.166—nine third-class cars with wooden seats and curtains drawn. A tenth car carried luggage. The train was jam-packed; estimating eight passengers per compartment for the ten compartments in each of the nine passenger cars, the total was at least 720 people. Among them were more than eleven children; one was two years old.

Montluc, Saint-Paul, and Saint-Joseph, Lyon's three prisons, were constantly full during Barbie's tenure, each new arrival entailing a new deportee. During the summer of 1944, trains departed at least three times a week, carrying an average of a thousand people per convoy to Drancy, Compiègne, or, as in this case, directly to Germany.

On August 11, at five in the morning, just as the sky lightened behind the ramparts of Montluc and the watchtowers of Saint-Paul and Saint-Joseph, names and orders resonated throughout the courtyards of the three prisons. Hundreds of prisoners were called out of their cells "with luggage." The reluctant were prodded with kicks and shoves. Two by two, resistants on one side, Jews on the other, they were loaded onto covered trucks and driven to the Perrache station. The Jews were in the first trucks, since they would be going all the way to the end of the line.

There is no telegram, no report signed by Barbie, concerning this operation in any of the German archives. But there is eyewitness testimony to suggest that he attended the "ceremony" from beginning to end.

Strapped up tight in his impeccable uniform, with his boots shined and a scornful sneer curling his upper lip, he barked out orders. His men promptly executed them with the help of pokes and insults. Those who did not climb from the trucks quickly enough were sent hurtling onto the platform, their meager belongings spilling out of their cardboard suitcases.

If I close my eyes, I can see my mother, tall and slender, as she boarded the train, her head held high, her blue eyes staring straight ahead, for fear of betraying the fact that they were full of tears.

The journey was infernal, even though these deportees were lucky enough to be loaded onto a passenger train instead of cattle cars. It seems there are gradations of horror, and the deportees of August 11 had it easier than their predecessors.

After a number of false starts, the train departed in the early afternoon, bound for Drancy, but sabotage and bombings rerouted it directly on to Germany. It took twelve days to cough its way to Birkenau, the Auschwitz station. During the entire trip, the deportees survived almost exclusively on the few provisions they brought with them. A few died on the way; those who made it were starved, dehydrated, exhausted, and yet, paradoxically, happy to have survived. They were still crowded on the ramp when the SS pulled all the children and elderly out of the group, lined them up, and led them straight to the gas chambers.

Aside from these three major charges brought by the prosecution, the court must also examine fifty-nine individual charges brought by people tortured, imprisoned, and/or deported by Klaus Barbie. Some of the plaintiffs were victims themselves, others are parents, siblings, and, most often, children of those who did not survive.

Simone Kadosche was arrested on June 6, 1944, when she was only thirteen. She was tortured by Barbie under the horrified eyes of her parents, who had refused to reveal the hiding place of their two younger children. She was then deported to Auschwitz, where she survived both her mother and her father.

Marcel Stourdze, whose surgical collar is a constant reminder of the beatings he received from Barbie on August 16, 1943, was also deported to a concentration camp from which his wife and mother-in-law never returned.

Joseph Touitou was arrested with his family when he was fifteen, tortured in order to get him to reveal the names of his Jewish classmates, and then deported with his family. He is the only survivor.

Alfred and Sarah Eberhard and their daughter Odette, newly married to a non-Jew, were arrested at Caluire on November 6, 1943, and gassed at Auschwitz the day of their arrival, December 12.

Esther Amram's fate can be summed up in three resonant dates: arrested on July 2, 1944; deported on July 31; gassed on August 5.

Professor Marcel Gompel, a Jew, was a lecturer at the Collège de France and a member of the "Combat" network. He was arrested on January 30, 1944, brought to the Ecole de Santé, where he was plunged into a tub of ice water, then placed under a scalding shower. Dragged back to the Jewish barracks in Fort Montluc, he was left to die under the eyes of his cellmates, who were unable to relieve his atrocious pain.

To these and other charges lodged and accepted during the investigation of the case, the Supreme Court's decision to broaden the definition of "crimes against humanity" will add many more. Only the survivors, and not those who represent a third party, will be called to testify. The spokespeople for thousands of disappeared victims, for the immense cohort of pathetic shadows that weigh so heavily on the conscience and memory of the world, these survivors are invested with a sacred mission: never to allow their companions to be simply counted among the profits and losses of war.

3

Two Careers

Saint-Etienne

In 1935, my father and his older brother, Pierre Kahn, co-owners of a steel business in Paris (the Société Outinat), decide to purchase another firm, the Siderexpor of Saint-Etienne, on the Loire, some fifty miles from Lyon. For both private and professional reasons, Pierre cannot leave the capital; but my father, newlywed, is eager to embark on a new adventure.

My mother, Jeanne, then twenty-three (two years younger than Robert), is not exactly enthusiastic about the idea of leaving Paris and her friends and family to go bury herself in a small industrial town in the center of France. A talented painter herself, she thinks she needs the richer Parisian soil in order to flourish. And at the beginning of the 1930s Paris is such fun!

Yet Jeanne is above all a woman in love, and would follow her husband anywhere. Robert is not particularly tall, nor especially athletic; but he is slim and long-legged, with smooth, soft hands, light brown hair (already graying around the temples), and sparkling green eyes. In personality he is easygoing, imaginative, witty, and, behind his joking facade, serious and shy.

"If I were to choose among Gregory Peck, Clark Gable, Humphrey Bogart, Cary Grant, and Robert Kahn, I'd still pick your father. He was the best," my mother will tell me years later, when those great seducers are melting the hearts of women around the world.

Robert loves the mountains in winter, even though he is a mediocre skier. He is also partial to Italian landscapes, Oriental cuisine, Dutch painting, and German music, especially Beethoven. Later, when I am nine or ten, I will walk unannounced into our sitting room to find my mother, her face hidden in her arms, sobbing uncontrollably as the room resounds with the last bars of Beethoven's "Emperor Concerto." It scares me to see my mother, who never reveals any weakness in front of her children, in such a state. She draws me to her and murmurs, "Your father loved this piece," but her sorrow only strikes me as self-indulgent such a long time after the war.

Robert comes from a well-to-do Jewish family which, though by no means Orthodox, believes in tradition. As is often the case in Jewish and Mediterranean cultures, the family comes first, and what keeps it together is the formidable influence of its elders.

I will never forget the New Year's parties in my paternal grandmother Angèle's living room. This is during the postwar years, when peace brings back a modicum of comfort and refinement. I remember the vast apartment on the Champs Elysées, with its crystal chandeliers, period furniture, painted wood paneling, and tall windows with muslin curtains. And the uninterrupted stream of uncles, aunts, cousins, and friends coming to pay homage to the tacitly acknowledged head of the family. The adults call her "Matko," which in Polish, her native tongue, means mother-in-law. But to the children she is "Grandmother."

Grandmother receives us in a Louis XVI armchair upholstered in white crushed velvet. She always sits in the same place, her bluish white hair gathered into a French twist, her cheeks discreetly rouged. The cook Marie's traditional chocolate cake is passed around with a cup of tea. Outside it is cold and, if we are lucky, snowing. At every ring of the doorbell we children—there are always at least half a dozen of us—rush to the door to cry "Happy New Year" to the new arrivals bringing us gifts. The living room vibrates with laughter, the rustle of wrapping paper, overlapping conversations, the clink of silver on porcelain.

The history of the Kahns is relived around the white marble dining table, its anecdotes told and retold. Each year it might be enriched by new additions—engagements, marriages, births, divorces—which by the following year are part of the family epic. Affectionate tales and recollections also make it seem as if those who have died are still with us: Grandfather Edmond, a frenzied gambler, who could win or lose his family's holdings in an hour; my Aunt Claudine, prematurely ravaged by cancer, whose nickname was "Three Apples"; and, naturally, my father, Grandmother's favorite, in all his legendary glow.

My mother wouldn't miss one of these reunions for anything in the world, even though, coming from a vaguely atheistic family of teachers, she always feels a little out of place with my father's family. When she married Robert, she had never been in a synagogue—or a church, for that matter. As far as Grandmother—who wanted a Jewish daughter-in-law—was concerned, Jeanne's only asset was her beauty, her only defense her arrogance. And my mother is always on the defensive around Matko. Saint-Etienne is, for Robert, a wonderful way to put some distance between the two women.

"We'll get a dog, we'll bicycle around the country, make jam, grow a garden. . . . I'll have a piano and a nice bright studio," Jeanne reassures herself. And off they go, Jeanne with her easel, her watercolors, and her music scores; Robert with his promise of a brilliant career; and both thinking that two or three children might fit nicely into the picture.

Jeanne and Robert's new home in Saint-Etienne sits on the hills of Cantalouette, or "Larksong," a lyrical name to which the grayness of the place does little justice. A region dominated by mining and heavy industry, Saint-Etienne is in turmoil with conflicts between workers and factory owners over paid holidays and other issues.

At Siderexpor, Robert institutes a very personal form of management, a compromise between paternalism and socialism. His employees are well paid and loyal; their employer is sympathetic but not a fool. Robert is aided by an efficient, discreet secretary, Philippe Frecon, who is devoted to his boss.

The rumors circulating about Nazi Germany are becoming more and more insistent. A house painter with a ridiculous mustache has been steadily rising to power in Germany, unopposed by foreign governments, which probably deem him too clownish to be a threat. Nevertheless, Adolf Hitler's ravings are radio-broadcast through France frequently enough during these years to turn initial curiosity into growing concern.

In September 1939, the war becomes fact. The call to arms reaches France's most remote villages. Jeanne and Robert have spent five radiant years together, without ever imagining that this would be all the time they would have to share their day-to-day lives. Now, like most French women—mothers, wives, fiancées, daughters—my mother is in despair. True to form, Robert jokes as he slips on his khaki uniform and camouflage cap: "Don't take it so hard, love. We'll go out for dinner as soon as I'm back. It isn't serious, you'll see."

Two months later, his son's birth brings him home on a short leave. He registers the child at the town hall, and though he and Jeanne had agreed on a name—Michel—long before, at the last minute Robert "titles" his son Paul-Emile. "Because General Paulus Aemilius won at Cannes," he jokes when Jeanne, dismayed, accuses him of having gone a little too far.

"Poor little Paul-Emile," Grandmother sighs when she sees him for the first time, though whether out of consternation over the child's complex name or his poor timing no one will ever know.

The first question is whether or not the child should be circumcised. More realistic than religious, the family lets caution decide. They have all read *Mein Kampf*. They are all aware that in Germany, by order of the Reichstag, Jews can no longer be given Christian names, must make a legal declaration detailing all their possessions, and must carry ID cards stamped with the letter "J." They know that things had been worsening throughout 1938, when, in the infamous November Kristallnacht, legal persecution suddenly gave way to violence.

In November 1939, France hasn't yet gotten to that point, but Jews feel threatened; the Germans have been systematically applying Nazi principles to every country they have conquered. In a few months, France will be brought to its knees, with the cooperation of Marshal Philippe Pétain, a hero of World War I who is installed as the Premier of France; and on June 17, 1940, the status of French Jews will take a turn for the worse. To circumcise a young boy in 1939 was tantamount to signing his death warrant.

Paul-Emile's circumcision is postponed. But most Jewish families continued to circumcise their newborn boys. If they hadn't, all the Jewish boys under five who were sent off to Auschwitz in 1944 might have been saved.

Not only will Paul-Emile never be circumcised, but after the war, in a moment of retrospective panic, we will both be baptized.

BERLIN

On September 26, 1935, a twenty-two-year-old German takes the SS oath. He has been accepted by this sacred brotherhood after passing the ultimate test—that of racial purity. He is enrolled under the regimental number 272284. For now he is just an SS member of promise, but he will soon distinguish himself for the speed with which he rises through the ranks.

He was a quiet, reserved child, arrogant and lazy. Born in Bad Godesberg, near Bonn, on October 25, 1913, he was christened Nikolaus, like his father, according to a tradition going back to the family's French Huguenot origins nearly three centuries before.

During World War I, Barbie's father, a primary school teacher, was lightly wounded in the neck at Verdun. After the war, he founded a small group which opposed the French occupation of the Ruhr basin and was dedicated to rousing anti-French sentiment with speeches, leaflets distributed among factory workers, and minor acts of sabotage.

Young Klaus Barbie had no respect for his father, whom he considered a failure. As he plodded through his studies in the laborious pursuit of his high school diploma, he vaguely thought of becoming a doctor or lawyer. He knew he was smart enough; but he also knew he was too lazy for years of study, even if he could afford it. His father was too busy drinking to be of any help.

Klaus Jr. was no longer on speaking terms with Klaus Sr. when the latter died in October 1933. Still, the father's death gave the son the chance to martyrize him. Klaus Jr. claimed that his father's death was a direct consequence of the wound he received at Verdun. An outrageous story, to be sure, but preferable (for this proud young man) to admitting that his father drank himself to death.

His biological father had already begun to be supplanted by an ideological father: Adolf Hitler. Klaus Jr. responded with uncharacteristic ardor to the birth of the Third Reich. He volunteered for the Hitler Youth, and in it attained his first position of power, as patrol leader of 120 children between ten and fourteen years old. He then joined the NSDAP, the Nazi Party organization in Trier.

A couple of months after his father died, his older brother died of a heart disease. The following year, Barbie volunteered for a Nazi work camp in Schleswig-Holstein. There he pledged himself to Nazism. In the secret service (the infamous SD, or Sicherheitsdienst, a section of the SS, the Schutzstaffel; expanded and officially placed under Himmler in 1936, the Gestapo was effectively absorbed into the SS and was ultimately merged with the SD under Reinhard Heydrich) of the Nazi Party—which was recruiting ambitious young men with strong nerves, hard hearts, and a taste for secrecy—Barbie found his next opportunity.

"For me, it was a means to enter public service with all the guarantees of work entailed," Barbie will explain during the investigation of his case in 1984. "I must admit that serving as an intelligence agent for my country and my Party seemed a job with an interesting future. I would be a public servant, but not a petty clerk."

So, on the chilly morning of September 26, 1935, at 8:00 A.M. sharp, in a spotless uniform with boots so shiny they sparkle, Barbie stands waiting to take the SS oath, his brow smooth, his gaze fixed on an exciting future.

"A special oath, quite different from the Wehrmacht's, in which we directly referred to Hitler. Unfortunately I cannot remember the precise text," he will tell the president of the Lyon Cour d'Assises at the beginning of his trial for crimes against humanity.

Barbie spends the next two years taking theoretical and practical courses at the SS school in Bernau. He is an SS Mann and proud to be one. He is part of the elite. He *is* the elite.

May 1, 1937, a workers' holiday in most of Europe, is the day Barbie rises one more rung on his career ladder by officially joining the Nazi Party. In Berlin, at the Charlottenburg officers' school, he is assigned to the SD of Düsseldorf, where he devotes himself to hunting down whores and homosexuals. Since it would be too easy, and not entertaining enough, to simply arrest people, he and his comrades beat them up first.

After three months of military service in the 39th Infantry Regiment (from September 5 to December 3, 1938: a brief formality) Barbie is appointed an *Oberscharführer* SS on April 29, 1939. A little over a year later, he marries the plump twenty-three-year-old daughter of a post office worker. Regine Willms hadn't gotten far in school, and had worked as an assistant cook and as a maid before finding the best way to rise socially—by joining the Party. Suddenly she became a professional, an assistant pediatric nurse. In no time, she was earning good money in a Düsseldorf nursery, which is where she met Barbie. He is half her size, and has a triangular face, blond hair, gray eyes, and a pale complexion. Regine is a true German woman, seemingly made to bring forth strong children. Among Regine's many assets, two in particular are of interest to Barbie—her docility and her apartment. As a nursery employee she has free lodgings, while Barbie has been shuttling from one tawdry furnished room to the next.

Five days after his wedding, Barbie receives a wonderful gift from his Führer: another promotion, this time to *Untersturmführer*, assistant company commander in the Einsatzkommando in Nazi-occupied Amsterdam. He is not yet a member of the infamous

Section IV of the SD, but he is being groomed for it in Section VI, its intelligence service. His job is to gather information about the political parties and Resistance movements in the Netherlands. He is thus directly connected to the Gestapo, which relies on such information for its own activities.

The Jewish community in Holland numbers 150,000 people, half of whom live in Amsterdam. As soon as Barbie's Section VI has taken a complete census of the Jewish population of Amsterdam, locating and identifying each of its members, the Gestapo can operate without hindrance. The first personnel report written about Barbie's performance extols his "enthusiasm, energy, initiative, effectiveness and honesty," and earns him a promotion to the rank of *Obersturmführer,* company commander.

By February 1941, everything is prepared for the systematic elimination of the Jews from Holland. Barbie's first mission involves a raid on an ice cream parlor managed by two Jewish refugees from Germany. Most of the twelve customers are wounded, someone's skull is cracked open. A few days later, Barbie "sweeps up" a building occupied by 425 Jews. All those arrested will be carted off to Mauthausen; only seven or eight will return. That evening, the SS celebrate their success with the leaders of the Dutch Nazi Party by getting roaring drunk.

A dozen Jews had dared resist arrest; Barbie has the honor of heading the firing squad that executes them. This earns him the second-class Iron Cross.

Raids on Amsterdam Jews become daily occurrences. Barbie's most impressive takes place on June 11: three hundred boys between fourteen and nineteen are sent to Mauthausen, where they will test the effectiveness of the gas chambers. While the boys are gasping for air in Mauthausen, their butcher's daughter, Ute, takes her first breath in Trier.

In June 1942, Barbie is transferred to Dijon in the Occupied Zone of France. His first summer there is quiet and restful, but the Nazis are worried. Hordes of "terrorists" are marauding through the free zone, pestering the Germans with various acts of sabotage, circulating underground newspapers predicting the fall of the Reich, and protecting Jews. In other words, the Resistance, centered in Lyon, is gathering strength; it must be stopped.

On November 11, 1942, German troops move into the free zone, and the demarcation line between Occupied and Vichy France is abolished. The Nazis place their best men in key positions, and Barbie is sent to Lyon to head the local Gestapo. He will make sure no one forgets his tenure there.

4 THE MURDERER AND HIS VICTIM'S DAUGHTER

MAY 1, 1987

Forty-four bunches of roses, each wrapped in cellophane and tied with a yellow ribbon, have been placed on the steps of the Palais de Justice. They will be changed several times in the course of the trial. They represent the forty-four Jewish children arrested at Izieu.

In the vast floodlit hall, people are taking their seats as if in a theater, amidst overlapping conversations and the folding and unfolding of newspapers. The mayor, the magistrates, and the guests of the prefect are led to the balcony that has been installed for the trial around three sides of the room. Journalists, witnesses, and civil parties sit in the orchestra. Some of the lawyers make a studied appearance for last-minute interviews. The tension mounts. This trial is a legal event of the utmost importance for France.

Four cameras have been installed at strategic points to record every moment of the proceedings: some two hundred hours. After the verdict, all the tapes will be sealed and consigned to the Chancery safes, where they will remain unseen for the next twenty years. And then, only historians, researchers, or novelists working on subjects related to this trial will have access to them. Not until 2037, thirty years after that, will the film be made available to the general public. By then, our as-yet-unborn grandchildren will be in their forties. What will Robert Kahn's great-grandchildren think and feel when, a century after their great-grandfather's death, they see the face of this old man who looks so little like a butcher and so much like a grandfather?

What am *I* going to feel when, in just a few minutes, I see Barbie for the first time? Trial reporters tend to be blasé, matter-of-fact. They go to court with briefcases under their arms, the way others go to their offices; at each trial, they meet their colleagues, their friends. They are as familiar with legal proceedings as a secretary is with her Xerox machine. Court rituals no longer impress them.

As a journalist, I have followed some twenty or thirty trials in this courthouse, sometimes indifferently, other times with interest. I have seen men who became murderers out of passion or for revenge: "She didn't love me anymore. I couldn't live without her . . ." I have listened attentively as kidnappers and child abusers told their stories. I particularly remember a very pretty young woman, nineteen years old, who had killed her father because he didn't like her boyfriend.

However, behind this cool front, even the most seasoned journalist can't help but respond to the public exposure of someone else's private life. Just as no two trials are alike, no two defendants are alike, and the feelings they elicit vary depending on the receptivity of their listeners. What moves me may well anger another reporter. Still, when the moment comes to put pen to paper, we are all guided by the same imperative: to preserve an objective distance, not to let emotion get the better of a story. We must mirror events, not judge them.

In my twenty years as a trial reporter, I've undergone many a crisis of conscience. At times I've sided with the victim; at others with the murderer. I've tried to put myself in a juror's shoes, or in those of the president, the defense attorney, or the public prosecutor. I've identified with the victim's parents, and with those of the accused. In other words, I've tried to play every role, to sit in every chair, to know and understand everything. And until now, I thought I had succeeded.

Though I've known since Barbie's return to France—several years ago now—that I would have to cover his trial, it has never fully dawned on me until just this moment that I would be face to face with my father's murderer. Now, suddenly, I must listen as attentively and take notes as precisely as I always have, while my insides are churning and my fingertips are frozen with emotion.

We are all standing in a complete, deathly silence.

The president orders us to sit and announces the beginning of the trial: "Guards, let the defendant in." The automatic cameras bend toward the hidden staircase connecting the defendant's box with a special room in the basement. As they gradually straighten, we can sense Barbie's approach even though we cannot yet see him.

He doesn't look nearly as old as I had imagined. Indeed, he looks quite a bit younger than most of those victims who will confront him. But he seems sluggish, broken, worn. He is seventy-four. I remember that among the Bron victims there was a seventy-five-year-old, Gustave Dreyfus. He was so famished and exhausted after a day of grueling work that he could not move. Barbie's men had to bludgeon him all the way to his grave. The head of the UGIF was also seventy-five. Throughout the proceedings, I will imagine those two ghosts standing beside the defendant's box.

Barbie's balding head is crowned with long wisps of dirty gray hair. His face is thin, with high cheekbones and sunken cheeks. Beneath his thick brows, his steely gray eyes glimmer like a freshly sharpened knife. His thin lips are forever tensed in an enigmatic smile, in which one can read just about anything: irony, spite, weariness, fatalism, cruelty, perversion. It is the smile of a man with many secrets, aware of the power this gives him. His eyes are colder than his smile, as if there was no connection between them. Indeed, these two parts of his face seem to belong to two different men. In a way, this explains why not one of the victims who will testify will have any trouble identifying the "Butcher of Lyon" in that face—a face at once impassive and tormented, impenetrable and sardonic.

Suddenly, as I stare at him in an attempt to understand what happened at Bron on August 17, 1944, an extraordinary calm descends upon me. My body relaxes, my mind stops reeling. The die has been cast. Barbie and I, the murderer and his victim's daughter, will coexist in the same space and time for a time. We will breathe the same air and see the same people (though we will see them differently), and listen to what they have to say (though each of us will hear different things). And all of his victims will be here around us: the two old men I have imagined standing beside his box, along with all the people he sent to be gassed, burnt, starved, or worked to death, and all the children he murdered, or kept from being born. They are all here, including Robert Kahn, closer than ever, so close I can whisper in his ear.

The photographers and cameramen focus their lenses on Barbie: his sharp profile, black suit, and wrinkled neck.

Through his interpreters he sets the tone: "My name is Klaus Altmann. I was born on October 25, 1913, in Bad Godesberg. I am a businessman residing in La Paz, Bolivia."

As long as he is present in the courtroom, he will calmly, but persistently, correct the president and the public prosecutor whenever they address him as Barbie. He insists upon being called Altmann. Though he admits he bore the name Barbie for a while, and that he was in Lyon between November 1942 and August 1944, he makes clear that the man who stands in front of us now is not the German Barbie, but rather the Bolivian Altmann. As such he cannot possibly feel implicated in crimes which, indeed, concern only Barbie.

The jury is introduced, and the witnesses are called one by one. After four hours of seemingly interminable legal procedure, Barbie's trial can now begin.

JUNE 1940

A perfectly blue sky is slashed only by the swift flights of swallows; wasps and bees buzz drunkenly in the wisteria that frames the front porches and in the rose bushes no one thinks of pruning; fresh grass grows wild all over the hills between Lyon and Saint-Etienne. In the early summer of 1940, the war marches on, but the countryside is so beautiful it makes you feel you're on vacation.

My mother has no idea how rapidly the situation has been deteriorating. But at the front, Robert is a daily witness to the swelling tide of refugees from Belgium and other parts of France: Normandy, Picardy, Paris and its environs. Uncharacteristically, he worries.

Toward the end of June, Jeanne is quietly doing her nails by her baby's crib when Robert, not yet demobilized suddenly appears, disheveled, sweaty, and covered with dust, riding a motorbike he has found God knows where. For once in their short life together he is not laughing. He tells her to collect a few things, only the necessities, and join his family at Amélie-les-Bains. "I'm scared," he admits. "Anything can happen, but for the moment it can only be bad. I'd rather know you're all together." And when my mother begins to object, he cuts her short. "Enough. Let's get going."

Three hours later, she is behind the steering wheel of her black Citroen, the very same model favored by the Gestapo. She pays for gas with carrots, eggs, and butter, valuable currency in these days of food shortage. Her mother and Paul-Emile are with her, wedged in among the suitcases, bags, and packages my mother has haphazardly filled with soap, toothpaste, medicines, condensed milk. Bonne-maman had fled Paris for Saint-Etienne in order to escape food rationing and the howling sirens that would wake her up in the middle of the night and propel her, heart pounding, out of bed, down the stairs, and into the closest cellar or metro station, clutching a few of her most precious possessions.

Bonne-maman was an upright woman—one of those who, though proud of having kept to the right path, might also regret never having had the courage to stray a little. Widowed young, she had spent all her life in a dreary apartment in a working-class quarter of Paris, devoting herself entirely to her two children. I adored her. She was the best storyteller I knew, especially when it came to telling stories of her childhood and early adolescence at the turn of the century—prehistory to me. In her frail voice, she sang old tunes: lullabies, sentimental love songs. She described dresses with trim waists and leg-of-mutton sleeves; a Paris where people traveled on foot or in a barouche; and spent Sundays on the banks of the Seine with young men wearing boaters, just as Renoir had painted them. I couldn't really believe she had ever been young, maybe because I had always seen her dressed in black with, at most, a hint of white. I remember a black straw hat she had, with a black-bird on the side and a black veil in front. She was austere in bearing as well as in mien, and her guiding principle was "thrift yes, avarice no." She often argued with her daughter, whom she reproached for having married "above her station." She felt ill at ease with my paternal family and resented my father for having lured Jeanne away from her. She suspected that his love for Jeanne was nothing more than a whim that would end as suddenly as it had begun.

My parents had met at Saint-Jean-de-Luz in August 1934. On vacation, each with no friends, they had both walked into the same bookstore on the same morning looking for the same thing: the company of a book. According to my mother, their eyes met as they were browsing through the classics. A banal but nevertheless fateful encounter for both of them. She left the bookstore fearing she might never again run into that lovely young man with those surprising green eyes. All they knew of one another was that they both loved books and went to the same bookstore. They both reached the same conclusion: same place, same time, the following day.

The day after that, they smiled at each other. The fourth day, he asked her advice: "If you were me, what would you choose, Victor Hugo's *Things Seen* or lunch with you on the waterfront?" "I would bring Victor Hugo along," Jeanne answered, despite her shyness. At home she fretted: "What if he doesn't like the sound of my voice, or my perfume, or this silly belt, or finds me stupid and ugly?" But Robert already liked everything in Jeanne.

The trip to Amélie-les-Bains is a nightmare. To feed and change the baby in the packed car is nearly impossible, and he expresses his discomfort by crying from the moment they leave until they arrive. It is a long trip. The roads are overflowing with the sluggish,

mournful tide of refugees: cars and mule-drawn carts, and since gas
is so hard to come by, there are wheelbarrows and baby buggies
filled with kitchen utensils, children, and old women. In the ditches
by the side of the road, cars hold people resting or seeking shelter
from the scorching sun. It is a depressing, pitiful, useless exodus,
with no clear destination other than to reach the free zone, if it is
still free, and there find some food and a place to sleep. Some give
up hope midway and go back home, only to find it pillaged down
to the last fork.

Amélie-les-Bains, in the Pyréneés-Orientales department, is a
chic spa, quite fashionable at the time of the Empress Eugénie, now
fallen on hard times. The entire Kahn family has taken up residence
in a rococo hotel which has clearly known better days but whose
staff still do their best to keep up appearances. Rutabagas, variously
seasoned, make up most of the menu; but they are served to tables
covered with starched white tablecloths by an impeccable maître d',
as if they were pâté.

Despite all predictions to the contrary, Grandmother and Bonne-
maman, both fiercely temperamental and as different from one
another as a peacock and a hen, manage to get along. My mother
breathes a sigh of relief. In August, my father is demobbed and
joins his family. After a few days of rest, he drives his wife, child,
and mother-in-law back to Saint-Etienne. It is time to make serious
plans: another baby is on the way, and the anti-Semitic laws are
getting stricter by the day.

This is when Robert decides to rent Villa Bénédicte in the small
village of Saint-Just-sur-Loire, a hamlet lost at the bottom of a
valley surrounded by thick chestnut woods; here, he thinks, his
family will be safe, and he will be close to his business.

Villa Bénédicte is a beautiful old limestone house with rounded
balconies and a red-tiled roof. Two rows of lindens lead from the
gate to a French window framed by wild holly. Under the nearest
tree there is a garden table with a marble top, a wooden bench,
and three or four wrought-iron chairs painted white. At the front
of the house there is a "pleasure garden" full of flowers of every
color and fragrance: roses, daisies, phlox. In June, the heady scent

of lilies hovers over everything else. My mother has a green thumb, unusual in a Parisienne, even one of peasant descent. The fruit trees and vegetables she plants in the garden at the back of the house will pull us through the worst days of the food shortage.

The year 1941 marks a turning point for both my parents. They gain a daughter and lose both their firms: Outinat in Paris and Siderexpor at Saint-Etienne. France's collaborationist government has made it illegal for Jews to own businesses. Outinat falls into the hands of a "loyal secretary" who, with her husband's help, steals all she can. Fortunately, Pierre and Robert have already taken the precaution of transferring all their Outinat shares into the names of a few trustworthy Catholic friends and relatives. Some of Bonne-maman's cousins, who hardly know my father, suddenly find them-selves the proud owners of sundry stocks and securities, which they'll tend carefully until Pierre returns from Dachau, after the war.

At Saint-Etienne, Marcel Guédras, an engineer, is named general manager of Siderexpor in October 1941. But the company he in-herits is only a shadow of what it was, as my father has taken all the account books and documents with him, after canceling a year's worth of steel orders. Later, in September 1943, Siderexpor will be sold to a mechanic for less than a third of its net worth—a deal not unusual at the time, when many people profited at the expense of the Jews. In 1945, Pierre will be able to recover all the shares of Outinat but only the walls of Siderexpor.

Back in Paris, the Kahns refuse to wear the yellow stars and cannot understand why other Jews don't do the same. Like everyone else in the occupied capital, they are going through hard times, even though Robert and Jeanne keep sending them food supplies from Saint-Just. Some arrive, others don't or come so late it's better not to open them. Jeanne has started raising chickens and sheep in her garden, and in the basement she has a pig my father has christened Herman, if for no other reason than to be able to say, "What a swine that Herman!" But Herman is not just any old swine; he keeps surviving his own death. His butcher, a neighboring farmer, assures his longevity by replacing him, every six to twelve months, with a younger Herman, while the senior Herman fattens

us all on hams and sausages. Meanwhile, in Paris, people stew all
the cats and dogs they can lay their hands on, and rats begin to
look quite appetizing.

In the course of 1942, the Resistance grows, and Lyon becomes
its center. France can now be said to have three capitals. Paris is
still its historical and geographic capital. Vichy is the new capital
of Unoccupied France, since what remains of the French government moved there under Marshal Pétain. And Lyon is the capital
of the Resistance. Lyon is the largest French city in the free zone.
The German army, which invaded it in mid-June 1940, left on July
7 by agreement with the Vichy government. Frenchmen who could
not stand living next to the Wehrmacht have moved to Lyon. The
city's geographical location offers several ways out: toward the Mediterranean, toward the Alps and Switzerland, and back to Paris, all
just a few hours away. In addition, it is easier to hide here than
anywhere else, thanks to an intricate system of courtyards and alleys,
known as "traboules," which connects all the buildings in the vast
center of the city.

Numerous Resistance groups form around the journalists, writers,
philosophers, and historians who have come to Lyon. Though these
movements share a common cause, on the whole they do not mix.
Underground papers crop up everywhere: *Témoinage Chrétien, Les
Petites Ailes, Le Coq Enchainé, Vérité.* They are slipped under doors
or into mailboxes at night, while graffiti denouncing collaboration
mushroom on the city walls.

Lyon is the meeting place for the leaders of the various underground movements, which, by and by, fuse into three main
groups—"Combat," "Libération," and "Franc-Tireur"—each with
its own paper. But their points of view are so similar that during
the winter of 1942–43 they will merge into a more powerful single
movement—Mouvements Unis de Résistance, the United Movements of the Resistance, or MUR.

The Lyon Resistance is not only fighting against the German
invaders; its main task, in fact, is to save Jews. There have already
been several raids on Jews in Paris, while in the meantime Jewish
refugees are pouring into the country from other parts of Europe.

They are welcomed, but advised to keep a low profile. Children are smuggled into Switzerland, often concealed at the bottom of empty barrels and then covered with coal or, better, manure to deter inspections. The smaller ones are hidden in old truck tires and bundles of fabric, or rolled inside rugs which are then tied to the roofs of cars. The easiest way to escape is still in groups, at night, across a loosely guarded border. But when this fails, it almost certainly means death. Many children will be saved by courageous friends, neighbors, and strangers during these years, but few compared to those who will be lost to Barbie and his Gestapo after the Germans return to Lyon.

NOVEMBER 1942

Lieutenant Klaus Barbie is twenty-nine when he first sets foot in Lyon, a dream city for epicureans and pleasure seekers alike. And Barbie happens to be both. There are no food shortages for the occupiers. Gastronomically speaking, these will be Barbie's two best years, while all around him France is starving.

His arrival in November 1942, when Vichy France becomes Occupied France, marks the beginning of a regime of terror for the city of Lyon and its environs which will make the trials of the earlier years of the war look like a joke. The fight against the Resistance will be ruthless and extremely bloody; Jew-hunting will become systematic. In Germany, the crematoriums need more fuel, and Barbie is glad to provide it.

Barbie, who has left wife and children in Trier, has been given carte blanche as head of the Gestapo in Lyon, thanks to his performance in Amsterdam and a very flattering record: "A leader who goes straight to his goal, loves action, and shows great taste and aptitude for intelligence service. His devotion to Nazi ideology is absolutely firm."

When Barbie and several hundred SS officers arrive in Lyon on the heels of the occupying Wehrmacht, they immediately requisition the Hotel Terminus to turn it into the regional headquarters of the Gestapo. Designed by Gustave Eiffel, the six-story building has 140 bedrooms, suites, living rooms, dining rooms, and a huge assembly room. The officers lodge in the rooms on the third and fourth floors. The rest of the rooms are turned into offices, and some twenty of them into interrogation chambers. It is here, in these well-appointed rooms with wall-to-wall carpeting, modern furniture, wall mirrors, and pastoral prints and paintings, that the prisoners from Fort Montluc are interrogated daily. None of the rooms is equipped as a torture chamber; Barbie's henchmen make do with what they have. For the *baignoire*, for instance—in which the victim is repeatedly submerged in a bathtub filled with icy water until his or her lungs are about to explode—they use their own bathrooms. And, of course, special rooms are unnecessary to flog prisoners or burn them with pokers or cigarette butts. By June 1943, the Gestapo will be operating above capacity, and will establish another branch at the Ecole de Santé on Avenue Berthelot. There it will conduct the harshest interrogations and receive often more than one hundred informers a day.

The efficiency of the Nazi hierarchy is directly dependent on the perks it provides its officers and collaborators: quick promotions, decorations, family subsidies, generous praise, and frequent parties to cement the esprit de corps.

Before Hitler, the organization of the German police was fairly simple: one division (called "Orpo") was concerned with maintaining law and order, and another ("Sipo") was in charge of security. Sipo was itself divided into two main sections: the criminal police, or "Kripo," and the state police, or "Stapo"—better known as the "Gestapo," a secret police-cum-intelligence service charged with suppressing espionage, terrorism, and other threats to the Reich.

In 1933, Hitler added his own small Nazi security service, the Sicherheitsdienst, or SD, so as to keep close tabs on the Gestapo. Three years later, to bring the police even more closely under his control, he put a loyal party man, Heinrich Himmler, in charge of all police services and merged Kripo, Stapo, and an expanded SD under the heading SIPO-SD, to be directed by Himmler's sidekick Reinhard Heydrich.

In June 1940, Heydrich established a Parisian branch of the SIPO-SD headed by Helmut Knochen, who immediately set up his offices on the prestigious Avenue Foch. It is Knochen who organized all the provincial subsidiaries under his command: the Einsatzkommando, EK for short. By the time France is fully occupied, there are thirteen EK across the country.

The Lyon EK covers ten regions, including the Jura, the Alps, a large part of the Center, and the Isère. Given its scope and the particularly recalcitrant regional character, this EK is indisputably the most important in France. After two unsuccessful bosses, the Lyon EK is placed in the hands of Werner Knab, a thirty-four-year-old lawyer (he looks ten years younger) who has been transferred to Lyon from Kiev, where he murdered Jews, Gypsies, and communists. Lyon is his reward.

Barbie, who has been there for nine months before Knab arrives, welcomes him with joy. He shares Knab's vision of the task at hand.

Barbie's team is, generally speaking, a counterespionage organization, intended to ferret out and repress communists, resistants, and Jews; and also to hunt down draftees for the compulsory work service (STO) who have either escaped from Germany or refuse to go. In November 1942, Barbie has twenty-five SS officers at his command and the Wehrmacht at his disposal for all major operations. The German soldiers are not by any means all Nazis; but those who refuse to carry out Barbie's orders will be immediately transferred to the eastern front.

Things start out slowly for Barbie, partly because the French still mistrust his men. But, little by little, people begin to cooperate, informing against their neighbors, their friends, their relatives. Informing becomes a career for the weakest and least scrupulous—a small army of some 130 people. Fifty of them make up Barbie's private regiment, a kind of bodyguard. They are an unmistakable symbol of his power. Even Werner Knab is a little jealous. "You may be the big boss here," Barbie tells Knab, "but you're not running half the risks that I am."

These French collaborators are headed by Francis André, who, because of a disfiguring accident, is better known at "Gueule Tordue," "Twisted Mug." "My war name," he never tires of explaining. André was once a communist but had a change of heart and is now Barbie's loyal right hand.

André creates the MNAT (Mouvement National Anti-Terroriste), whose motto is "terror for terror." Under the cover of anti-terrorism, the bandits of the MNAT blackmail, steal, loot, pillage, and murder with impunity. The job of Antoine Saunier, the treasurer, is to divide the booty taken from private apartments and shops between the MNAT and the Germans. By the beginning of 1944, the MNAT will have become such a powerful branch of the Gestapo that it will be officially stationed at the Ecole de Santé, where André's offices will abut Barbie's.

This is not the only group of French collaborators. There is also the "Milice" (Militia), the brainchild of Joseph Darnand, a loyal disciple of Marshal Pétain. Its targets are "bolshevism, the Jewish leper, and freemasonry." Its followers, all civilians, wear a black uniform with a beret and paramilitary boots, which makes it easy to spot them from afar. They are recruited from the uneducated lower classes and use the power invested in them by the Militia to take revenge on the rest of society. They never act alone.

The Lyon Militia, one of the strongest, is headed by Joseph Lecussan, a navy captain, blindly devoted to both Barbie and André. It is Lecussan who, on January 10, 1943, will arrest Victor Basch, the eighty-year-old president of the League for Human Rights, in his own apartment, and kill him and his wife. He will then abandon their bodies in the street with a sign that reads "Terror for terror. Jews always pay."

Klaus Barbie was not just a butcher. He was also a shrewd tactician and manipulator. And he firmly believed in tangible results. If it is true that the Gestapo never would have gotten anywhere without the consent of the French people, it is also true that Barbie and his henchmen did their best to inspire such acquiescence.

In the eyes of France and the world, Barbie is most notorious for arresting and murdering Jean Moulin, president of the Conseil National de la Résistance, and General Charles de Gaulle's special envoy. Yet it is almost certain that someone in the Resistance collaborated in Moulin's arrest.

Jean Moulin—with his ironic smile, a soft felt hat overshadowing his right eye, a schoolboy's scarf flung over his shoulder—is legendary in France. As a young government prefect in 1940, he refused to sign a statement issued by the new German authorities alleging that Senegalese sharpshooters were responsible for German atrocities. Shortly thereafter, he was thrown into a ditch and bludgeoned to a pulp. Later he slit his throat open with pieces of broken glass for fear that at the next beating he might sign that statement after all. (The scarf he always wore in the years following concealed an ugly scar.) Recovered from his wound and dismissed from his government post, Moulin joined the Resistance.

Meanwhile, from his exile in England, General de Gaulle was orchestrating the unification of the Resistance, then made up of several disparate and often conflicting groups. De Gaulle proposed a coordinating committee involving an equal number of representatives from the three major movements—"Combat," "Libération," and "Franc-Tireur"—chaired and mediated by an independent party answering only to him: Jean Moulin.

Accompanied by practical assistance, the proposal was enthusiastically accepted. Through Moulin, de Gaulle managed to parachute not only money but radio equipment, technicians, weapons, and other supplies into Occupied France. By the end of 1942, Jean Moulin was the key man in the French Resistance.

However, the Gestapo was also increasing its efforts to dismantle the Resistance, with greater and greater success. On June 10, 1943, General Charles-Antoine Delestraint, chief of de Gaulle's secret army, was supposed to meet "Didot," the leader of the network in charge of sabotaging the French railways, at a metro station in Paris. (In civilian life, Didot was René Hardy, the author of an internationally acclaimed novel called *Bitter Victory*.) The Lyon Gestapo heard about the meeting and passed the information on to Paris through a double agent; Delestraint was arrested at the metro station. Didot never showed.

He had good reason; he had been arrested three days before.

Oddly, however, the day after Delestraint was captured, Didot was set free.

Generally, only three kinds of people were released by the Gestapo: those who could prove beyond any doubt that they were arrested by mistake; those who agreed to inform on the Resistance; and those the Gestapo set free as bait for larger prey. These last usually realized what was going on, and they either managed to warn their contacts or found themselves forced to leave the Resistance. But when René Hardy resumed contact with his group just a few days after his release, he told them nothing about his arrest—a flagrant violation of Resistance precautions.

Delestraint's arrest, given his high rank, sent the Resistance into turmoil. Jean Moulin decided to restructure the entire system, and he hastily set up a meeting of its main leaders.

The meeting was an open secret. Those who had been invited boasted about the privilege. "Lots of people who weren't supposed to know about it knew," my Aunt Edmée admitted to me last spring. "Jacques Baumel, my boss, was very miffed at not having been invited. And your Uncle Jacques, who had nothing to do with it, knew both the time and the place."

The meeting took place on June 21, at the home of Dr. Frederic Dugoujon, a Resistance sympathizer. No precaution was taken to protect the house from unexpected visits; no one was stationed outside to sound the alarm in case of danger. While the doctor tended his patients on the first floor, the resistants arrived one by one. Some walked directly up to the second floor; others, such as Jean Moulin and Raymond Aubrac, mixed with the small group of patients waiting downstairs. When the Gestapo showed up, led by Barbie himself, many of the participants had yet to arrive. Nonetheless, eight Resistance leaders were arrested.

Barbie did not know which was Jean Moulin; they all had false papers. The only man he could identify was René Hardy. The eight were handcuffed and led to the Gestapo's black Citroens. In the shuffle, one of the prisoners managed to escape through the garden, miraculously dodging the Gestapo's heavy gunfire—"heavy" perhaps but, according to most witnesses, not aimed at the fugitive. This lucky man was René Hardy.

The remaining seven prisoners were driven directly to the Ecole de Santé and tortured for two days. Barbie wanted to know which was Jean Moulin, and he figured that if he didn't confess, one of the others would. At least one resistant was placed in front of a firing squad three times in a row.

No one knows who spoke; maybe Jean Moulin himself did, to spare his companions. In any case, the six other prisoners were quickly deported, while Klaus Barbie concentrated on making de Gaulle's emissary talk.

By that evening, Moulin had been worked over so thoroughly he was in a coma. But he wasn't dead, not yet. The Gestapo knew how to keep people alive, when necessary. If Moulin refused to talk to the Lyon SIPO-SD, he would talk to the Paris Gestapo, even more powerful than Barbie.

But Jean Moulin would never talk. He could no longer speak, let alone write anything with the paper and pencil they kept handing him—along with a couple of slaps, even though they knew he was already as good as dead. Moulin would never recover, the German doctors who visited him at the beginning of July were sure.

Jean Moulin died on July 7, 1943, at forty-four, and two days later was cremated at the Père-Lachaise cemetery so that no one, aside from his butchers, would ever see what state he was in. His ashes were transferred to the Panthéon in 1965. "To great men their grateful country," reads the inscription on the pediment of the monument where rest, among others, Victor Hugo, Rousseau, and Voltaire.

Hardy was tried twice after the war, first in 1947 and then in 1950, and acquitted both times for lack of evidence. The critical witness, Klaus Barbie, was missing. But the mystery of Moulin's betrayal haunts France still. When Barbie was brought back to Lyon, everyone thought his trial would solve that mystery, but Barbie has repeatedly contradicted himself on this issue. René Hardy died at the beginning of 1986, in utter misery, taking his secret with him.

5 THE CARDPLAYERS

MAY 12, 1987

André Cerdini, fifty-eight years old, has been the president of the Cour d'Assises of the Rhône department since 1984. As he well knows, he owes his appointment in Lyon to legal politics. The Chancery wants him there for the Barbie trial.

Despite his rather ordinary appearance, Cerdini is a remarkable man. Slim, with thinning hair and discreet spectacles, he is deft at balancing the more sensational elements of such a trial with the requirements of the penal code. He keeps things under control without curtailing the freedom of the press, as French judges often do. He is accessible to journalists, but never betrays any of his feelings about the trial. He agrees to pose for press photographers, even though he hates having his picture taken, but firmly refuses to pose in front of the thirty volumes constituting the Barbie file. "You must understand," he explains, "I don't want there to be any confusion." He is well aware that a suggestive caption can distort the meaning of even the tamest snapshot.

Cerdini has been preparing for the Barbie case since the beginning of the year, reading books on the Occupation, the Gestapo, the "final solution." He has pored over the transcripts of the 1952 and 1954 trials, as well as those of the Nuremberg trial and the 1961 Eichmann trial in Tel Aviv. Two weeks before the trial, he put aside his books to devote himself entirely to rest and exercise, "so as to be in top form."

The public prosecutor, Pierre Truche, is fifty-seven and an eminent figure in French legal circles. He has already proved himself innumerable times in some of France's most highly publicized trials. A socialist and member of the magistrates' union (otherwise known as "the pink judges"), he irritates his right-wing colleagues, many of whom would love to discredit him. His reputation is untarnished, however. With his mane of white hair, piercing blue eyes, broad shoulders, and relaxed manner, Pierre Truche is a very seductive character. He will have to grapple with a formidable adversary, readjusting his firing line every time he thinks the defense is trying to shift the focus of the debate; bringing the court back to earth each time it threatens to become lost in arabesques of legalese. And he will have to address his closing speech to the world.

Lyon is Truche's birthplace, and he has long wanted to return. After practicing in Bordeaux and Marseille, he is finally transferred there, like Cerdini, specifically for Barbie's trial. To those who ask what tack he is going to take, he smoothly answers, "It's just another trial."

The defense attorney, Jacques Vergès, is sixty-two, and the perfect devil's advocate. He is best known for the skill with which he holds society and its political regimes responsible for his clients' crimes. He does not defend individuals so much as an idea of individuals manipulated by the system.

Haughty, cynical, and sharply intelligent, Vergès is both hated and admired. He likes to threaten, to be feared. His defense of Barbie promises to be almost entirely political. His client is charged with crimes against humanity, but Vergès claims that he will show that what France did to itself is far more serious than its enemies' crimes. He plans to turn Barbie's trial into that of the Resistance and its failures; he intends to shake the foundations of French history.

Throughout the *instruction*, Vergès has repeatedly asserted that his client was not afraid to appear in court; that on the contrary, he would welcome the opportunity to tell the world about the cowardice of the Resistance. Vergès claims that Barbie knew nothing about the "final solution" or the concentration camps. For months he has been maintaining that his client could only profit from a trial that would finally offer him the chance to exonerate himself.

According to Vergès: (a) Barbie did not order or participate in the UGIF raid, nor did he authorize the one in Izieu; (b) the telegram bearing his signature supposedly sent to Paris the evening of the Izieu raid is a fake; and (c) Barbie was not present at the departure of the last train from Lyon, on August 11, 1944, since his boss, Werner Knab, was fully responsible for that operation.

As a lawyer, Vergès has one major flaw: He is more effective outside a courtroom than at the bench. The sentences his clients get are often heavier than the ones requested by the prosecution. But he doesn't seem to mind; the stricter the punishment, the more persuasive his point. In case his clients have not fully grasped the subtlety of his arguments, their sentences prove that they are indeed victims of the state.

Despite all the bravado Vergès has displayed during the four years of *instruction* (a period of pretrial investigation of a case), he will often show himself capable of humility, modesty, and even discretion in the courtroom. His trial of the Resistance has yet to materialize.

Ute Messner, Barbie's daughter, asked Vergès to represent him. A rabid anti-Zionist, Vergès is known to have ties to Middle-Eastern terrorists and barely refutes the accusation that he is anti-Semitic. He is a mysterious man who disappeared for eight years, from 1970 to 1978. Some say he was in Cuba, others that he was in East Germany, still others that he was in Cambodia with his friend Pol

Pot. Is he a secret agent? A conspirator? His only answer is a cryptic "Who knows?"

Serge Klarsfeld, fifty-two, is a historian by training, with a degree in political science. His presence in the court, where he represents the forty-four children of Izieu, marks the end of his long pursuit of Barbie. Without the efforts of Serge's wife, Beate, Barbie might still be living peacefully in La Paz. Born in Bucharest and escaped to France with his parents, Serge was only eight when the Gestapo knocked on the door of their apartment in Nice. His father barely had time to hide his wife and children in a closet before answering the door, only to disappear forever in the smoke over Auschwitz.

"I have no particular vocation for the law, but I want to defend my cause, and put an end to the impunity of the Nazi criminals who worked in France," Klarsfeld declares. President of the Association of Sons and Daughters of Jews Deported from France, Klarsfeld is the author of several books on the implementation of the "final solution" in France. The most recent, *Les enfants d'Izieu*, documents the short lives of those children.

It is Klarsfeld who found, in the archives of the Contemporary Jewish Documentation Center, a copy of the telegram Barbie sent Knochen on the evening of the Izieu raid. Unfortunately, the original document has disappeared and this copy, authenticated by the Nuremberg Military Tribunal, amuses Vergès, who calls it "a fake created for the occasion."

These are the trial's main actors. In supporting roles are all the interpreters and court clerks who take turns recording every word uttered in the course of the trial. Among them is Jean-Michel Viout, the deputy state prosecutor, who every evening patiently reinterprets the day's proceedings for the foreign press, as well as for the numerous French journalists who have trouble finding their way through the intricacies of their own legal system. Then there are the thirty-nine lawyers representing different plaintiffs; and the jurors, four women and five men. The oldest, fifty-one, is the only one to have some memory of the Occupation. The others are in their forties and are for the most part white-collar workers. For two months, until a verdict is announced on July 3, these men and women will live on the margins of both their private and professional lives. They will not be able to return to their jobs until the beginning of July; and during that time they will be paid a daily allowance which is for most of them a fraction of their usual salary.

And last but not least, there are the witnesses: survivors, "historical witnesses"—Jacques Chaban-Delmas, Raymond Aubrac, Elie Wiesel.

The reading of the bill of indictment, listing all the charges brought against Barbie and redefining the crimes for which he is going to be tried, takes up most of the day. Barbie, who has already read the entire document in his cell, listens politely. But Vergès immediately protests:

"This trial cannot take place. My client was already tried in absentia for all his activities in Lyon in 1952 and 1954. Those sentences are prescribed, and no new legal proceedings can be brought against Mr. Barbie, since the law does not allow the same defendant to be tried twice for the same crimes. Therefore, I suggest that this court set Mr. Barbie free at once."

"If it can be proven," Truche calmly responds, "that some of the actions for which Mr. Barbie has already been judged have slipped among the crimes for which he is being tried now, I will be the first to request that they be removed from the file. It is a fact that, in 1954, some of the actions that should have been qualified as crimes against humanity were presented as war crimes in the course of the trial. I am referring to the Bron massacre and other executions of Jews simply because they were Jews. There is nothing we can do about that now. The laws of the Court of Criminal Appeals are clear: One cannot question the authority of a previous judgment. On the other hand, Maître Vergès is mistaken when he asserts that in 1952 and 1954 his client was tried for the totality of his actions in Lyon. He was not tried 'globally,' but for very specific actions, which could not possibly be the same ones with which he is charged now for the simple reason that the crimes which are the subject of this trial were brought to light only after 1954. Who in the course of those earlier trials spoke of Dr. Gompel's atrocious death? Who brought up deportation? Incredible as it might sound, the sight of those living relics returning from concentration camps did not move anyone to start an investigation and initiate legal proceedings. In any case, Maître Vergès, let me reassure you: The court does not intend to waste time reconsidering any of the events that were already judged thirty years ago."

But Vergès does not give up easily:

"I again maintain that in 1954 Klaus Barbie was tried for everything that happened in that region, including what happened to the Jews. Barbie knew that they were being transferred to Drancy, Compiègne, Romainville, but he did not know their final destination. That was determined in Paris, not in Lyon."

Barbie then takes the stand and, through the feminine voice of his interpreter, makes his statement:

"Yesterday, when I heard what I was accused of, I couldn't believe my ears. I thought I was in front of the Military Tribunal in Nuremberg. For a moment, I almost believed I had behaved like a madman in Lyon, chasing, arresting, torturing all the Jews, as if I owned the city. In fact, we were all, one hundred and five men— an entire unit of which I was not the head—dependent on the Wehrmacht. A few days ago, in Der Spiegel, I read that the President of the Federal Republic of Germany was sentenced to seven years in prison for having signed a letter advocating the acceleration of Jewish deportation. . . ."

But all this is quite beside the point, and President Cerdini has no intention of letting the court get bogged down. We move on to Barbie's curriculum vitae: his childhood, adolescence, early devotion to the National Socialist Party, and his intelligence work for the SD and the Party, all the way up to 1940, just before he is transferred to Amsterdam.

"At that time, your superiors considered you one of the best agents in the SD," says President Cerdini.

"I wouldn't know," Barbie modestly responds. "All the files were secret, I had no access to them." But he does know the documents in question; he saw them while preparing his defense. They say that he was "an irreproachable comrade. An exemplary SS officer, both in service and off duty. A devoted follower of Nazi ideology."

"The people who wrote those things about me knew me well,"
Barbie concedes. "Obviously my superiors could not be wrong."

Now, could Barbie tell the court something about the "Nazi
ideology" he was so devoted to? Aware of the larger implications
of this question, Barbie responds:

"Your Excellency, I could not possibly explain what National
Socialism was in just a few words."

At which point the court adjourns until tomorrow.

November 11, 1942

If Lyon is the capital of the Resistance, Saint-Etienne is one of its
headquarters, and Barbie knows it. The Gestapo move into Saint-
Etienne the same day they arrive in Lyon, on November 11, 1942.
They immediately settle into the best hotel: the Nouvel Hotel,
near the train station, where the town's leading families celebrate
their weddings and communions, and businessmen hold their meetings. There my father entertains his clients, celebrated both his
children's births, and plans to throw a party on the day of a Liberation he believes close at hand.

Barbie is in contact with his Saint-Etienne team daily. At first
the team is quite small: five SS officers of various backgrounds—
an ex-brewer, an armaments engineer, a clothier, a salesman, and
an idler with a knack for public relations. The idler is handsome
and friendly and speaks French fluently; he likes to spend money
on women. Before the war, he sold household appliances in the
southeast of France; most likely he took a job with the Gestapo so
as to remain in France. His name is Gustaf Neumann, but he goes
by the name "Armand Bernard." His knowledge of French slang
and manners has earned him a number of "friends" who, unaware
of his German origins, occasionally confide in him.

When, in 1943, Barbie realizes that the roots of the Resistance
run deeper than he thought, he asks Paris for reinforcements and
forms the "Neumann gang" to keep an eye on every district of the
city and its surroundings. The Gestapo of Saint-Etienne alone soon

consisted of some twenty-five German officers and one hundred thirty French recruits; more or less the same ratio as in other parts of France.

Among Neumann's most zealous recruits are three who deserve particular mention: a member of Doriot's PPF (the Parti Populaire Français, the only French fascist party officially recognized as such); a short, skinny Militia man still bitter about being declared unfit for service and better known as "the skunk"; and an ex-resistant. These three are responsible for most of the arrests in the area. They kill so as to have the opportunity to loot and steal, though their reports invariably state that they "were forced to shoot, since the suspect refused to show his papers and tried to escape." To prove his loyalty to Neumann, the ex-resistant denounces his group, and over thirty people are arrested. Some are questioned by Barbie himself and promptly "retired"; others are sent to Auschwitz or Buchenwald under two main labels: resistants and Jews.

The "skunk" spends his evenings drawing up lists: the names of the Jews in Saint-Etienne, followed by lists of their possessions (known or suspected) and a few lines of commentary: "X gets home regularly at 6:30 every evening. He rents the house where he lives with three children, his wife, his grandmother, and his parents-in-law. He has two servants. He has another house in the Ardèche where he keeps his most valuable possessions: original paintings and family silver. But how can we act in a region that's not under our jurisdiction?" It was the "skunk" who reputedly first informed Barbie about the children's home in Izieu.

However, Barbie doesn't seem to appreciate the "Neumann gang" as he should. "They stink," he says. Meanwhile, Neumann and his sidekicks despise the Germans at least as much as they are despised by them, and they are always trying to keep the Gestapo from getting credit for their actions.

The Kahn brothers join the Resistance in 1942. They haven't done so earlier only because they didn't know how to go about it. Mistrust and compartmentalization make contacts difficult. Pierre is the first to find a way in. A friend of his sister's, a Jewish lawyer, introduces him to Serge Ravanel. Ravanel is actually Serge Asher,

one of the masterminds of the "Liberation" network, along with
Lucie Aubrac and Emmanuel Astier de la Vigerie. Ravanel sizes
Pierre up and offers him a position creating and managing a service
producing forged documents. Pierre accepts. In 1943, people
haven't yet fully grasped the advantages of a false identity, but
Pierre immediately understands its importance. By the following
year, when "Liberation" joins the MUR, he is nationally known
by the nickname "False-Papers Pierre."

Pierre is one of the best-organized persons I have ever met; under
his management, an inefficient system of document forging becomes
a factory of false ID's in just a few months. Based on the identity
of people who have disappeared but have not yet been declared
dead, Pierre's ID's are utterly convincing. On the side, he also
produces food stamps, transportation passes, textile tags, anything
in demand. No one around him can complain of hunger or cold.
He is the king of counterfeiters. When he is arrested, on May 18,
1944, in Paris, he is both "Alias," the head of the MLN's national
service of forged documents, and "Plutus," the MLN's treasurer.

In the winter of 1942–43, the Loire region's branch of the MLN
(Mouvement de Libération Nationale) is looking for a leader. Robert Kahn has a house in the country, a business in Saint-Etienne,
and an easygoing manner which effectively conceals his patriotic
spirit. All these qualities make him an ideal candidate for the post.

In order to circulate freely and make some money on the side,
Robert, with the help of his ex-secretary, Philippe Frecon, manages
to secure a job as a salesman for a line of household products called
"Solitaire."

Robert does not discuss his Resistance activity with Jeanne. He
hates to keep secrets from her; "but it's for your safety and the
children's safety," he explains. "The less you know the better. Never
ask me what I do and whom I see. Be cautious. Don't talk to anybody
you don't know, and don't be too personal even with those you
know well. If anyone seems overly interested in you, let me know.
Let me know if you notice anything strange."

Everything seems strange to my mother these days: a new car
crossing the village, a stranger casually met at the bakery. She is

beside herself with worry. She even locks the gates to the garden, which she used to throw open every morning to let a neighbor's goats graze. Early one morning she refuses to open the gate to a very handsome young man with Aryan looks who wants to talk to her husband. She curtly informs him that her husband is away on business, and she does not know when he is coming back. He insists. She treats him harshly until Robert himself comes to open the gate. The man is just a neighbor.

Off at dawn, back late at night, Robert's lifestyle is beginning to look suspicious. Jeanne starts the rumor that she and her husband have separated and she is living alone with the children. People feel sorry for her and go out of their way to be kind; a glass of milk for the children, goat cheese for her, wool. Only after the war, when she goes back to Saint-Just before leaving it forever, will my mother understand the real reason behind these attentions: Most of those neighbors were working with Robert.

The guest room of Villa Bénédicte is always ready, as now and then Robert brings guests home. Jeanne is not supposed to know. They never leave the room except at night, when they go down to the dark kitchen to have a bite. They may stay one, two, or three days, and then they leave in the middle of the night. Fortunately, the only neighbors we have, the Chevalliers, live across a field; and their son, Pierre, gives Robert a hand whenever he can.

In 1942, Grandmother Kahn moves to Lyon under the name of Madame Mahé. She settles in Rue Cuvier, where she is soon joined by her son, Pierre Mahé, and a young friend of the family, a certain Mademoiselle Helene Rougerie: my Aunt Edmée, on her way to spend a few months with a handsome young man named Gaspard Jacquemin—my Uncle Jacques. Helene and Gaspard will return to Lyon to join the Resistance in 1943.

I have only two clear images of our last summer in Saint-Just. The first involves my discovery under a head of lettuce of a porcupine, which Bonne-maman gingerly dropped into her apron and brought into the kitchen. The other image is of a long, dark staircase with a carved banister that stretched from the hallway to the second floor. It seemed monumental (though my mother assures me it was quite average) to me as, two and a half years old, I played on its steps.

Meanwhile, my mother is more and more worried. She knows that the Lyon Gestapo is headed by a ruthless Nazi named Klaus Barbie. She knows they murder resistants under the pretext of reprisals, and has even heard of the cruelty of their interrogations. She begs Robert to abandon his activities and hide in Auvergne or Dordogne or anywhere else until the war is over. But he is intractable. "Go, if you want, with the children. You have reason to go, and I would feel better knowing you're safe. But I'm staying. You must understand: it is my duty as a Frenchman and a Jew."

She stays, but she can no longer stand being alone all day and asks Bonne-maman to join her over the holidays.

Like most resistants, my father was extraordinarily disciplined in his daring: "Risks can only be taken within the most rigorous guidelines," he had explained to my mother. "I'll never spend a single night out without your knowing beforehand. No matter what I do, I'll always be home for dinner. The day I'm not, it will mean something has happened to me, and you'll have to take care of yourself." But he had concluded with a jaunty smile: "I'm only telling you this because I know nothing'll ever happen to me."

Now night has fallen and Robert is not home. Bonne-maman gives us our dinner and then rushes us off to bed while our mother moves from one window to the next, peering into the darkness of the garden. Outside, the dense silence of the country is undisturbed. Hours go by. Steeped in moonlight, Jeanne sits on the steps of her porch drinking black tea. She has sent Bonne-maman to bed. She needs to be alone, alone with him whether he comes back or not. The hoot of an owl, the roar of a car engine fading away in the distance, the creaking of a branch, a dog barking, and she runs to the gate. By dawn, Jeanne, exhausted, has to give in. Either Robert has been in an accident, in which case she couldn't possibly be informed, since his identity and address are false, or he has been arrested. But why? As a Jew? As a resistant? As a resistant and a Jew? For an answer she must go to Saint-Etienne. She leaves us in

Bonne-maman's hands, along with all the money she has and the keys of the safe, just in case. With a pang of anguish, Bonne-maman watches her pedal away on her bicycle.

In three days, on September 6, Robert is going to be thirty-five, and in four days, on September 7, Jeanne will be thirty-one. The coincidence of their consecutive birthdays amused them when they first met, and every year they did something special to celebrate it. Once Robert surprised Jeanne by whisking her off to Florence. On her twenty-sixth birthday he gave her as many presents as she had years. It took her ages to unwrap them all, from cashmere sweater to nightcap.

She has been walking the main streets of Saint-Etienne since 8:30 A.M., trying her best to look like an average housewife taking her time shopping. Her patience soon pays off. Around ten o'clock a young man walks by and whispers, "Follow me at a distance." He is Fernand Levy, a friend and colleague of my father whom she has already met a couple of times. He walks on and she follows him, always leaving two or three people between them. Inside an apartment, Fernand tells her that Robert has been arrested and is wounded.

Late the previous morning, Robert was playing cards with three comrades in the back of a bar in Saint-Etienne. It was a pretext for a bimonthly meeting, fixed long in advance, during which the participants exchanged important information using the jargon of the card game. In addition to learning the game and all its terms, they also had to master a look and an attitude. They wore old clothes and caps, slouched in their seats, and told bawdy jokes like typical cardplaying Frenchmen. Behind this facade hid a business-man, a dental technician, a furrier, and a representative from a neighboring MUR network who had identified himself by showing half of a five-franc note the other half of which was in Robert's pocket.

They had been playing for barely a quarter of an hour when a group of armed civilians broke into the bar, sent by the Gestapo. The four men escaped through the back door of the bar. In vain.

My father was caught on the staircase of a building and stopped by a bullet in his left thigh as he was desperately trying to reach the roof.

Fernand falls silent. This is all he knows.

But I can imagine the scene clearly now: a dreary little bar with no sidewalk café, four small windows, and a narrow door letting in barely enough daylight to illuminate the dingy interior; worn wooden tables, a chipped counter, and behind the counter a tarnished, fly-specked mirror. The place reeks of cheap wine, stale tobacco, and the wet sawdust that the owner scatters on the gray tiled floor each morning.

At a rear table, four resistants play cards. They gather here about twice a month, order anisette or draft beer, and set themselves up with an oily pack of cards. Maurice, the owner, doesn't know where they come from or what they do. He senses they are no Nazi lovers. He isn't either, but lives by the maxim "The less you know, the better off you are."

That afternoon, the four barely have time to sit down before a group of armed civilians bursts through the door. The resistants rush to the back exit, which opens onto an alley. They run for the side streets, but in minutes they are caught, handcuffed, and shoved back into the bar, where Maurice is furiously mopping the counter.

Renaud has been shot in the thigh; blood is seeping through his trousers. At the moment of our father's capture, my brother and I are taking a nap barely twenty-five kilometers away, while our mother putters in the garden, trying to take her mind off her fears.

Many had tried to remind my father that, as a Jew, he was already in danger enough, and urged him to think of his wife and children, but his answer was always "Luck's on my side."

I was two and a half. My brother was going to be four. We would never see our father again. We wouldn't even remember him.

Fernand tells Jeanne what he can. He stands, places a hand on her shoulder. He is only twenty-four but looks older and more mature than she. He must leave the city immediately. He is himself in danger and fears for the safety of his parents. He wishes her the best of luck, and they hug. They leave the house separately. Under the name of Berton, Fernand goes to join my uncle's group in Lyon. He will then follow Pierre to Paris, where he will be arrested with him on May 18, 1944. Fernand will be among the nine hundred people who died of thirst and exhaustion on the train that left Compiègne on July 2, carrying 2,400 people to Dachau.

6 JUSTICE'S HONOR

Barbie will never define Nazi ideology. To do so would make it difficult for him to plead ignorance as to what happened to the trainloads of Jews he sent to Drancy. Instead, he reminisces about his various decorations and recommends that we look at the events of those days "in their proper context."

"I know that in one of the evaluations of my service there is a note concerning my abilities as an intelligence agent, and my responsibility in the dismantling of numerous enemy networks. . . . One of those reports describes me as 'Extremely dependable.' But I was only doing my duty. . . . I executed the orders I received. I behaved like any other SS officer."

The pages of Barbie's life after the end of the war are turned quite rapidly, up to the point where he was expelled from Bolivia and officially arrested in French Guiana: "My extradition is illegal. It is a violation of the Bolivian constitution. I do not consider myself a prisoner of France but its hostage. The Bolivian Supreme

Court is currently examining my appeal. Your Excellency, I would like to make a declaration."

Vergès passes him a note. With the spare, deliberate gestures of an old man, Barbie unfolds the piece of paper and irons it out with the palm of his hand. The president, who already knows what is in store, admonishes him: "Please, be brief."

Barbie reads: "I would like to tell my illustrious judges, and the ladies and gentlemen of the jury, that I am illegally detained in Lyon, since I am the victim of an abduction. Despite all the respect I have for you, Mr. President, Mr. Public Prosecutor, ladies and gentlemen of the jury, I must inform you that I am a Bolivian citizen, and that I find myself here before you because I have been illegally expelled from my country. I therefore no longer intend to appear before this court, and would very much appreciate it, Mr. President, if I could be taken back to the Saint-Joseph prison. Despite the climate of vengeance and the lynching campaign led by the media against me, I leave the whole matter in my attorney's hands. I trust him with my defense and justice's honor."

The courtroom is in an uproar. Former deportees suddenly find themselves deprived of the chance to confront their persecutor face to face. And the journalists have lost the chance to use that confrontation to dramatize their stories.

The rumor of Barbie's possible defection has been buzzing around the press box since the beginning of the trial. This is why, though disappointed, the journalists are not surprised by this coup de theatre, which they dub "the Abdallah precedent," after the Lebanese terrorist, Georges Ibrahim Abdallah, for whom Vergès had used the identical defense tactic just three months before.

Commotion is at its peak in the tiered rows where the plaintiff's attorneys sit. Their black gowns swell like waves in a storm, their voices overlap in their expressions of outrage and disgust. A couple of them stand to speak: one, Roger Souchal, says: "My words are neither motivated by hatred nor by a thirst for revenge, even though, when I was seventeen, I was tortured by the Gestapo. Still, I would have liked to see you face our witnesses with courage and look them straight in the eye. You are a coward."

But Henri Noguere, another attorney, adds, "This trial will lose none of its importance without you. Had you stayed, we would certainly have had to listen to a pack of lies. Your absence will spare us that."

There is no doubt in anybody's mind that Barbie is fleeing in fear. Pierre Truche, the public prosecutor, expresses the general sentiment well:

"There are several ways to question a man. It can be done the way it was done here, in Lyon, some forty-five years ago, with the questioned having no right to tell his questioners that he would rather not answer, that he would rather go back to his cell. It is to justice's honor, which you yourself have just invoked, that an accused have the opportunity to state his case and question his own accusers. But you prefer to play the role of Herr Nein, Mr. No. I understand that the name of Barbie must be a very heavy burden to bear. I even understand that he may not wish to confront what he did in the past. . . . The French legal system grants him the right not to. . . . [But] could it be that the triumphant Nazi is in fact only a shamefaced Nazi who doesn't dare face his past?"

Without answering, Barbie is escorted from the courtroom.

Barbie's judges could force him to attend all the proceedings, but they will only require his presence on three occasions: twice to confront victims who did not have the chance to identify him during the *instruction,* and the third time to hear the verdict.

Meanwhile in the courtroom it is the psychiatrists' turn to take the stand. Barbie has been examined by three experts—Dr. Didier Weber, Dr. Daniel Gonin, and Professor Jacques Vedrinne—and they have found him "an ordinary man, difficult to reach, unflinching in his sense of duty, loyal to a rigid ideology which forbade questioning, intolerant of any situation he may be unable to control." This may explain why he has chosen to leave the courtroom: Barbie the Gestapo chief was in control; Barbie the defendant is not.

The three doctors have spent long hours with their "subject," who, in his attempt to manipulate his interlocutors and to impress them with the image of a sensitive and highly cultured man, has ended up revealing aspects of his personality which belie his words. He has spoken of the war as a harsh, dirty affair in which military men had to fight against a bunch of faceless outlaws—this is how he saw the Resistance. "Those people were inveterate liars. We couldn't possibly treat them as soldiers," he told his doctors, concluding his remarks with this barb: "You are a decadent country, and you will remain one, since you refused the ideology we offered you."

"He is intelligent, sociable, with a marked Nazi outlook on at least two major issues: work and birth. Obsessed with social norms, he makes no distinction between genealogy and race. He is constantly invoking morality, but a morality of which he is the only worthy representative," Dr. Weber notes. Professor Vedrinne, instead, emphasizes another aspect of his subject's personality. "Barbie is convinced that all the problems of our age are a consequence of the disintegration of the family. He says that as a result today's youths don't read, and are indifferent to geography and history."

Dr. Gonin sees Barbie as "a man who believes himself capable of knowing all there is to know about people if given time. He manifests a radical refusal of otherness, which essentially means that he does not want to give of himself for fear of losing control over the other, and he is peculiarly unemotional."

In his cross-examination, Vergès tries—unsuccessfully—to have Dr. Gonin state that "What psychologists call lack of emotion is known as modesty in everyday language."

SEPTEMBER 1943

On her way back to Saint-Just, Jeanne begins to panic at the thought that she has left her children and her mother alone. She pedals faster; she wants to be with them when the Gestapo comes for them.

At the end of the driveway everything seems calm. She hears the children's voices beyond the wall and that of Bonne-maman calling them for lunch. Jeanne's knees are weak. At least they are still with her, but for how long?

Jeanne calls Lyon to inform Matko, rather, Madame Mahé. They speak in code: "Good morning, Madame Mahé, this is Jeanne speaking. I was planning on paying you a short visit today but I'm afraid I've been sick and must stay home." At the other end, her mother-in-law, who has already been informed, answers in a strained voice: "I'm so sorry. Yesterday evening my son told me he saw the doctor stop by your house. We all hope it's nothing serious. We think of you and hope we'll see you very soon."

On that dismal evening, Jeanne believes there is still hope. If the Germans haven't come for us yet, they probably aren't coming. While Bonne-maman takes care of us, she shuttles back and forth between Saint-Just and Saint-Etienne, and visits the foundries and steel mills of Bernay every morning, to see Philippe Frecon. In front of the workers they talk business, but in the privacy of the boss's office Philippe tells her whatever news he has gathered.

Robert has been brought to the Gestapo headquarters in Saint-Etienne along with his comrades. He has been interrogated. He has been beaten, but he is alive. My father has a number of false identities, but his "true" Resistance name is Renaud. That name is not on the SS's lists. The man must be an outsider, the Gestapo decides, but not an innocent one, since he tried to escape. They question him, and when he refuses to answer, they whip him, systematically, from the back of the neck down to the knees. Robert says nothing until the second day. Then he lies, or rather reveals part of the truth the better to conceal the whole. The SS hasn't suspected that he might be a Jew. He doesn't look Jewish. He is circumcised, but they haven't bothered to check. My father knows what it means to be a Jew in 1943, but he also knows that to be a member of the Resistance, now that the Gestapo is intensifying its efforts to wipe it out, is worse. So he tells them he is a Jew, and that he has assumed a false identity to save his skin.

The risk is enormous, but Robert's ploy works. Suddenly the Gestapo loses interest. He is of no consequence. They are not going to waste any more time on him. And they think he's single, so he can rest assured that Jeanne and the kids are safe. But he has to find a way to get out. He alone knows how to reach dozens of people whose lives are in great danger. He must establish some contact with the outside world. But how? While waiting to find a way, he asks to be transferred to Bellevue Hospital, as the bullet is still in his thigh, and the wound is getting infected.

On September 5, a uniformed police officer rings the bell at Jeanne's gate. In a booming voice, he informs her that he is taking a census of the non-native population of the area, of which Jeanne's family seems to be a part. Uneasily, my mother lets him in. Once in the kitchen, his tone of voice changes. He is one of my father's men. He is also one of the guards in the hospital's prisoner ward. He has seen my father and his companions. Some have bullet wounds and all have been tortured.

"But none of them has squealed," he reports proudly. Then he pulls a piece of paper from his pocket and hands it to Jeanne: a note from Renaud. While he discreetly walks to the window, Jeanne fumbles with the note. It is Robert's writing: "Don't worry. I am doing what I can to get out of here. The MUR is taking care of it. But the children must be protected. A woman who works for the MUR will pay you a visit. Trust her. She will take your mother and the children to your aunt's in Angers. It is the only solution. I am sure she will be glad to help them. Don't worry about them. They'll be safe. As for you, act as normally as you can. Show your face around, go shopping, go visit the farmers nearby, and wait for my notes. You'll soon be told what to do."

Jeanne puts herself in the MUR's hands. Bonne-maman packs a few bags and gets the kids ready for the trip. The following evening, an unknown young woman arrives at the door. Bonne-maman and my mother hug in silence. My mother squeezes us in one big hug, and then watches us joyfully climb into the car. We are so excited, we don't even turn to wave goodbye.

The trip from Saint-Just to Angers goes smoothly. After the young woman's car, we ride through the country in three different trucks. When Aunt Léontine sees us, she doesn't seem too surprised, but she is worried. Her meager food rations are not enough to feed three more. But Aunt Léontine, a widow with a firm hand and masculine voice, is a resourceful woman. She knows there are people in the country who can neither read nor write. She will keep their books and write their letters in exchange for food. And she quickly sends her sister to City Hall to try to get more coupons.

Bonne-maman waits in line in front of the food stamp window for hours. Eventually she faces a bald, stocky man who is sweating and looks as if he has no neck. When, with her shrill little voice, Bonne-maman starts explaining her situation to him—"I am a refugee. I am in charge of two smalll children I can't declare as my dependents, since their father has been arr—" —the man cuts her short. "Shut up! I don't have time to listen to your life story. Leave me your name and address, we'll take care of the rest." Bonne-maman doesn't understand. If she weren't so flustered, she would give that rude city servant—he doesn't even dare look her in the eye—a piece of her mind.

Fortunately, the man has a conscience, and he registers us under false identities as "health refugees." The food stamps and other coupons arrive in time and will keep being renewed until we leave, after Liberation.

Back home, Bonne-maman can't even wait to take off her hat before giving her sister a detailed account of what happened. She is surprised when her sister doesn't compliment her. On the contrary, Léontine looks horrified. Two children whose father has just been arrested for being a Jew—and whose mother cannot prove she is an Aryan because in her atheist family children have not been christened for generations—are two doomed children.

"Augustine, you didn't! You did not tell him that!"

"Of course I did! How could we manage otherwise!"

"Do you realize that in five minutes, maybe an hour, they will be at the door asking for the children? And it will be your fault? You're so self-righteous you don't even realize that half of France is collaborating with the enemy and that if your grandchildren are found out they'll go straight to hell."

Bonne-maman turns pale. She suddenly sees the possible consequences of her indiscretion. There isn't a minute to waste.

Aunt Léontine has a daughter who lives in one small room, right across the street from her. We are going to trade places. Our cousin is going to move back with her mother, and the three of us are going to squeeze into our cousin's room. We'll move back only when Aunt Léontine is sure that her sister's blunder has had no effect. But the citizens of small provincial towns are curious and love to talk. We must not be seen or heard, and it is not easy to keep two small children from screaming, crying, or laughing. So Aunt Léontine decides to bring us, as soon as she can, to her brother, Uncle Valentin, who lives in the country where both he and his wife, Madeleine, are teachers. Pruillé is a small village whose schoolyard and big round-headed chestnuts I will never forget. Aunt Léontine has a brilliant idea: What better way to hide children than mixing them up with other children?

Meanwhile, Jeanne's first and last night alone in Saint-Just is harrowing. The house creaks. In the morning she finds an envelope by the garden wall. The note inside tells her to pack a few things—the minimum, so as not to attract attention—and all her jewels and money, and go to the Andrezieux station, either during the night or at dawn. There, she must take the train to Saint-Etienne and find her way to the headquarters of a road transport business managed by a woman named Dora Founier. That night, Jeanne follows the instructions to the letter. One last look at the moonlit garden, one last twinge of regret, and she is on her way.

It is still dark outside when Dora, who is already waiting in her office, hears footsteps on the sidewalk. She looks outside and sees a hesitant young woman with a traveling bag. The streets are still deserted under the steady drizzle; quickly, Dora lets Jeanne in. They look at each other for a moment, then they hug.

Dora leads Jeanne to a small room where there is only an old sunken sofa and a strong smell of bleach. Jeanne must sit there alone in the dark. Nobody must know she is there. The moment Dora has news she'll let her know. Jeanne is shivering and can't keep her teeth from chattering. Dora brings her a sedative: "Sleep, Jeanne," she tells her gently. "It's the best way to kill time."

In the middle of the afternoon, the door bursts open, jolting Jeanne out of a heavy, troubled slumber. The sun is filtering in through the closed shutters. Dora is radiant as she hands Jeanne an apple. "It worked. You must run to Lyon. Robert is waiting for you at nine Rue de Silly, second floor to the left." Jeanne twists her ankle while hurrying to the station and is limping when in the evening she reaches the sparsely furnished apartment where Robert, his mother, and Uncle Pierre are waiting for her. They open a bottle of champagne, a relic of better times preserved for just such a great event. The champagne is lukewarm, the glasses are old coffee cups, but who cares. Snuggled in Robert's arms, Jeanne listens as he tells the story of his escape. . . .

The day after Robert Renaud's arrest, Lucie Aubrac, the head of the "Libération" network, pays a visit to False-Papers Pierre to keep him posted about the escape plans for her husband, Raymond—who, under the name of Claude Ermelin, was arrested with Jean Moulin at the famous rendezvous in Caluire. She finds Pierre terribly upset. She knows nothing about Robert's arrest, but Pierre tells her what little he knows.

Lucie and Raymond have a son roughly Paul-Emile's age, and Lucie is expecting another child. A history teacher in the girls' high school on Place Edgar-Quinet, she has been part of "Libération" from the beginning. She knows everyone. Through a friend's friend who is a prison guard, and through another friend who is related to a police officer, Lucie learns that all four prisoners are currently in Bellevue Hospital. Not too promising, but it could be worse. Only last spring, Lucie and some friends freed three comrades from the Antiquaille Hospital by posing as Gestapo officers. The action itself is nothing compared to its preparation. Lucie contacts Ravanel, the man who introduced Pierre to the Resistance, who had helped her with the operation at the Antiquaille. He is ready to act; he needs the exercise. He says, "It's good for the circulation." He offers Lucie three cars and three young men who immediately assure her of their commitment.

Lucie pays a visit to a Dr. Riva to borrow a white smock, white cap, and stethoscope. She will commute to Saint-Etienne every day to "play doctor" in the corridors of Bellevue, shuttling between the ICU and the surgery room, checking patients' records, expertly reading the progress reports attached to the foot of every patient's bed. In less than three days, she is known by all the nurses and hospital staff, and no one questions her authenticity. By then, she knows where the prisoner ward is.

One morning, Lucie strides past the guards into the room, walks up to the first bed, and, leaning over the patient, says, "Tell Pierre's brother that I'll be back." That afternoon she finds two new guards. They also let her pass. Once inside, Dr. Aubrac takes her time. She soon figures out who the four resistants are. Fortunately, they occupy contiguous beds. She takes their blood pressure, then leans over their bare chests, moving the stethoscope slowly from the navel to the armpits while she whispers, "We are coming to get you tomorrow or the day after at the latest. Officially, we will be taking you to the Gestapo. Protest. Raise hell. But don't overdo it."

The next day, Dr. Aubrac and six men leave Lyon in three black Citroens with fake license plates and a few German stickers on windshields and rear windows.

As soon as they get to the hospital, Lucie rushes up to the ward to make sure everything is in order. One of the cars waits outside, while the other two enter the courtyard. Two Gestapo officers climb out. One informs the hospital administrator, with a perfect German accent, that he has come to fetch the four prisoners, and rattles off their names. The administrator protests and tries to stop them. Meanwhile, upstairs, Dr. Aubrac, who is pacing nervously up and down in front of the ward, sees a doctor and two male nurses approach from the other end of the hallway. They march straight into the room and soon emerge carrying Robert on a stretcher. Robert and Lucie look at each other questioningly. Suddenly the two Gestapo officers, followed by a gesticulating administrator, appear at the top of the staircase and block the way.

"We have come to take this man and his three companions," the one with the perfect German accent announces.

"As you can see," the administrator protests, "you can't possibly take this man. He is on his way to surgery. If you really want him, you can come back tomorrow."

But the officers are determined to carry out their orders. Brandishing their guns, they kick Robert's stretcher. He struggles to his feet and then, much to everyone's surprise, asks the administrator to let him go, since clearly the Gestapo is not taking his protests too kindly.

While the four prisoners are driven off in the two cars that waited in the courtyard, Lucie changes her clothes in a bathroom and quietly leaves the hospital. All three cars are waiting for her just around the corner. It is an emotional ride back to Lyon along deserted mountain roads. At Dardilly, the cars separate. Robert gets in with Lucie. His wound is causing him a great deal of pain, and her pregnancy is making her uncomfortable and tired. They hold hands like old friends. By the time they arrive at Grandmother's apartment, Lucie is the one who needs attention the most.

That day, my father forgot to thank her. He probably thought he had a life's worth of thanksgiving ahead of him.

7   Carte Blanche

May 14, 1987

The testimony this afternoon is devoted to Barbie's extradition from Bolivia. Gustavo Sanchez Salazar—Bolivia's Minister of the Interior in the leftist government that came to power in 1982 under President Heman Siles Zuazo—is the first to take the stand. Squat, slick, and tan, and wearing a very rumpled linen suit, Mr. Sanchez (an agricultural engineer since the fall of Zuazo's regime) speaks volubly and energetically about Barbie's activities in Bolivia.

"When General Banzer seized power in 1971," he explains, "Klaus Barbie was given carte blanche to organize a system to get rid of opponents of the new regime. [It was a system composed of] prisoner camps, tortures, and executions. France's 1972 extradition request was hopeless, because judicial power was then in the service of the military. It is because of this affront to freedom, this shameful past that we decided to do all we could to ensure that the Butcher of Lyon, whose service record we knew well, be judged at the site of his crimes."

The ex-minister goes on to describe Barbie's contribution to

Bolivia's military dictatorship: "On August 4, 1981, I was at the military barracks in Cochabamba, where I saw Barbie, or Altmann, call him what you please, it doesn't matter since he is the same man. He was in charge of suppressing the insurrection in Santa Cruz. . . . On that particular day, thousands of workers were killed and hundreds of civilians were arrested. It was the darkest day in Bolivian history, and Barbie played a very active, a prominent role in it. In our land—which is not his—he created a squad of mur-derers, Los Novios de la Muerte, the 'Fiancés of Death,' a sort of superpowerful militia that came to the aid of the official army whenever they had their hands tied, or when they balked at using more radical methods. . . . This group drew most of its resources from the drug trade, with the blessings and protection of the gov-ernment of General Luis Garcia Meza. His Minister of the Interior was Colonel Arce Gomez, otherwise known as 'Mr. Cocaine.' Gomez was very impressed with Barbie. What I am offering you here is sheer speculation. I cannot prove that Barbie was also directly involved in the drug trade, but given what I have just told you, we are quite sure he was.

"He acquired Bolivian citizenship under a false name and birth date. His naturalization was therefore flawed from the start. . . . According to Bolivian law, a presidential decision is enough to validate an expulsion. Our duty was to hand Barbie over to those who wanted him, that is, you."

Maître Vergès tries to shake up the witness by calling him "Mr. Five Thousand Dollars" in response to "Mr. Cocaine." He asked him whether his "democratic conscience had anything to do with the greenbacks stuffed in your pocket" in 1972, when he helped Serge Klarsfeld and Regis Debray organize an attempted kidnap of Barbie.

"Yes, it is true, I received money for it, and it didn't work. But democracy cannot be bought. That money was supposed to be used solely for the kidnap, and was in fact spent entirely on its prepa-rations."

The jurors take notes.

The Bolivian witness is followed by Erhard Dabringhaus, a German-American university professor now retired in Florida. In the years immediately following the war, he worked as a civilian agent for the American Counter-Intelligence Corps (CIC) in Germany. There, on June 15, 1948, he met "two important informers whom I was asked to move from Kempten to Augsburg. They were Josef Merk (a.k.a. Kurt Merk) and Klaus Barbie. The latter nonchalantly introduced himself as a former officer of the German SD. It sort of shocked me, since I was well aware of what the SD had been during the Occupation; I felt humiliated for having to work with that kind of person. The other, Merk, told me he was an ex-captain in the Abwehr, the intelligence service of the German army—a more respectable outfit.

"Captain George Spiller, who had introduced me to Barbie, confidently told me that if one day the French were to find the mass graves Barbie left in his wake, not even Eisenhower would be able to protect him. I passed all I knew along to my superiors. They said, 'We know, but Barbie is still too useful to us. We'll hand him over to the French as soon as we no longer need him.'

"I also heard someone say that, for a while, Barbie had spied on the French secret services in Germany," Dabringhaus continues. "It's quite possible. He poked his nose into everything. If he spied on the French it was probably to find out where he stood with French justice. In fact, the only thing that mattered to him, in the intelligence work he did for us, was to accumulate dollars, more and more dollars. There is nothing he wouldn't have done for American dollars. He would palm off as scoops stories I had already read in yesterday's papers, or he would resell stuff he had bought at our commissary—coffee, chocolate, cigarettes—on the black market for a big profit. He was a shameless opportunist. I was delighted when I heard he had fled through the Rat Line to South America, I found it very appropriate. You see," he goes on, obviously ill at ease, "we were instructed to tell the French we knew nothing about Barbie's whereabouts. But if I had been told exactly why they were looking for him, and how many people he had actually killed, then I would have told the French, 'Follow me, I'll take you to him.' "

For several years, Dabringhaus tried to get the American media to focus their attention on Klaus Altmann's past. But no one wanted to publicize the fact that the CIC had employed ex-Nazis. When Barbie was handed over to France, however, Professor Dabringhaus appeared on almost every network.

"I brought my evidence, but public opinion resented me for having sullied the name of the American army. . . . In a two-hundred-and-eighteen-page report published in 1983, Allan A. Ryan, Jr., the head of the Special Investigation Bureau of the U.S. Department of Justice, confirmed everything I had said. He encouraged the American government to present its apologies to France for having so long hindered the due process of its justice, and to offer its help to the Cour d'Assises of Lyon."

In his testimony yesterday, Barbie claimed he had been blackmailed to work for the U.S. "To force my hand, the Americans held my son, Klaus Junior (three years old at the end of the war), hostage for almost two years in the house of a midwife who lived in Kassel. My first condition, when I accepted their offer, was that they immediately free my child."

SEPTEMBER 1943

At the little reunion in Lyon, Robert looks deathly pale. He suddenly feels very tired; the strain of the last few weeks is catching up with him. The stinging memory of his arrest, and the beatings that followed, mingles with the pain his wound is still causing him, and his excitement at finding himself free again with the people he loves—his mother, his brother, and his wife. Pierre realizes that it is time to leave and, complaining of hunger, manages to drag his mother away.

Jeanne and Robert are alone at last in that little apartment, with a can of sardines, Grandmother's rabbit stew, grapes, and some candles. After the war, candlelit dinners will become very chic, but in 1944 they are a necessity for people in hiding. The flickering flame casts a magnified shadow of their entangled bodies on the wall. Jeanne is caressing her husband's back when suddenly her fingertips wander across strange bumps and furrows. His moans are not of pleasure. She brings the candle closer: Robert's back is one massive bruise.

The following day they must get down to business and find a new apartment, since the tenant of the one they are in, a school administrator who spends her weekdays in Grenoble and comes back to Lyon for the weekend, does not know they are there. She always leaves a set of keys with her neighbor, who is a member of Pierre's group. As a result, the comforts of her apartment are often appreciated by fugitives who come and go while she is away. Her neighbor is not sure enough of her political leanings to dare ask her for a service she already performs so well unawares.

Robert and Jeanne must clear out of that apartment as soon as possible and find something discreet away from the center of Lyon. To go back to Saint-Etienne or Saint-Just is unthinkable. "We'll create new memories and we'll buy new furniture, but for now we have to save our skins. We can't waste any time looking back," Robert admonishes Jeanne.

Jeanne agrees. Not only do they have to find a new place, but they have to forget who they are. They must masquerade as an average working-class couple with little education, with Jeanne playing the role of a proletarian housewife. Robert doubts whether she can pull it off, and Jeanne is ready to prove him wrong when they both hear a knock on the door, and freeze. The knock is followed by a whisper. It is Pierre; he says he has brought the plumber. Why a plumber? There are no leaks in the apartment. Jeanne gingerly opens the door. With Pierre is a little man in overalls and sandals, carrying what looks like a heavy tool bag. But his hands are white and well manicured. He walks in and quickly shuts the door. "Don't worry, I'm a doctor. I've come to get his bullet out, but he will have to be brave because I have very little anesthetic, barely enough for a local shot." As he talks, the physician opens his bag and starts pulling out his tools: a wrench, rubber washers, tubing, pipe cutters, a hammer. "Hey, Doc, you may not realize it, but I'm not a faucet," Robert jokes while the doctor removes the false bottom to reveal a set of shiny surgical instruments. Willy-nilly, Jeanne must play nurse.

Fortunately, the bullet hasn't traveled too far, and the doctor has all the anesthetic he needs. At last he brandishes the little metal object like a trophy. Maybe Robert wants to keep it as a souvenir? "No, thanks," Robert replies. "It belongs in the garbage."

"Are you nuts?" the doctor exclaims. "When everybody is rummaging through it in search of something to sell or eat? It belongs in the toilet!" With his hammer, he flattens the bullet beyond recognition. Then he gives Jeanne some medication to disinfect the wound and an ointment for Robert's back, and he leaves.

Robert already feels better, convinced more than ever that he was born under a lucky star. He has regained his freedom and his Jeanne. He misses his children, but knows they are safe in Angers, thanks to a brief message: "Aunt Léontine has received the package with the cake, the cheese-spread, and the coffee."

Back in Angers, Bonne-maman sighs. "Ah, my poor children. When is all this going to end?" Puzzled, we climb into her lap, subconsciously knowing that she needs our warmth as much as we need hers. "Where are Mommy and Daddy?" we ask. "They're working. They're very busy, but they're coming home soon, very soon." This is, indeed, what Bonne-maman hopes: that her son-in-law will stop playing soldier and bring Jeanne to Angers. Isn't the place of a husband and father by his family's side? More patriotic than Bonne-maman, Léontine is infuriated by this sort of argument.

"Do you want to become German? Don't you see your country's going to hell? Don't you know what they're doing to the Jews? Do you at least know whom your son is fighting against and what he's fighting for? You should be proud of him!"

It's no secret that Léontine adores Robert, and that the feeling is reciprocal. But Bonne-maman is not stupid. She knows exactly what her sister is talking about, yet she trusts her feelings.

"I know you're right, Léontine. Believe me, I feel the same way. I can't stand hearing German spoken all over the city, seeing Germans downing our best wine as if it were beer. It hurts. And I can't understand how they can exterminate Jews as if they were cock-roaches. It's incomprehensible. But I just have the feeling that something awful is going to happen, and I want Robert and Jeanne here, with their children."

Léontine shrugs. While they bicker, Poumi and I lie on the kitchen floor, drawing a picture with a few crayons and a used piece of packing paper. It is "for Mommy and Daddy," but it will never be sent. Bonne-maman and Aunt Léontine don't know where they are. If anything happens to us, Bonne-maman must send a cable to Philippe Frecon saying that "Celestin House Expects Visit Regional Business Manager," and he will get a message to Jeanne and Robert.

The day after the doctor's visit, Jeanne and Robert start looking for an apartment. Jeanne remembers a distant cousin of her mother's who manages a grocery on Rue d'Anvers, the Dock Lyonnais. She pays Elise Pardou a visit while Robert follows another lead. Elise, a hardy woman fresh from the country, knows a young couple right across the street who have to leave Lyon and are looking for someone to take over their apartment. She gives Jeanne a rapid once-over: auburn hair, fashionably cut and curled, a freshly polished leather bag, tailored dress, perfectly tended nails. Elise shakes her head.

"On second thought, I'm not sure it's your kind of place. You're not used to this sort of neighborhood; you're going to stick out like a sore thumb."

"Don't worry," my mother answers. "I can do without lots of things, provided I have some water to wash and a comb for my hair. I don't even need running water; I can adapt to just about anything."

The apartment is on the second floor of a dingy little house. The dark hallway looks like a bowel, the steps are slimy. Three doors open onto each landing, those of two apartments and a third, left ajar, and exuding a powerful stench: the common toilet. My mother feels queasy. Do they really have to live in such a hole? She knocks on the door. An emaciated middle-aged woman opens it with reluctance mixed with mistrust. My mother will never forgive herself for giving such little importance to the expression on a woman's face.

The apartment consists of two rooms, with cracked walls smeared with saltpeter. There are large water stains covering the ceiling, and the only faucet sits high above an ancient sink black with grime. The kitchen is lit only by a small skylight. The place is filthy, musty, smelly—horrible—but for that very reason ideal. Nobody would think of looking for Robert here. They can move in immediately. The next day they bring along gallons of bleach, scrub brushes, mops, and rags, even though they don't intend to stay long.

These days, all the members of the family living in Lyon meet at my grandmother's for tea every afternoon. It is the best way to make sure everyone is all right, and it is the only place where Grandmother's two sons—who are close both as brothers and as best friends—can see each other. Outside, they are strangers. Robert wouldn't miss one of these meetings for anything in the world. Going to Grandmother's afternoon tea is like "checking in at work," he says.

Since Robert's arrest, "Madame Mahé" has been living in constant fear. Pierre is also worried, and tries to make Robert understand that since his escape his position has become much more precarious. Barbie and his Gestapo must be wondering who Renaud is, and why he is so precious to the Resistance. Pierre tries to persuade him that he is needed in Paris, or in Marseille to work in the false papers business. My exhausted mother agrees with her brother-in-law. To force Robert's hand, she buys two tickets for the Lyon–Marseille train that very same evening, September 21. It is a night train, the safest.

For once, Grandmother and Jeanne agree, but to no avail. Robert's mind is made up. "I'm not leaving. Jeanne, you're free to go when you want to. I'll join you as soon as possible. But first I have to get in touch with my successor in Saint-Etienne."

Jeanne cannot understand how Robert can be so selfish, so insensitive as to put his duty as a Jew and a resistant above his love and concern for his own wife and children. If he's killed, the Resistance will find someone else to take his place; but his children will be fatherless.

Tempers run high that evening in the dingy apartment on Rue d'Anvers. Jeanne and Robert go to bed angry. The next morning they are calmer but still far from reconciled. They barely look at each other over their toast and bowls of ersatz coffee.

My mother has some shopping to do, and an old lady to visit— an arthritic piano teacher who lives at the other end of the city. My father is still at home when she leaves. They are still so miffed they don't even bother to say goodbye when they part; they know they'll see each other that afternoon at Grandmother's tea.

It is a gray, rainy day. When Jeanne reaches Rue Cuvier fairly early that afternoon, her feet are soaked. By and by, the others arrive. The first is Uncle Stanislas Feintuch, one of Grandmother's brothers. He lost four of his five children in the July 17 raid on the Vélodrome d'Hiver in Paris over a year before, and he has had no news of them since. Then Pierre. Edmée, "Mademoiselle Helene" for the neighbors, is in Paris with Jacques Baumel, her boss, helping to organize the fusion of all Resistance networks from north to south.

Only Robert is missing. The tea begins to get cold, and the conversation flags. Five-thirty P.M., six P.M. Everyone's head is bowed.

By six-thirty there is no more hope. Jeanne feels drained from within; miracles don't happen twice. She borrows a dark hood from her mother-in-law and, protected from the rain, runs to Rue d'Anvers. Everything looks calm there; the windows of the apartment are closed. Before going home, Jeanne passes in front of the Dock Lyonnais. Elise, who is helping a customer, stares at her meaningfully and waves a finger from right to left. Jeanne understands. She must not go up; Robert has been caught.

As Jeanne will learn later, when the Gestapo broke into their apartment around noon, they were looking for the previous tenant, Roger Moreau, a communist they had been after for a long time. Instead, they found someone who showed them papers in the name

of Robert Renaud. But as far as the Gestapo officers, accompanied
by two Militia men, were concerned, Renaud was Moreau, and as
such they hauled him off to the Ecole de Santé.

Elise saw the Militia men shove him into a van and drive away.
She does not know whether the Gestapo are still in the apartment.
She tells all this to Jeanne while pretending she is helping her
choose some merchandise. But Jeanne is visibly shaken, and so is
Elise. Jeanne is already out the door when, feebly, Elise tells her,
"If I can help you in any way, let me know."

Jeanne has nowhere to go except to her mother-in-law's. But she
won't be able to stay there long. With Robert newly arrested, the
entire family will have to disperse. In the meantime, however,
everybody has been anxiously awaiting her return. When she finds
herself surrounded by all those questioning eyes, the strength she
was able to muster in the trolley and in the street dissolves in a
torrent of tears. Shaken by sobs, she can't say a word, but she
doesn't need to.

8 NIGHT AND FOG

<u>MAY 15, 1987</u>

This first week of the trial ends with a session that would delight only an archivist: readings of documents, some concerning Barbie's civilian past, most documenting his role as the head of Section IV of the SIPO-SD (the acronym for Hitler's combined police services) in Lyon. Meanwhile, the plaintiffs' lawyers are arguing over whether or not to let Barbie skip the rest of the trial. Some think it's best to let him be; others, prodded by their clients, are determined to persuade the president to invoke an article of the penal code which would force the prisoner to confront his victims.

"Didn't we use force to bring Barbie back to France? And now you are afraid to use force *legally?*" argues Maître Alain Jakubowicz, counsel for the International League Against Racism and Anti-Semitism.

Maître Gérard Welzer, representing three victims, ponders the implications of a forced appearance:

"If we force Barbie to be present at his trial, it will be a victory for him which he will know how to exploit. Just think of what would happen if he were suddenly ill and unable to come to court for several weeks. We would have to suspend the hearings until some later date. This trial has been proceeding smoothly, let's not hinder it."

Again, it is Pierre Truche who takes the stand to put an end to this debate:

"This trial is still in its abstract phase. It is easy, at this point, to wonder whether we should have held it at all, since, after all, we are now allies of Germany. On the other hand, the civil parties, the only victims, have reason to be angry for having to participate in a depersonalized debate. It's true, we could force Barbie to attend. But what for? What would we gain by having someone who refuses to speak in the defendant's box? We can force Barbie to be physically present in the courtroom, but we cannot force him to speak. No doubt, there will be times when we'll want him to come and confront the witnesses. And what will we see then? An old man in a wheelchair. His refusal to attend this trial is everything you say: an excuse, an escape, a shame, a defeat, a failure. But it is above all a victory for his victims. I have no desire to watch him play the martyr. We will soon move on to the more concrete phase of the proceedings, the testimony of the victims. Then we won't need Barbie's presence for the world to realize that there was a time in our recent history when it was decided that all men were not equal."

Maître Vergès mumbles something to the effect that if his client is forced to appear, he himself will resign. The final word is left to President Cerdini. He sees no reason, "for the time being," to force the defendant to attend the proceedings.

Meanwhile, the court must determine the actual limits of Barbie's powers as head of Section IV of the SIPO-SD in Lyon between November 1942 and August 1944. The first SD commander for Lyon and the region was Werner Knab. As head of Section IV, Barbie was second in command. Section IV was divided into six subsections, or bureaus, one of which, IV B, run by Erich Bartelmus, was exclusively in charge of Jewish affairs. The question is whether this subsection operated autonomously, as Barbie maintains, or whether it was under his direct orders. Barbie has repeatedly contradicted himself on this point, as evidenced by the declarations President Cerdini now reads aloud:

February 24, 1983: "Jewish affairs were the responsibility of the regional commanders—the regional commander in Lyon was Werner Knab. They were directly appointed by Eichmann. I had nothing to do with the work of this subsection and its deportations."

March 24, 1983: "I had authority over subsection B, in charge of Jewish affairs, through my subordinate [Otto Wolfgang] Wenzel, who was later replaced by [Erich] Bartelmus. But they also received their orders from other quarters: from Kurt Lischka, of the Paris Gestapo, and from Eichmann in Berlin."

March 30, 1983: "Werner Knab received his orders from Paris and then passed them on to me, and I, in turn, passed them on to the subsection in charge of Jewish affairs."

March 18, 1986: "I was in command of all the subsections of Section IV . . . except for the one in charge of Jewish affairs, which was autonomous."

Once Barbie's position as leader of this section is established, the court must move on to examine the role he played in the Gestapo raids on the UGIF offices and on the children's home in Izieu.

Three documents implicate him in the former. One is the Lyon SIPO-SD report sent to Helmut Knochen in Paris on February 11, 1943. The report is signed *"Der Leiter des Einsatzkommando, SS— Obersturmführer Klaus Barbie."* In March 1983, Barbie admitted having signed the document but quibbled about the "by order of" preceding his title and signature. He claimed that Knab was absent, and that he, as second in command, had to sign in his place. Later, however, after learning that the document was provided by the Contemporary Jewish Documentation Center, a private organization, he even questioned the authenticity of his signature. He also questioned the authenticity of the other two documents: one a telegram sent to Knochen the day after the raid, specifying that "the Jews arrested are in the care of the Germans and will be shipped on to the appropriate camps," and the other a telegram concerning the escape of two of the prisoners. Confronted with this last document during the *instruction*, Barbie first authenticated the signature, then questioned it, then maintained it was not his.

The bailiff pulls a third telegram from its plastic envelope with extraordinary delicacy, this one incriminating Barbie in the raid on the children's home in Izieu. It reads:

Lyon, 4-6-1944. 8:10PM.
Re: children's home in Izieu (Ain).

Early this morning, the Jewish children's home, the "Children's Colony" in Izieu, was closed down. A total of forty-one children, aged between three and thirteen,* were arrested. Besides them, all the Jewish personnel—consisting of ten people, including five women—were also arrested. We did not find any money or other valuables. Their transport to Drancy will follow on 4-7-1944.

DER KDR. DER SIPO UND SD LYON ROEM. 4B 61/43—
I.A. GEZ. BARBIE SS-OSTUF.

This is probably the most serious of all the charges brought against Barbie. Throughout the four years of the *instruction*, Barbie has insisted the telegram is a fake, and a bad fake at that; after all, it comes from the Contemporary Jewish Documentation Center. The defense refuses to accept this document as evidence because:

1. It is not signed in Barbie's own hand.
2. The mention I.A. (*Im Aufrag*), literally, "by order of," means that Barbie sent the cable in somebody else's place, as in the case of the telegram dated February 11, 1943.
3. It is printed on the back of a map of England.
4. The postmark is in French and not in German.
5. On April 6, Barbie was fighting against the Maquis in the Jura.

---

*Three fifteen- and sixteen-year-olds are numbered here among the adults. With the help of some of Robert Renaud's old cellmates, I can reconstruct only a fragile outline.

Judge Christian Riss refutes the defense's objections point by point:

1. Of course the signature is not in Barbie's hand; the telegram in question is the one received by Knochen in Paris. It would have been hard for Barbie, who was in Lyon, to sign a document in Paris. On the other hand, Barbie's name, faithfully typed by the employee who received the text, is followed by the official abbreviation of the sender's rank: Barbie SS-Ostuf (*Obersturmführer*).

2. The letters "I.A." are an SS formality indicating that the person in question is communicating within the scope of his own responsibilities. If Barbie had sent the telegram, as he maintains, in the place of a momentarily absent or indisposed superior, he would have used the letters "I.V.," that is, *Im Vertretung*, "on behalf of."

3. The paper used by the telegram receiving services, on which are glued the typed strips spewed by the machine, was indeed the back of maps representing part of Great Britain. Whole stocks of such maps had been printed in Germany in 1940, in view of an imminent invasion of England, and had soon become obsolete. But the scarcity of paper in France, which forced the Germans to use whatever they had, had put them back into circulation. Several other telegrams, including one sent the very same day from Marseille, were pasted on the back of such maps at the SIPO-SD Parisian Communication Services.

4. The French postmark is at least as frequent as the German one on all official correspondence. Sometimes both were used together.

5. How could Barbie have been absent from Lyon on April 6 when the legal investigation has discovered an official pass which Barbie processed in Lyon that very day?

MAY 18, 1987

In the courtroom, we journalists are getting to know each other, becoming friends. This week we will hear the first of many witnesses. There is some tension in the air, mixed with impatience and fear.

By now, all the plaintiffs, with their gray or white hair, their wrinkles, and their uncertain steps, have become familiar. I am anxious to see them again and in the last sixty hours have often wondered how they were spending their weekends. With their families? Alone, besieged by memories? Mentally preparing to take the stand? Most are in their seventies, a few in their eighties. The only exceptions are those who, like Simone Kadosche-Lagrange, were still teenagers when they were deported. Even the eldest seem intellectually alert and absorbed in the trial despite all the legalistic jargon and procedure.

The president needs a few more hours to go through the investigation file, sheet by sheet, as if he were peeling an onion. The defendant's box is, of course, empty.

A few lawyers are still trying to fill it, however. Maître Alain Feder makes a persuasive argument on behalf of Professor Gompel's daughter:

"For the last forty years, this woman, the daughter of a Catholic mother and a Jewish father, has lived in the hope that one day she would confront her father's butcher. Professor Gompel went through the *bagnoire* torture, was hung from the feet over a basin of ammonia, whipped unconscious, and then dipped into boiling water and flayed alive. His daughter has never seen the man responsible for these horrors. If he does not attend his trial, she wants her attorneys to spend the time we would normally devote to our pleas in silence, as a sign of protest."

Since Nicole Gompel was not herself a victim of Barbie, and therefore, does not have to identify him, her appeal is denied.

This afternoon, the court will have to determine Barbie's role in the departure of train 14.166, the last deportee convoy to leave Lyon on August 11, 1944. Then, it will have to answer a critical question: When Barbie ordered the deportation of all these people—the Jews of the UGIF, the children of Izieu, the prisoners on convoy 14.166—did he know where he was sending them? Was the "final solution" to him an abstraction or a concrete reality?

The prosecution has no written proof of Barbie's connection to this last deportation from Lyon: no letter, no telegram, no memo. But some of the Montluc prisoners called out of their cells at five in the morning saw him in the prison courtyard; and later, others saw him on the platform of the Perrache station. When in 1984 Judge Christian Riss read Barbie their testimony, Barbie shrugged his shoulders, rolled his eyes, and snapped, "They don't know what they are talking about. They have lost their minds. On August 11, 1944, I had already retreated to Dijon."

But the Einsatzkommando and the SIPO-SD did not leave Lyon until August 22, two days after the massacres of Bron and Saint-Genis-Laval. Even assuming the man in the prison courtyard and on the station platform was someone else, wasn't it Barbie who ordered the deportation? Barbie claims that the deportations were not the responsibility of Section IV, but were ordered by Section II. In this, however, he was contradicted by Helmut Knochen, whose deposition (taken in Germany, where he resides) is very clear on this point: "Section II had nothing to do with deportations."

All the trains Barbie sent off were bound for Drancy, the point of convergence for rail convoys from all over France. However, when the train of August 11 was diverted from Drancy because of sabotage, the commanding officer on board knew enough about the deportees' final destination to head directly for the concentration camps, dropping male resistants off at Rothau, from where they would proceed to Struthof, the female resistants at Ravensbrück, and the Jews at Auschwitz. If he was so well informed about the destination of each group, how could an SS officer who was his superior both in rank and responsibility not have known?

Testimony gathered during the investigation implies that Barbie knew all too well. As Ferdinand Hahn was leaving on the rail convoy of June 6, 1944, Barbie sneered at him: "Where I am sending you is worse than death." Hahn did not understand what Barbie was alluding to until he saw it with own eyes.

"Yes, I knew all those people were gathered in concentration camps," Barbie responded to Hahn's testimony during the investigation, "but I didn't know what happened there. I never had the opportunity to visit one, and, as you well know, lots of deportees came back."

Yet this "devoted follower of Nazi ideology" could hardly have been ignorant of Hitler's master plan. Nor could he have been unaware of the decree of September 7, 1941, better known as *"Nacht und Nebel,"* "Night and Fog," which prescribed the internment of "all people guilty of crimes against the Reich"; that is, resistants, communists, socialists, trade unionists, Gypsies, and Jews.

Soon after this decree, Field Marshal Wilhelm Keitel circulated a memo pointing out that "life imprisonment will be considered a mark of weakness," that is to say, encouraging the elimination of camp prisoners. However, the means had to be kept secret. "The Führer's aim is to produce uncertainty concerning the fate of the people imprisoned in the Reich [the deportees], so that their families, unaware of their death, won't get the idea of demonstrating." This was the kernel of a memo circulated by Knochen, dated June 24, 1942. It seems unlikely that Barbie, a direct subordinate of the author of these orders, knew nothing about them.

But there is more. Theodor Dannecker, head of the Jewish Affairs Bureau of the Paris Gestapo and a rabid anti-Semite, often discussed the Jewish question with his colleagues quite openly. Dannecker wrote a great deal, thanks to which we know that all of his colleagues who held any position of responsibility in the Nazi hierarchy knew about the "final solution." On July 20, 1942, three days after the raid on the Vélodrome d'Hiver, Dannecker, somewhat disappointed by the outcome (the raid yielded 12,884 people, including 4,115 children) wrote the following note to Helmut Knochen: "The Jewish community must have understood that all Jews in the camps are doomed to total extermination." This somehow got back to Berlin, which immediately sent a telegram to Knochen to remind him that deportees were to believe they were being sent to work camps like any others, to avoid any possible revolt that might hinder operations.

"I believe we have satisfactorily demonstrated that even German officers of the lowest ranks knew that the deportees were doomed to die," President Cerdini concludes as he closes the file.

SEPTEMBER 1943

Jeanne spends the night of September 22 at her mother-in-law's. Needless to say, no one sleeps. But this is only a temporary solution. Jeanne cannot stay there; it is too dangerous for everybody. Fortunately the family has put some money aside, and Philippe Frecon, who is taking care of Robert's business, can always give her some more. All Jeanne has is what she is wearing: a worn pair of sandals, a pair of socks, her blue polka-dot dress, and her white sweater, knitted by Bonne-maman.

Without a second thought, Jeanne decides to go back to Villa Bénédicte to get some of her things. She takes a train, a bus, and before long she is standing in front of her home, basking in the sunset. The air is heavy with the sweet and sour smell of linden. The leaves of the poplars are already starting to yellow. Jeanne and Robert loved the fall above any other season. To this day, she cannot think of that house without pain. But then, her first reaction was fear: fear of being there all alone, with her memories and her sorrow; fear that the Germans have found out Robert's true identity and are waiting for her. Suddenly the house looks hostile, and Jeanne decides to glean some information from the neighbors before she enters.

The Chevalliers, the farmers next door, welcome her with open arms. Madame Chevallier leads her down to the cellar, where Jeanne finds all her silver and other valuables wrapped in old newspapers and, hidden under a pile of trash, her ivory and silver vanity set, my father's vermeil cigarette case—now used by Poumi with something akin to religious devotion. "My son Jean did this, in the middle of the night. He stored everything he thought might be important to you," Madame Chevallier explains. Jeanne cries with gratitude. She had forgotten such kindness and generosity existed.

The Chevalliers sit Jeanne down at their table and tell her that one morning in early September, shortly after Robert's escape, the Germans broke into Villa Bénédicte. They stayed only a short while and apparently didn't steal anything, but they left a big mess, particularly in the kitchen. "Madame Robert," as the Chevalliers

call my mother, should be aware of this before she walks into her
house. "Had I known you were coming," Madame Chevallier apologizes, "I would have cleaned it up." My mother reproaches her
for even thinking such a thing: "Don't you think you have already
done enough for me?"

That night, accompanied by Jean, she sneaks into the house
through the little cellar door, right below the cherry tree. This is
the path Jean followed on his rescue operations. In the kitchen,
my mother shudders with disgust. The floor is covered with human
excrement. They find more in the hallway and on the staircase.
The walls still bear the marks of shattered jars of gherkins and
brandied cherries. The Germans also smashed wine bottles against
the Dutch armoire, the Louis XV bureau, the piano.

Missing from the top of the piano is Jeanne's photograph, taken
at Studios Harcourt. Jean did not take it; in fact, he never saw it,
which is strange, since he rescued a number of things from that
room. Jeanne blanches. Obviously the Gestapo has it.

She fills a knapsack with a few clothes and other necessities and
is out in no time. The last glance she casts at her home is not one
of tenderness, but rather one of bitter regret.

Jeanne knows that, thanks to the stolen portrait, the Germans
can now recognize her. She remembers what my father told her in
between his two arrests. The Gestapo in Saint-Etienne believe he
is a Jew, consequently, his wife is also a Jew unless she can prove
the contrary with a certificate of baptism, which Jeanne does not
have. Instead, she has a false ID card in the name of Marguerite
Lindet, a rather poorly executed document, like most of False Papers
Pierre's earlier products, but better than nothing. With it she goes
to Paris to pay a visit to the priest of Saint Paul's parish, in the
quarter where she was born—the very same church where her
mother refused to have her christened, and where she attended the
communion of all of her classmates. She is sure the priest will gladly
grant her the certificate, since it is a matter of life and death, and
he is her last resort. But the priest refuses. The Church cannot be
involved in a lie, he says. My mother insists, protests. To no avail.

"If you follow my course of religious education I will christen you according to the rules of the Catholic Church," he tells her. "But first you must give me proof of your faith."

Jeanne cannot believe her ears. Still, she swallows her anger, and renews her pleas:

"Please, Father, I promise when the war is over I'll take it as a sign of God. I'll come back. I'll take all the courses you want me to. But now there's no time. Don't you understand? My husband's been arrested. I must go back to Lyon to figure out what they've done with him. I'm in danger myself, Father, in great danger. If they arrest me, it will be as the wife of a Jew. They'll deport me, and I may never come back. I have two young children, Father. You're my only hope."

But her prayers remain unheeded. Finally, Jeanne leaves. She swears she will never set foot in a church again for the rest of her life.

Since Jeanne cannot go on without news of either her husband or her children, she decides to risk paying us a visit.

She arrives in Angers just as the city is being bombed. Later she will joke, "I dropped in on you like a bomb!" But once she realizes that her children are all right, she is unable to sit still. Bonnemaman and Aunt Léontine do their best to discourage her from going back to Lyon, telling her she will risk her life for nothing; that if she stays where she is, Robert will know where to find her when he is freed. After all, her place is with the children. But in her mind, she is already in Lyon, in the shadow of Fort Montluc. Robert needs her, the children don't. If anything happens to her, she knows they are in the best possible hands.

Jeanne chooses her husband over her children, and even though I am not sure that I would have done the same thing, I cannot blame her for it.

It is a cool October in Lyon. Jeanne sleeps wherever she can find a room to rent for a night or two: sometimes in a slum, other times in a sumptuous bed, once in a child's room amidst dolls and teddy bears. Most people have learned not to ask questions, but in any case, she must take her chances. During the day, she knocks on the doors of all the friends she has in Lyon, but they are all packing.

Lyon has become a trap. Grandmother and Uncle Pierre are getting ready to return to Paris, and then try to persuade her to go with them. But Jeanne cannot leave. She has learned that the indefatigable Lucie Aubrac is working on a crazy new rescue mission, this time to free her husband, Raymond Aubrac. She has persuaded the Gestapo—who, of course, don't know who she is—that she is carrying Raymond's illegitimate child, and that she wants them to force him to marry her before he is executed. And the Gestapo, unusually sensitive when it comes to maidenly honor, have agreed to bring Raymond from Montluc to the Ecole de Santé for the wedding. Lucie's plan is to attack the van transporting him.

Jeanne tries to glean as much information as she can in the farfetched hope that Robert may once more benefit from Lucie's daring, that Raymond Aubrac will probably not be transferred alone.

On October 21, Raymond Aubrac and fourteen other men get free after a rescue operation in which four German soldiers are killed. But Robert is not one of the freed prisoners.

Jeanne has very little hope left. She knows that the Red Cross distributes packages in the Lyon prisons and prepares one for Robert in which she tenderly packs a sweater, socks, handkerchiefs, underwear, toiletries, condensed milk, and, shrewdly, a sausage, so that if the Germans open the package they won't suspect Robert is a Jew. Then, instead of writing a love note, she dampens her hands with her usual perfume and rubs them on his clothes. This is her way of telling him, "I am with you, my love. I think of you and love you." She addresses the package to Robert Renaud, and leaves the rest to God.

This is all she can do for the moment. Alone and helpless, Jeanne has to surrender. Her mother and her aunt were right, her place is with the children. Her money is dwindling. She spends her days walking so as not to be caught in a raid, and eats very little. Soon she can no longer pay for lodgings if she wants to save enough money for a train ticket to Paris. But there is still cousin Elise at the Dock Lyonnais.

Elise welcomes her, though cautiously. Jeanne can only come and go at night to avoid arousing the suspicions of the neighbors.

9 TANGIBLE PROOF

Today, two world-renowned magistrates, specialists in the history of war crimes and crimes against humanity, are going to take the stand. Alfred Streim is the director of the Central Judicial Services for the Investigation of Nazi Crimes, created in Ludwigsburg, near Stuttgart, in 1958. His office contains 1.3 million documents, plus the complete records of the trials of 6,480 Nazi criminals held in West Germany since 1945.

Rudolf Holtfort is the Attorney General of Cologne and an expert on the implementation of the "final solution" in France. Together, he and Streim answer general questions concerning the authenticity of documents in Barbie's file, some of which they have already seen as they have circulated from trial to trial since Nuremberg.

"The mention '_ohne Vorgang_' ('without reference') on the telegrams concerning the Izieu and UGIF raids proves that they were both personal and local initiatives; otherwise they should have borne the mention 'on behalf of' or 'by order of,' " Streim explains.

"No question about that," Holtfort continues. "At this point, however, one may wonder whether Barbie's name could have been used unbeknownst to him by someone else in the Lyon Einsatzkommando, someone who may have wished to incriminate him in those raids. Theoretically, it's possible, but in practice it's unthinkable. . . . The hierarchy and the particular duties assigned to each and every member did not allow for this sort of confusion."

Starting from the general principles of National Socialism, the two experts gradually make their way to Barbie's particular case.

"The thesis according to which 'an order is an order'—the *Führerprincip* that bound the SS as well as every Nazi administration and the Wehrmacht itself—was used by the lawyers of war criminals for a very long time, starting with those at the Nuremberg trial," Streim explains. "But it was just an alibi which has gone out of fashion since 1960. Soldiers, as well as civil servants and SS officers, could refuse to obey an order if they deemed it criminal. Several SS did, and were sent to the Russian front. This is what happened to Major Hannibal, who withdrew from a particular operation with his entire battalion because he refused to kill Jews. Nonetheless, he had a brilliant military career and was decorated for his actions on the Russian front. Similarly, Ernst Heinrichson, an SS officer stationed in Paris, was transferred to the Russian front for having expressed his disapproval of extreme anti-Jewish measures. Germans were not executed for disobeying the *Führerprincip*, but because they had deserted or otherwise abandoned their post."

Ill concealing his emotion, Holtfort examines the implementation of the "final solution": "Until January 1942, when they were clarified, Hitler's instructions concerning this plan were transmitted orally by means of a coded language only known by some leaders, who could then pass the appropriate orders on to their subordinates without having to get into details. The instructions concerning France were transmitted by Heydrich's office in Berlin directly to the head of the Paris SIPO-SD, who then passed them on to the heads of the regional bureaus. Barbie, by virtue of his position, was part of this select group of initiates. In any case, this is how seventy-four rail convoys carrying 75,000 Jews left France bound for German concentration camps. . . . The fact that so many people were dead by the time they reached their destination is enough to suggest that their fate had been decided before the trains left the station, and that the very conditions of their transport were a form of preselection. In other words, their extermination was under way the moment they boarded the trains."

As for Barbie's authority over the subsection of Section IV in charge of Jewish Affairs, Holtfort declares:

"He most certainly had authority over that subdivision since all the SIPO-SD headquarters in France followed the same model: Each subdivision of Section IV answered to one person, and this person, in Lyon, was Klaus Barbie. Even on the rare occasions when special commandos were sent from Paris or Berlin to conduct anti-Jewish actions in other cities, they placed themselves under the authority of the heads of Section IV. In the spring of 1944, the SIPO-SD in Paris sent a note to all its regional headquarters to encourage them to take the initiative both in arrests and deportations without waiting for instructions from the main office. This is why the Izieu raid can only be considered the responsibility of the man who ordered its execution."

MAY 20, 1987

The first survivors called to the stand are those who will testify about the raid on the Union Générale des Israélites de France.

Among them is Michel Godot-Goldberg, forty-eight, a victim's son.

"My father was twenty-one when he became a French citizen in 1938," he begins calmly. "A decorated soldier, he was demobbed in 1940 and left Paris with his family in 1941 because life in the capital had become impossible for a Jew. We moved to the outskirts of Lyon. Thanks to some courageous neighbors, I was immediately provided with a false ID under the name of Godot, the name I have kept next to my father's. On February 9, my father told my mother, 'I'm going to the UGIF to see what they have. I'm bringing Michel along.' But it was snowing, and I had no boots, so my mother refused to let me go. And that's the only reason why I'm still here."

He clutches the bar in front of him so tightly his knuckles whiten, and goes on: "So I did not go to the UGIF with my father. I didn't go with him to Auschwitz either. He disappeared without a trace: a few ashes drifting in the German sky and then dropping, like snow, on German soil. All the people who disappeared and died there, they are all abstractions. They have no bodies, no graves, no cemeteries. And we, the sons and daughters of the victims of Auschwitz and other extermination camps, we haven't even been given a chance to mourn them. This trial is, to me and many others, a tribute to all those anonymous dead gathered into a number that means nothing: six million. In a way, it lends some life to those nonexistent victims, our unburied dead, our abstract losses."

All his companions, all the victims' children, including me, stare at him, mesmerized. He expresses something we have all been feeling for a very long time.

So this is what it means not to know one's father, not to have a grave to go to. I begin to wonder if my own insensitivity to my father's death—the fact that until this trial it had always seemed so distant and unreal—has to do with this, the absence of a grave.

"By the end of the war," Michel Godot-Goldberg remembers, "everybody knew Klaus Barbie was responsible for the raid. When in 1974 I heard that Bolivia refused to extradite him, I was flooded with anger, frustration, a craving for revenge. I decided to kill him. By then, I had three children and was the executive manager of the South American branch of an international firm. . . . First, I took a reconnaissance trip. Then on Easter 1975 I went a second time, pretending I was a journalist. Barbie received me without the slightest hesitation. We talked for an hour. He seemed very self-assured. [Bolivia] had proven it would protect him. Even then, he claimed what he is claiming here: The Jews were not his responsibility; his task was to get rid of communists. He was quick to deny the authenticity of all the documents bearing his signature. According to him, they were all fakes or pieces of paper he signed without knowing what he was signing. There were several other people present at the interview; in front of them Barbie couldn't help bragging, 'I was only an *Obersturmführer*, but I had more power than a general," he declared, banging his fist on the table. . . . 'With Jean Moulin's arrest, I changed the face of the world. He was so intelligent that, had he lived, he would have taken General de Gaulle's place and France would have become a communist country.' I had trouble affecting a journalist's impartiality. But I didn't kill him. I didn't kill Barbie, as I'd planned to do for such a long time.

"Whether Barbie was present or not at the UGIF raid is not important. What matters is that he was the head of the Gestapo, and the Gestapo was there. In other words, he is the only recognizable link in the chain of events that sent my father to Auschwitz. Neither I, nor my children, nor any of my descendants will ever know whether he died in the ovens, or in the mines, or of typhoid fever, or whether he was shot. In fact, we will never even know whether he died at Auschwitz or during its evacuation.

"In any case, Barbie's impunity struck me as an insult to all the UGIF victims. I wouldn't have fled after killing him, because I wanted to be tried in Barbie's place, since he seemed to be above justice; at least I would remind the world of all our dead. But then I met Barbie, and all of a sudden lost my will. France had already proven itself too halfhearted in its extradition requests to succeed. Obviously, back in 1975 my country was not yet ready to face its own shames and failures, as it is doing now. Had I killed Barbie with my own hands, I would have done a great service to all those who wanted him to remain silent. Furthermore, I had no official mandate, no mission to fulfill other than a very private, personal one. Besides, I found Barbie despicably mediocre and full of contradictions. I didn't feel the rush of hatred necessary to pull the trigger. I no longer hated him enough. I would have had to commit a cold-blooded murder, and I could not do that."

Michel Godot-Goldberg leaves the courtroom so quickly that I don't have time to ask him whether he felt relieved after that interview, or whether he was haunted by his unfulfilled goal.

I call my mother often while I'm in Lyon, reporting on the trial.

That evening I tell her that, like some of the witnesses I heard that day in the courtroom, I am sorry there is nothing left of my father, no memorial plaque, no grave, nothing.

"But your father has a grave," my mother interrupts. "At the beginning of the fifties, someone wrote to tell me that all the people who died for France during World War II would be buried in the military cemetery, and that my husband was among them. I don't know where it is because I have never wanted to know. Somewhere in Lyon."

I am surprised and furious at the same time. How could she have known all these years and never told us? It's hard for my mother to comprehend my anger.

"I didn't want to upset you for no reason. We lived in Paris then, and your father was buried some four hundred miles away. It wouldn't have changed anything. There were times when I thought I should tell you, but somehow it was never the right moment. It's not that easy to tell one's children, even when they're grown up, 'By the way, I should probably tell you . . .' over a cup of coffee or in front of the TV. Besides being afraid of upsetting you, I was afraid you might not care. It was easier not to say anything."

Not only did I not know my father had a grave; I had never even wondered whether he was buried somewhere. For me, he had simply disappeared and never come back. My mother has always disliked cemeteries. "Your dead are within you, not out there," she claims.

I have no trouble locating the military cemetery at La Doué, a suburb of Lyon. It looks like an American cemetery, with its perfectly mown grassy knolls and neat rows of identical white crosses. The caretaker, the only living being in that expanse of white and green, is trimming a boxwood hedge. He doesn't know where Robert Kahn's grave is. Visitors are rare, and that name has never come up. He hands me a stack of yellowed cards. "Have a look at these," he tells me.

I quickly find the one I am looking for: "Robert Kahn, a.k.a. Renaud," somebody has written along with the name of a path and a number. It is the first grave in an endless row that runs along the base of a hillock. The journalist friend who has accompanied me stands back as I approach the stone engraved with my father's name. For the first time in my life, I have tangible proof of my father's existence. The earth bears his trace.

NOVEMBER 1943

I know little about the interrogations my father must have been subjected to, or many other details of his stay in Montluc. Nor do I wish to fill that void with my imagination. But with the help of some of Renaud's old cellmates, I can reconstruct a fragile outline of those eleven months.

At first, the Gestapo doesn't connect the man arrested on Rue d'Anvers in Lyon to the runaway of Saint-Etienne. They don't know that Renaud is an important figure in the Resistance and, given his Aryan looks, don't even suspect that he is a Jew. So they leave him alone, relatively speaking. He is locked up with other "political prisoners" in a section known as "the refectory," a huge hangar divided into tiny cells where men are packed together like herrings. At the SIPO-SD, his file is quickly buried under several others.

After a few weeks during which various cellmates come and go, Renaud encounters an old acquaintance, Augier, the printer in Saint-Etienne.

"You know, I'm getting out in two or three days. They've promised," Augier tells him. "They haven't been able to find anything except the tracts I printed last March and April. I told them I had to make some money to feed all my kids, that I didn't even read them, since it was my assistant Mussburger, the Alsatian, who did the job. You see, I'm sure Mussburger is their stool pigeon. After all, they speak the same language. Anyway, they checked my story and believe I'm clean. This morning, after the third interrogation, they were even nice to me. They said they still had a couple of things to check, and that in the meantime they were going to place me with 'good people.' That's what they said, pal, and here I am, with you."

Augier and Renaud chat about this and that. Augier keeps trying to broach the subject of the Resistance, but Robert is inscrutable.

"I don't have anything to do with it. They think I'm some communist I've never even heard of. I'm waiting for them to realize I'm not the guy they want."

Augier changes the subject and begins asking about family. Renaud must have a wife, since he's wearing a wedding ring, right? My father looks at the thin white-gold band around his finger and sighs.

Augier stares at him, waiting for an answer.

"Yes, I have a wife. Of course I have a wife. She sent me a package at the beginning of the week, and I can't even let her know that I received it."

"If you like, I can tell her. That is, if I leave before you," Augier offers. "If you have any messages for her let me know."

"Maybe," Robert answers, still on the defensive. But when the following morning a guard opens the cell door shouting, "Augier, you're out of here," my father doesn't want to miss his chance. While Augier laces his shoes, Robert bends over him and whispers: "My wife might still be around. If so, you may find her at the Dock Lyonnais, on Rue d'Anvers."

"You can count on me," Augier answers with a friendly pat on Robert's shoulder. "So long, pal!"

Augier is freed on Thursday, November 4; Jeanne has just bought a train ticket to Paris for that night. She barely has time for a cup of real coffee with Elise, who slips a bag of cookies and dried bananas in the outside pocket of her knapsack. Yet Jeanne is still hesitating, looking for excuses to stay in Lyon. Attacks on the railways are getting more and more frequent, trains are stopped for hours. It might be safer if she left in the morning. Unconsciously, she is trying to delay the moment when she has to put more distance between herself and Robert. Finally she makes up her mind: "Elise, let me stay one more night. I promise I'll be gone by the morning. I'd feel better traveling in the daytime."

At five o'clock the following morning, the Pardous are jolted from sleep by screeching tires, slamming car doors, and loud bangs on the wooden shutters of the Dock Lyonnais. Jeanne knows immediately that they have come to get her.

Moments later, she finds herself in the back of a black Citroen surrounded by German civilians and an armed Militia man.

It is still night when the car reaches Montluc. Stunned, Jeanne is escorted to a cell that reeks of mildew and excrement. Jeanne feels nauseated. She realizes this is to be her new home. Her pale cellmates can read the disgust in her face.

"We all felt that way when we first got here. But you'll get used to it. One gets used to everything; even the worst things are never quite as bad as they could be," a prisoner with graying hair informs her, making room on a cot. At the back of the cell there is a slop pail. One of the women goes to sit on it. An old coat hanging from a string partly conceals her from the others' eyes, if not from their ears. They all bow their heads in shame, shame for themselves having to live like animals, shame for her whose needs have proved stronger than her dignity. Worse is the problem of menstruation; as the prison offers no means of "protection," the women must sleep on bloody sheets and wear clothes covered with dry bloodstains.

Life in prison is full of surprises, as Jeanne will eventually discover. She thought she was hungry when she was scouring the streets of Lyon in search of black bread and potatoes. But now all she gets is a bowl of soup in the evening, when they don't forget to bring it around, and provided there have been no alarms to suspend its distribution. The soup is a thin broth in which float a few unidentifiable objects, and it tastes like dishwater. "But at least it's warm, salty, and liquid," she's told on her first evening by a very proper woman, Madame Maze Censier, who drinks it as if she were enjoying a cup of Lapsang souchong in a smart English tearoom. At first my mother is full of disdain. But soon she realizes that camaraderie and a sense of humor are her only weapons against despair.

My mother has never been gregarious. In fact, she has always disliked crowds, whether in a subway or at a dance. Now all of a sudden she finds herself cooped up with ten women she would never

have associated with under normal circumstances. But these are
not normal circumstances, and Jeanne pulls Elise's bag of cookies
out of her knapsack and passes it around. The women seem astonished and stretch out their hands timidly. Before Jeanne knows it,
the cookies are gone and she has made ten new friends.

She will soon get to know fleas, lice, and bedbugs as well. It
happens to all newcomers. For the first few days they fall prey to
a sort of Saint Vitus's dance that makes them twist, turn, and wriggle
in the hope of shaking some of the bugs off. The only other remedy
is to scratch one's back against a wall until it bleeds. In her agony,
she often remembers magazine pictures of Africans whose faces and
eyes are covered with flies, which they don't even seem to notice.
Like them, she will have to learn stoicism, if not resignation.

When they come to fetch her to be interrogated, her companions'
eyes follow her, full of sympathy. She is driven to the Ecole de
Santé in a van. There she is escorted to an office where she finds
a man whose face is hideously covered with scars. Back in her cell
she will learn that he is Francis André, "Twisted Mug," Klaus
Barbie's French acolyte. He holds my mother's false papers in the
name of Marguerite Lindet, and sneers as his eyes shift to the
photograph stolen from Villa Bénédicte, now standing on his desk.
Obviously, she is the wife of the Jew Kahn. Where is he?

In a flash, my mother realizes that the Gestapo has still made no
connection between the missing Robert Kahn and the prisoner
Robert Renaud. She wants to scream with joy.

Instead, she plays the role of the deserted wife. "Ask around.
Everybody knows it. My husband left me alone with my two children." No sooner has she spoken than she bites her lip. Thanks to
her, they now know about the children. Francis André takes some
notes and leaves the office for half an hour.

"It looks as if you are telling the truth," he tells her when he
returns. "That sort of behavior is not surprising in a Jew. They are
all bastards. Are you also Jewish?"

No, she is not a Jew. She is not Catholic either, nor Protestant.
She is nothing at all, she has no religion. Religion doesn't matter
where she comes from. At this point, a little man with a thin smile

and narrow eyes enters the room. He is German. His name is Klaus
Barbie.

Jeanne speaks German. She thinks this will impress him. She
has never heard of Barbie before and doesn't know who he is, or
that nothing and no one can impress him. Insofar as he is concerned, if she is a Jew's wife and is not a Catholic, she is a Jew and
should be treated as one. But first of all, he wants her to tell him
where her children are. He wants to nip those future seeds of
Jewishness in the bud. He knows there are two of them, a boy and
a girl, and demands to know where they are hiding. Jeanne hesitates.
The two men grab her by the shoulders and shake her. Then, pulling
her hair, they jam her neck against the back of the chair. She
bursts out crying with fear and pain. She believes every word she
invents for them: Her children have been taken away, to Switzerland, and she has had no news of them since. She is afraid they
might be dead, or caught by the Gestapo. Her babies, her darlings,
she will never see them again. Her sobs intensify. She really believes
her children have forever disappeared beyond the Alps. Klaus Barbie
slaps her a couple of times "to bring some color to her cheeks" as
he puts it. Jeanne's cheeks burn, but in her heart she rejoices because
she knows they've bought her story.

Finally, they bring her back to her cell, which looks so much
friendlier now. There is that crazy Madame Censier, who keeps
pretending she is a guest at some chic reception, bestowing smiles
and "dahlings" right and left. But why shouldn't she, if it keeps
her going? And then there is Carmen, an eighteen-year-old girl
who doesn't hesitate to say out loud what others don't dare think:
"If I've got to eat Krauts to get out of here, I'll shut my eyes and
choke them down."

Jeanne keeps bemoaning the fate of her children, lost in Switzerland. She wants to know where her husband is, but must go
about it discreetly.

A month later, in mid-December, a tiny miracle happens as the
women are coming back from their "walk": a half hour in a courtyard
with a large tub. Every day Jeanne looks forward to the moment
she can wash, even though the water is icy. She pushes her com-

panions to join her: "It lifts one's spirits. Washing means refusing to let oneself go to seed. It means you want to go on living." Still, most of them don't dare. "The Germans look at us, we don't want to be naked in front of them." Jeanne's arguments don't convince the others: "German soldiers are not men. It's like washing in front of a pair of old shoes."

As the women are returning to their cells, their group crosses a line of men coming back from work. They are covered with mud, and since their guards don't want them to look at the women, they are all facing the wall. All but Robert, who instead stares deep into Jeanne's eyes as she walks by. They are close enough to touch. Quietly, he tells her that he loves her. As quietly, she tells him that the children are safe.

Jeanne returns to her cell with the distressing image of a thinner, paler Robert, his face furrowed with wrinkles and overgrown with stubble, his eyes shrunken and sad. He looks awkward in a bulky fur-lined jacket she has never seen before. He has probably borrowed it or inherited it from someone. It should keep him warm, at least. But it hurts her to see him looking broken, aged.

Prisoners are made to change cells frequently to prevent complicity and, they say, homosexual relationships. In fact, it is one more cruelty aimed at breaking the prisoners' morale by constantly pulling them away from what's familiar. But as she moves from one cell to the next, Jeanne meets a few extraordinary women: the one who never speaks and is always dragging a fox-fur blanket behind her; Madame de Graff, who after the war became Madame Gramont, the inventor of the stroller; Denise Clairoin, a translator and literary agent. Clairoin is a dynamic woman with an extraordinarily calm, reassuring voice in spite of a terrible experience she alludes to but never talks about.

And then there is Dora, an Austrian guard, a big woman with a pretty face and an unusually kind manner. She shouts at the top of her lungs when she is within earshot of the Germans, but otherwise is quite friendly and warm. She delivers messages from cell to cell and on occasion even between buildings. A few days after Jeanne and Robert's meeting in the courtyard, just as the women are filing out of the cell for their "walk," she seizes my mother firmly by the arm and, pretending she is reprimanding her for the disorder of the cell, forces her back. Once they are out of sight, Dora slips a piece of bread into Jeanne's hand, and a message from Robert scribbled on a piece of cheese wrap. "It was a shock to see you here. I didn't know. But don't worry, I think we'll get out of this." Clearly his optimism has been blunted—normally he wouldn't have said, "I think."

Jeanne gets rid of the note by swallowing it. But there will be more messages in both directions thanks to Dora's complicity. Nor is Jeanne the only prisoner she helps. Dora does all she can to alleviate the distress of detention by giving prisoners a few kind words, something to eat. Though she's taking a big risk in delivering messages, it's not for ideological reasons. She doesn't care what side people are on, she just doesn't like to see them suffer. The Gestapo will make her pay for her generosity by shooting her in front of Fort Montluc just before they flee the city.

But Dora is the exception. Frau Aufhäuser, for instance, is a sadist. She is weak and afraid of her superiors, but her cruelty is directly proportional to her fear. Jeanne manages to win her over by asking her for a "Sanderson," a big German grammar. Thus she kills two birds with one stone. The German she perfects at Montluc will be of great help to her in Auschwitz. Jeanne also sews, both for Frau Aufhäuser and for herself, which is why every cell she stays in is seldom short of cookies or fruit—distributed by the Red Cross for the prisoners but inevitably sifted through by the German guards. Of this winter Jeanne will remember mostly the nights broken by constant machine-gun fire and other explosions: partisan attacks, German reprisals, executions. All it takes to face a firing squad is to be strong-willed; to have bright eyes, or a proud stance; to lag behind in one's work; to be weak, or sick, or depressed. Her captors are not particular.

10   MONTLUC

Michel Kroskov-Thomas is too polite to be honest, too garrulous to be clear, too precise to be exact. All the witnesses we have seen and will see take the stand are simple people leading simple lives, extraordinary only in that they survived the most brutal expression of racism. Not so Michel Kroskov-Thomas. At seventy-three, perfectly tanned, with a porcelain smile, and "golden chestnut" hair (very fashionable in the best salons), he reminds one of Ronald Reagan, who keeps looking younger as he gets older.

A naturalized American, Kroskov-Thomas is the general manager of several language schools in the United States, and lives in New York. He was born in Poland and moved to France in the 1930s, when he was in his teens. There, he first joined the Maquis of the Isère, then the intelligence service of the First Alpine Division; he was soon transferred to the special services of the First French Army, and finally to the American army, with which he participated in the liberation of Lyon. He speaks impeccable French and brings some comic relief to the tense courtroom. He claims he saw Barbie in the UGIF offices, but his colorful delivery leaves one skeptical even though his story is plausible.

"Having dodged the STO, I came to Lyon from Grenoble, where I was an officer of the secret army, in September 1942. I was on a mission: to recruit young people for new fighting units. Thinking that young Jews might wish to fight the occupier more than anyone else, I got in touch with the director of the UGIF. . . . He wasn't too eager to cooperate because the aim of his organization, as he put it, was to help and reunite dispersed families, not to promote the Maquis. So, on February 9, I decided to go to the UGIF myself; I knew I would meet people, since it was assistance day. I wanted to explain what deportation really meant to all the young people who knew nothing about it. I wanted them to be able to choose between hiding and deportation, and fighting.

"On the staircase, I had a sense of foreboding, but dismissed it as cowardice, and forced myself to climb to the third floor. I stopped at the door, struck by the total silence behind it. I should have been hearing voices, the clicking of typewriters, steps on the wooden floors, the usual office noises. My intuition told me not to go any further, but I did anyway. As soon as I opened the door I saw a pair of black boots. I was about to retreat when an arm seized me and pulled me in. I pretended that I could not speak any German and had come to the wrong address. They led me to another room which was crowded with people, the children very quiet and well behaved. At the back of the room there was a table behind which sat a rather short man, clearly in command. I was dragged in front of him, where I continued to play the idiot and to pretend I spoke no German. One of the Gestapo officers who stood behind me drew his gun and placed the barrel right against my left ear. Turning to his superior, he said calmly, 'Better do away with him. Shall I shoot him in the nape of the neck, or in the ear?' I forced myself to stay as still as possible.

"The short man at the table, who was none other than Klaus Barbie, signaled his man to lower the gun and then shouted something in German. He clearly wanted to see my papers. Naturally, I had a fake ID supplied by the Vercors Maquis. It worked. Barbie

turned to me and in French, which he spoke fluently, asked me
what I was doing at the UGIF, since obviously I was not a Jew.
When I was on a mission, I generally brought along a sketchbook
with a few of my watercolors as an alibi. I told him that I had an
appointment with a gentleman who wanted to buy some of my work
to decorate his office, and that I must have come to the wrong
building, or maybe the wrong floor. Meanwhile, more people had
joined the ones already crowded in the office. I recognized some of
them, and was afraid they would show they knew me. But they
didn't. They were so stunned and scared they had lost the ability
to react.

"I stood there, facing Barbie, for some three hours. He was in
charge of the whole thing. He had a strange way of moving his
fingers, with his pinky always sticking out in a very effeminate way.
Every second of my interview with Barbie, that angel of death, is
engraved in my memory, like a deep scar that will never heal. It
was a profoundly traumatic experience that marked me for the rest
of my life. I will never forget that monster hiding in the shape of
a man. I will never forget that sarcastic, cynical, sadistic smile, the
smile of a man who enjoys seeing other men suffer. I will never
forget those piercing, shifty rat eyes; the face of a man who, for
three hours, had power of life and death over me.

"Barbie doesn't want to confront his few surviving victims, he
wants to flee justice. Too bad. I would have liked to see him one
more time. I would have also liked to show you the very peculiar
asymmetry of his ears that so struck me then.

"At last he let me go, convinced I was telling the truth. I left
the office very calmly, but once out I did my best to warn other
people. . . . This is my story. It lay buried at the bottom of my
heart until in 1972, leafing through *Time* magazine, my eyes fell
on a photo of Klaus Barbie during the war. It was like an electric
shock, it shook me up so. It was as if all the wounds I had received
had suddenly reopened and blood was pouring out. It literally
drowned me in sorrow. The photo was the photo of the man I had
faced for three hours at the UGIF on February 9, 1943. I have no
doubt about it. Some wonder how one can be so sure after forty

years. They say his face has changed. It may be easy to forget a person casually met in the street several years earlier, but it is impossible to forget a man you faced for three hours as he played with your life. That man you'll never forget."

Why is such vivid testimony so embarrassing, so unconvincing? Michel Kroskov-Thomas is no doubt sincere, but he is so theatrical, so grandiloquent! In a few days, another witness will evoke the asymmetry of Barbie's ears, and the affectations of his pinky, and he will be believed on the spot.

Meanwhile, Gilberte Lévy, a seventy-four-year-old retired teacher and grandmother—a small, frail woman with silvery white hair and a lovely face—has taken the stand.

"I had been a social worker at the UGIF since November 1942," she begins. "The Germans arrived in the early afternoon and took everything we had away from us. The only thing I managed to keep was my wedding ring. . . . They loaded us into a truck and took us to Fort Lamothe, where we stayed for two days in the most awful conditions, without cots, blankets, water, hygienic supplies. . . . On February 12, we were sent off to Drancy. . . . [There] we were deprived of everything . . . the bread was stale, there was no soap. We lived in filth and were forced to sleep on pallets teeming with bugs that crawled all over us, even inside our ears. The floor was covered with excrement and vomit. The courtyard was covered with ashes. I saw horrible things there. Once they stripped some men naked and made them crawl, yes, crawl like worms from one side of the courtyard to the other. The other prisoners had to watch if they did not want to incur a worse punishment. . . . There were lots of children in Drancy who desperately clung to anyone, since they no longer had their parents, and knew, by some uncanny sort of intuition, that they were going to die."

Gilberte's crystalline voice cracks. She pauses awhile to swallow her tears, but refuses to sit down.

"I had become friends with a few other women prisoners. Friendship can be very strong among people who know they are doomed. On March 23, we learned that we were going to be deported the following day, and we knew what it meant. But at the last moment

I was pulled out of the group and had to watch my friends leave: Régine, Madeleine, Juliette, Marcelle. I will always remember the courage with which they walked to their deaths, their heads held high. Believe me, Mr. President, ladies and gentlemen of the jury: It was harder to be left behind than it would have been to leave with them. They had such courage!

"But I was left behind, and so I devoted myself to the children. I was the only thing they had. They were waiting to be deported and, in an excess of sadism, had been placed in a wonderful room where there was a large mural representing the fables of La Fontaine. They were all very young, between four and six. I never spent more than one or two days with them, barely time to get attached to them before they were whisked off on the morning convoy. . . . Then I was sent to the Levitan warehouses to sort out all the things that had been taken away from the Jews. The best were carefully packaged and sent to Germany. I was deported in July, to Bergen-Belsen. Before leaving, I had heard that my brother-in-law had also been deported, and that my sister had been shot dead in the street. My other sister had been sent to Auschwitz, where she had been gassed upon arrival.

"Typhus and dysentery were rampant in Bergen-Belsen. People died like flies. In our barracks, we shared our pallets with the sick. I was assigned to a work commando and spent my entire days weaving plastic and dying of cold and hunger. Toward the end of our stay, they gave us practically nothing to eat, at best half a raw potato. One morning I thought I wouldn't have the strength to walk down the three steps that led to the workshop. But I was wrong. Our survival instincts somehow allow us to survive on nothing and find energy where there is none left.

"I would like to tell you about the filth in which we lived. We looked like monkeys picking lice out of each other's furs. As soon as we had some free time, we pulled off our rags and ran their seams between thumb and index finger to squeeze out the vermin. Now and then we had the right to take a shower, but it was real torture. They waited for us to be all soaped up to turn off the water, and we were left covered with an abrasive film that dried on our skin, causing the worst itching. Other times they would suddenly turn off the cold, or the hot water. The crematory ovens were going around the clock, filling the air around us with a smell I won't forget until I die. To this day, I cannot stand the smell of grilled meat.

"Then, in April 1945, as the Americans approached, the Germans, not wanting to admit defeat, evacuated our camp. We were loaded into the 'hostage train' fleeing east; ours was an open car vulnerable to every whim of the weather. It was a shock treatment which, however, prevented us from getting typhus. We were on this ghost train for almost three weeks, wandering through Germany, having nothing to eat but thistle, with which, somehow, we managed to make a soup. Some of us took advantage of a curve, or of the train slowing down, to jump off, but I don't know whether anyone managed to escape for good.

"Then one day the train stopped at a small village station where, much to our surprise, we saw a Soviet soldier on a horse. . . . We were on the other side of the Elbe, and the Russians were setting us free. It was the beginning of May. On May 21, 1945, I was back home."

The entire courtroom breathes a sigh of relief; we have all been holding our breath. Not a sneeze, not a cough, not a sniffle has interrupted the absolute silence in which Gilberte Lévy's words hovered.

Victor Sullaper is one of two brothers who were at the UGIF when the Gestapo raided the offices; he, unlike his brother, managed to escape.

"It's not easy to be that lucky," he admits. "I was twenty-three then, Rachmil was a few years older. We were waiting our turn in a long line of people. [The Gestapo] crashed into the office like bulldozers, guns in hand, all wearing civilian clothes. They kept shouting, 'Hands up! All against the wall!' as if we were dangerous criminals. . . . They immediately locked all exits, doors and windows, and ordered the telephone operator to tell all callers that she could not explain anything on the phone, that they had better come to the office as quickly as possible. Rachmil kept his true identity, which is what finally got him deported. I had a false one, in the name of Victor Sordier. . . . My brother pretended he didn't know me. I was kept aside for a while, and then released. I tried to warn the people I met on the staircase as well as I could. . . . I rushed to Place des Terreaux and immediately sent a telegram in Hebrew to the Israeli community center in my district: 'Sir, UGIF in trouble, warn everybody.' But my brother was still there."

Two brothers, two friends. Edith Grinzpan, thirty-one, and young Hélène, then fifteen, were laughing as they climbed the steps to the UGIF offices that afternoon, Edith carrying her four-month-old baby. All three were spared: Hélène because she was too young, Edith because her child wouldn't stop crying. Exasperated, a Gestapo officer pushed Edith out the door, telling her to "go give something warm to the brat."

We will hear one more story of a "lucky" man.

"Here's what happened to me," Elias Nahmias, a burly sixty-one-year-old says as he launches into his tale. He was eighteen when a Gestapo officer stopped him as he was going to mail a letter.

"He must have thought I looked suspicious. In any case, he took me to one of his superiors, who later turned out to be Klaus Barbie—at least, this is what my cellmates told me when I described him. Anyway, he didn't torture me, though he questioned me twice. I saw the most unbelievable things in Montluc, the way people were tortured! I saw a man screaming with pain and shame after they had burnt his testicles. . . . I don't exactly remember when I left Lyon to get to Drancy's camp, but I know I left for Auschwitz on July 31, 1944. There were four hundred children in my convoy. The people of Paris, who had begun to figure out what deportation really meant, were demonstrating in front of the camp. They demanded that the children be surrendered into their hands. But the guards threatened them with their machine guns and they had to disperse. A few men were crying helplessly as we walked to the train. The head of the Toulouse Resistance was with us. He told them, 'Come, come don't behave like babies. I've got the key to detach the cars.' But either it was the wrong key, or he simply said it to make us feel better.

"As soon as we got to Auschwitz, the children were sent to the gas chamber. But first we had to get out of our cars. If you have seen a seal hunt, you know what it was like. They literally bludgeoned us out, and we had to drag the corpses out as well. Then they prodded us in line with the handle of a pickaxe. . . .

"I was lucky enough to be the last one to be left. They spared me, only me. The rest of the convoy was murdered that very same day. It's incredible. I don't even know how I can utter such things, they are so far beyond human understanding. And yet, that is exactly what happened. I was the only one to be spared. I was young and very stocky. They stripped, shaved, disinfected, and tattooed me, and then placed me in a work group which immediately went through another selection. I was again lucky, since they kept me. They gave me a pair of clogs, overalls, and a cap. The cap was critical. We had to have it on our heads during the innumerable and useless roll calls, else *kaput*. My job consisted of loading and unloading carts in a mine, at Mutzen. Galley slaves must have been treated better than we were. Every day men died at work, and every evening we had to bring their corpses back with us to match the morning's body count.

"Now and then, in the middle of the night, our guards wanted to have fun, so they woke us up with the butts of their guns, and forced us to split stones. It was unclear what for, but we never asked. I can't tell how many nights we spent standing at attention because in the evening we hadn't brought back any corpses. That meant the system wasn't working. . . . So they hoped a long, tense night would do the trick. And it did. After a couple of hours, men would start falling flat on their faces, like bowling pins—dead even before they hit the ground.

"Then there were the forty Russians who had planned to escape. They were hanged right before our eyes, you see, to serve as an example. . . . The Krauts hung on to their legs to speed up their deaths. The last people in the line kicked the stool away themselves to avoid this last humiliation. On January 17, they brought some women to our barracks. One of my comrades recognized his wife. . . . He asked the guard whether he could go kiss her, and the guard gave him permission. . . . He started running toward her and then, as they were about to touch, he was shot in the back. But at least he died happy.

"A few days later, the camp was evacuated. I don't know how many we were when we started. All I know is that we lost twelve thousand on the way. My uncle was with me all the way to Lübeck. He was aboard one of the ships that were sunk in the harbor. The few survivors were led to another camp, near Grossrosen, next to which the previous one was like a kindergarten. This time we had to push wheelbarrows full of cement as they whipped us along. We were forbidden to help those who fell. So we watched helplessly as they reeled and dropped right into that gray paste, which swallowed them like quicksand.

"One day I received a package, which was a dubious blessing, because they had threatened to kill anyone who got a package. . . . I managed to trade a pack of cigarettes for a place in the work unit assigned to digging potatoes, but they caught me. To save my skin I gave a piece of chocolate to the kapo. I was lucky. I owe my life to a candy bar.

"Day after day, all we had to eat was a bite of bread each. People kept dropping dead under my eyes. I was always sure I would be the next one, and every time I woke up in the morning I was surprised. I'd tell myself, 'Well, if it isn't this morning, it'll be tonight.'

"Then they crammed us into a train bound for Lake Constance. At one point, it stopped in front of some silos full of potatoes. Without even thinking about it, we started running for them. But as soon as we got to them, the Germans turned their machine guns on us. I got hit in the leg, but once again I was lucky. I crawled under my companions' corpses and played dead. Next to me was a young man who did the same thing, but not convincingly enough. The Germans noticed that he was breathing. Through the corpses above me, I saw a pair of boots slowly approaching and stopping right above my living comrade. Then I heard a shot.

"I waited for a very long time, until I was sure that the silence around me was only the silence of death. When I pulled myself out of that bloody tangle, I was alone with the crows. I bandaged my wound and ate some potatoes. I had difficulty swallowing, but they tasted delicious. Then I must have fainted, come to, and fainted again. I don't know how much time went by. Two hours? Two days? In any case, at one point I found myself sandwiched between the Americans and the Russians, approaching from opposite sides. Bullets crisscrossed over my head. Yes, I was lucky. And that was the end of my nightmare.

"I would like to add one more thing," he continues. "Often I hear the most disgusting things. People who say the gas chambers never existed. In Dachau, the crematory ovens worked like a fac-tory: as efficiently and with as little feeling. When I was there, at least two thousand people were gassed and then burnt every day. I saw fathers so distraught at having been unable to protect their children, and so dismayed at the thought of how they died, that they ran into the barbed wire to electrocute themselves. They were left there for days to wither like leaves in the fall. Others would simply walk toward the watchtower to be shot by the sentries. It never failed. What kept me alive through all this was my youth, the youth I lost, and a promise I made, which today I have kept.

"During the death march following the evacuation of our camp, I found myself walking next to an old man. Maybe he wasn't that old, but down there even a man in his forties looked like an old man. He whispered to me, 'You're young, you're strong. You're going to make it. You'll be one of the few who will survive. You must tell everybody how we died, and you must also ask them why.'"

JANUARY 1944

The study of German and sewing help Jeanne kill time and earn her a good reputation. She's known as the one who doesn't fall to pieces, keeps her chin up, and doesn't complain. When she asks to be moved to the barracks (a sort of hangar hastily built to solve the problem of overpopulation), she is immediately granted permission. There are only thirty women in the barracks and a sink, where in the evening they can wash without being seen. And it is closer to Robert.

One day in February, a woman who has just come back from a day's work dismantling railroad tracks tells Jeanne that her husband is at a third-floor window and would like to talk her. Jeanne is so well thought of that she's even allowed to step outside for a breath of fresh air more or less whenever she wants, without asking permission. She walks into the courtyard and leans against the wall, her head tilted back as if to feel the warmth of the wintry sun on her face. She pretends her eyes are closed but through the curtain of her lashes she scans the third-floor windows. Behind the bars of one, she sees a face. A hand waves; it's Robert's. He looks unsteady. No doubt he is perched on somebody's shoulders, since cell windows tend to be set very high. Telegraphically, they manage to communicate that they are fine, that they think of each other, that they are cold and hungry. "Don't worry. The worst is over," Robert tells her, whether he really believes it or is simply trying to reassure his wife, who, seen from above, must have looked so small and lost.

This is the last time my parents see each other. Jeanne has attained such a privileged position that she tends to forget that she is a prisoner. When a guard reprimands her for some minor infraction, she responds insolently and in no time finds herself back in a crowded cell. In one blow, she loses the barracks, the sink, the courtyard, and the possibility of seeing and talking to her husband.

One afternoon in March, she sees a large group of people dragging themselves through the courtyard. They are all young, in their twenties. It is rumored that they are members of the Maquis of the Ain, or of the Isère, and that Barbie has defeated the Resistance outposts in the mountains. Rumors spread quickly through the prison, but they are often inaccurate; this one, however, is at least partly true.

In the spring of 1944, Barbie launched a campaign to clean up the Maquis. In order to encourage denunciations and force them into the open, he pillaged entire villages. He didn't seem to care who was a *maquisard* and who wasn't. Here he got rid of the mayor and the blacksmith; there a family, grandmother and newborn included; elsewhere he randomly selected fifteen people out of a crowd of terrified villagers and had them shot in front of their friends and neighbors. But the Resistance remained impenetrable, at least until March 7, when they arrested "Chatoux."

Chatoux, a resistant from Lyon, was in close contact with the leaders of the major Maquis of the region. No sooner was he captured than he was immediately handed over to Barbie himself and the man at the head of subsection IV-B, Erich Bartelmus. Chatoux was subjected to the *bagnoire*, his face was kicked in, he was flogged until there was no more skin left on his back. Half dead, Chatoux talked. Before the week was over, 110 people—his entire network—were caught.

Among them was Albert Chambonnet, a.k.a. "Didier," a Resistance leader in charge of the regions of Alsace, Jura, Haute-Savoie, and Ain, whom Barbie has been pursuing for over a year. A few months later, after a foiled attack on the Gestapo's favorite restaurant, Le-Moulin-à-Vent, Barbie would decide to retaliate by executing five Montluc prisoners. He would put Bartelmus in charge of the selection, which would include Chambonnet; the five men would be shot one by one right in front of Le-Moulin-à-Vent, and their bodies left to rot on the pavement for two days before an order is given to "sweep up that garbage."

The prisoners my mother sees in the courtyard are the 110 Maquis of Chatoux's network, including Chambonnet. They are frail, worn, silent. Some drag their legs, others are wounded and bleeding through their bandages. Those unable to walk are supported by their companions. They file by with heads bowed. The Vichy government calls them bandits, terrorists. And every day brings more.

One morning, a small blond woman is thrown into Jeanne's tiny, overcrowded cell. Her knees buckle and she crumples to the floor, unconscious. She is twenty-one, her name is Irène—she was arrested that very morning and has just gone through a special session in Barbie's office at the Ecole de Santé. She has been thoroughly beaten. When she comes to, she is unable to say a word. Her mouth is bleeding. Her cellmates have to wring a wet rag over her lips to help her to drink.

Soon the prison regime stiffens. Roll calls ring through the court-yards at the crack of dawn. More often than not, they are lists of Jewish names. The prison is too crowded. To make room, trainloads of Jews and resistants leave daily for Dachau, Ravensbrück, Auschwitz. The infernal machine is going full tilt.

The summer heat only worsens the already intolerable situation. Typhus and dysentery wreak havoc among the prisoners. Montluc becomes a cesspool. The guards hold their noses whenever they have to open a cell. It is a huge pigsty, with one main difference: sty troughs are kept cleaner, and the animals are fed.

11 A Vase with a Rose in It

At the Barbie trial, no sooner do those of us in the audience feel that, word by word, we have reached the limits of the nightmare, than we realize we have been optimistic. It has no limits.

Only two weeks ago, we thought Barbie would be the focus of his trial. Instead, his victims, our witnesses, have a presence that quite eclipses his absence. Among those we will hear today, Friday the 22nd of May, is Irène Clair, who is sixty-five. A retired teacher, she now has time to take care of her garden and her grandchildren. But in 1944 she was only twenty-one, and her name was Irène Fremion.

"I joined the Resistance quite naturally. I thought it was the right thing to do. I was the secretary of one of the department leaders, Lucien Bonnet, otherwise known as 'Gilbert.' My work was mainly to receive and transmit information, orders, and instructions from London. I received coded messages, decoded them, and passed them on. On March 9, I had an appointment. We knew our network was in danger and we were to move that same evening.

I arrived at the apartment we had been using as our headquarters around five P.M. and fell right into the trap. . . . Several of my comrades were already there, held at gunpoint. We were taken to Gestapo headquarters and I was literally shoved into Klaus Barbie's office. Lucien Bonnet was already there, chained to another member of our group. Barbie looked very angry and kept calling us terrorists, assassins, bandits. I don't know what got into me, but I was very young then, and nothing scared me, so I just burst out laughing. Barbie glowered at me, then he called a Militia man, gave him a whip, and turning to me, said, 'As for you, blondie, we are going to tame you.' At this point they brought in another one of our liaison officers who had been arrested the previous day and tortured. He looked dreadful. Then they brought us down to the cellars, where we spent a hellish night. I could hear the howling and groaning of the prisoners who were waiting to be shot; I could hear the dogs growling and the screams of their victims, men and women.

"The following morning we were transferred to Montluc, where they locked eight of us up in tiny cells meant for two people at most. A week later, Barbie summoned me back. He wanted me to see Lucien Bonnet, though I had trouble believing this old wreck was my dynamic thirty-four-year-old boss. All his teeth had been knocked out, he was twisted and bent with pain. I burst out crying. They left us alone for a few minutes. In a whisper he told me, 'Irène, you'll have to be brave. That man is Klaus Barbie. He is mad and a sadist. I'm afraid he might want to talk to you.' He told me about electric shocks, beatings with a truncheon, various forms of hanging and stretching, having one's genitals burned. He could no longer stand. Barbie wanted me to identify him as Lucien Bonnet, my boss. I denied it. I told him my boss was in Paris, that I'd never seen that man before. For two months they hit me with a riding crop across the back of my neck. Barbie showed me the photos of people he wanted me to identify. He wanted to know where we kept our money, our weapons. But I didn't give in. Then, one day, he told me, 'I'm done with you. You're going to take a trip.'

"That same evening I left Montluc for Romainville, a transit camp on the outskirts of Paris. It was May first. Until then, May first had always been a lovely day; the air always smelled of lilies of the valley. It's silly, I know, but that thought made me terribly sad. On May 18, I left for Ravensbrück. There were thirty-five or forty of us—men and women, old people and adolescents—crammed into a cattle car with little air and no water.

"When we reached our destination, we couldn't believe our eyes. I had been glad to leave Montluc, but suddenly I wished I were still there. To understand, one has to have seen those walking skeletons, and the dense smoke produced by the crematoriums which some pretend never existed, but which I saw puffing away day and night. One had to have breathed the smell of grilled flesh that clung to our skin and choked our throats. At some station along the way, the Red Cross had given us some packages containing sweets: gingerbread cookies, dried fruit and such. The guards took everything away from us, emptied it in the middle of the courtyard and trampled it. It was a terrifying gesture, a hint of the meanness and cruelty to come.

"We were led to a room where we were stripped of all we had. Our heads were shaved. . . . We were stripped of our gold chains and rings—even our gold fillings. Then they ordered us into the showers, and we all thought it was the end, since other prisoners had told us about the gas chambers. We finally ended up in a barracks where there were only women, with little or nothing to eat. We picked all sorts of herbs, including one that tasted like sweet spinach. We often found worms in our soup, and though I was literally starving, the mere sight of one made me nauseous. But the worst thing was having nothing to drink. Duchess Yvonne de la Rochefoucault, who was a doctor, made us drink our urine. She'd tell me, 'Irène, hold your nose and close your eyes. It's a liquid, and you must drink or it'll be the end of you.' It is, in part, thanks to her and her advice that I can now tell you about these horrors.

"We were evacuated to some sort of hospital which specialized in vivisection. I saw horrible things there, pieces of women scattered here and there. I arrived with a bad ear infection. It was very painful, but they gave me nothing to relieve the pain. I thought my head would burst. Here again, I owe my life to Yvonne de la Rochefoucault and Geneviève de Gaulle. Geneviève stole medicine and gave it to Yvonne for me. When I think of what could have happened to them had they been caught, I break into a cold sweat. The toilets were regularly strewn with bodies. Some of them were still breathing when they were carried to the crematorium.

"Klaus Barbie was a bloodthirsty beast. He tortured people both directly and indirectly. All I went through, from Lyon to Ravensbrück, is thanks to him. When I had to face him during the investigation of the case, I shook with fear. And yet our roles were reversed: he was the prisoner and I was free."

Lise Lesevre, the next witness, has often had the opportunity to tell her gruesome story to the media. She is carefully made up and coiffed, and wears a fashionable dark silk suit. Her back is bent, a vestige of her torture. As a result, she leans on a cane, but proudly refuses the chair the usher has hastened to bring her.

"I worked for the Resistance and was arrested by Klaus Barbie's men on March 13, 1944. They took me to Montluc. I had numerous papers and documents on me, as well as some photos for false ID's. But, more crucially, I had an envelope addressed to 'Didier,' the liaison agent in charge of distributing mail within our network. I knew that for months the Lyon Gestapo had been vainly tracking a very important regional leader, Albert Chambonnet, also known as 'Didier.' Barbie was convinced that my Didier and the one he wanted were one and the same. Which, of course, was not the case, but the more I denied it the less he believed me. The first evening he left me more or less alone. Things started getting rougher the following morning, when I was brought back to his office. He was holding a riding crop in his hand, and was surrounded by several men. Francis André, the notorious 'Twisted Mug,' was among them. I was hung from the ceiling by my wrists and flogged. Then my hands were cuffed in spiked manacles that bit through my flesh, drawing blood. Then I was again hung, but this time with my arms spread apart. And every time, I would faint, come to, and faint again. Barbie soon realized I would not speak, so in a mellifluous voice he told me, 'Very well then, we are going to get your son and your husband. I bet you'll talk in front of them.' This was pure sadism. It was awful to see my husband and son there, awful. . . .

"Then I was treated to the *bagnoire*. I had to strip and get into a bathtub full of freezing water. They pinched my nose and poured water down my throat. Then they tied my hands behind my back and attached my feet to a bar running across the bathtub. When they yanked the bar, I automatically went under, and they kept me there until my lungs were about to burst. Every time I came to after passing out, I was afraid I might have talked, but their faces always told me otherwise.

"This went on more or less without interruption for nineteen days. Even at night, I was often forced to sleep with my hands chained to my feet. Fortunately, my jailer was humane enough to detach the chain so I could sleep for a few hours.

"Finally, I was condemned to death by the so-called German military tribunal and was locked up in a special cell in Montluc. On one of the walls were a few words of farewell signed by one of my Maquis comrades. When they came to look for me, I thought it was to bring me in front of the firing squad, but I was wrong. I had another appointment with Barbie. His command had just carried out an operation against the Maquis in the Jura Mountains, and one of the partisans they had captured had revealed my name. It was during this last 'interrogation' that they wrecked my back. I was strapped to a chair on my stomach, with my head and arms dangling on one side, and my legs on the other. Barbie was there with 'Twisted Mug' and another man they called 'Big Max.' They started pounding my back with a handle at the end of which was attached a steel ball studded with metal points. I quickly passed out.

"When I regained consciousness, I was sitting in an armchair in the middle of an elegant drawing room. On a nearby table there was a vase with a rose in it. I thought I had lost my mind. Barbie was kneeling at my feet, telling me that he admired my courage but eventually I must give in, like everybody else. Then he started reciting a litany of names, obviously hoping that I would cave in and admit that I knew them. But soon he realized it was useless. He stood up and, snapping his fingers, ordered his two French watchdogs to get rid of me.

"My back hurt horribly, whether I stood, sat, or lay down. There was nothing I could do to relieve the pain. Ten days later, I was transferred to Romainville, which, to me, seemed like a haven of peace, since there were no SS there, only the Wehrmacht. But it didn't last long. We were soon loaded into a train, up to a hundred people per car, and sent to Ravensbrück. As soon as we arrived, we were brought to a dentist who extracted our gold fillings. But I was lucky enough to find an ex-cellmate from Montluc, Madame Léger, who had gotten there just a few days before me. Together we felt stronger. We were both sent to work in an arms factory specializing in anti-aircraft shells. Of course, we did all we could to sabotage their products, helped by a German foreman, an anti-Nazi, who was later hanged for having participated in the Munich putsch [sic] against Hitler.

"My husband caught diphtheria in Montluc. I saw him when he got back from the hospital, just before I was deported. My son and I left on the same convoy. I was even able to hug him, thanks to the 'greens,' who were much better than the SS. But then my son was sent to Buchenwald, where he caught tuberculosis and was treated by a Lyon doctor, Dr. Florens, who had been able to save forty Jewish children from Auschwitz by having them transferred, I don't know exactly how, to Buchenwald. But when they found out what he had done, he and the forty children were hanged from butchers' hooks. My husband, already sick when he left Montluc, died of typhus in Dachau."

At no point has Lise Lesevre's voice wavered, though both magistrates and jurors have occasionally had to bow their heads. No wonder most survivors are so reluctant to talk about their experience in the camps; there are no words powerful enough to render what they went through, let alone make it believable. Only here, supported by the memories of others, could their voices really be heard.

• • •

Simone Kadosche-Lagrange takes the stand. She is in her fifties, the matriarch of a large family whose members alone have shared her secret until now. Her son is with her. He is thirteen, exactly his mother's age when she was deported.

"My parents and I were arrested on June 6, 1944, while the Allies were landing in Normandy. We had been denounced by a French woman who was with us when the Gestapo came to get us," she remembers with closed eyes. "They took us to Place Bellecour. As we were climbing the steps leading to Barbie's office, I heard the German who was pushing us from behind tell another German, '*Kaput.*' One didn't have to know German to know what that meant. We stood facing the wall, but were ordered to turn around when Barbie walked in. He wore a gray suit and kept caressing a cat coiled in his arm. I took that as a good sign. He couldn't be that bad if he was so nice to an animal. Besides, he was smaller than the typical SS. . . . First he walked up to my father, considered him for a while, and then walked over to my mother and asked her, 'Do you have other children?' My mother was very scared, but she was able to answer. 'Yes,' she said, 'I have two more, but they're in the country, I don't know where.'

"He didn't insist but, setting the cat down on the floor, returned to me and asked me the same question. Fortunately, I didn't know where my siblings were, otherwise I might have told him. As none of us answered, he grabbed my hair and, pulling my head back, slapped me across the face. My parents had never slapped me. . . . It may not sound like much, but my parents were devastated.

"Then we were transferred to Montluc. My father was put in the Jewish barracks, and my mother and I were locked in a cellar. It may sound stupid, but I was afraid of rats. I spent the night looking through the basement window. I saw several trucks arrive carrying Jewish children. Around nine, the door opened, and Barbie himself stepped into our cell to get me. He asked me again where my brother and sister were. I couldn't figure out why he cared so much, but obviously he did because he kept beating me to get an answer, and when I fell to the ground, he kicked me until I got back up. My face was covered with blood. Then he had someone go fetch my mother and when she walked into his office he pushed me toward her saying, 'Look what you've done to her!' Every morning, for a whole week, he would beat me on top of the wounds I'd received the previous day. But my physical pain was nothing compared to my mother's psychological torture. . . .

"After about a week, Barbie had me transferred to another cell, and my mother thought I was dead. As for me, I thought she was being tortured in my place and I cried in despair. Barbie was my first torturer, others followed.

"On June 23, I left for Drancy, where I was lucky enough to be reunited with my mother. Those few days we spent together were very happy compared to what we had gone through and were going to face. Then, on June 30, we left for Auschwitz, on train number 76. On the platform, there was a group of children holding hands. I saw them climb into their train car quietly, sadly. I could have been among them, since some were my age. We were so many in each car that we had to sit on the floor with our legs wide apart so that someone else could sit in between, like the pieces of a puzzle. But I was relatively lucky, since I sat near the door. Until then, modesty had been important. Mothers and daughters never saw each other naked. Physiological functions were strictly private. And suddenly . . . for days we had to live in our excrement and relieve ourselves in front of everyone. . . . Yes, we were dirty, but no dirtier than the souls of those who put us through this. A few sick children screamed relentlessly. A man died the day after our departure. We placed him at the back of the car, and every morning the number of corpses increased. We cried for them, but, in a way, we were glad to have more room to breathe. As our journey progressed, the screams and howls of the children became more and more haunting. I still hear them at night, echoing in my skull. . . . I have been taking tranquilizers for the last forty-two years in order to sleep, but I still have nightmares.

"My vocabulary is inadequate to express what Auschwitz was like. I can only offer you a few images, a few facts. My first trauma was being shaved. I know it is not that serious, but it was painful to see all those women, especially my mother, so completely naked. The tattooing session was not much better. To this day, I cannot understand how some people can pay to be tattooed. I immediately rubbed my arm and the last number, a four, sort of smudged off. But a guard saw what I had done and, naked as I was, lashed me ten times. That's when I first realized I had no more identity, no more personality. I was number A8624, waiting to die. The kapos enjoyed keeping us posted about the fate of our companions. That's how we knew that the people who had been taken away by truck had been gassed shortly thereafter. From the start we knew what fueled the tall flames rising from the smokestacks. Put in words, it sounds absurd, I know, but there is worse. Women lined up at the door of the gas chambers, holding their children by the hand and singing lullabies to assuage their fears. All those who have visited the gas chambers have noticed how the walls are scratched, because even though one may be mentally resigned to death the body revolts down to the last second.

"I don't want my children or my grandchildren ever to go through such a horror. This is the only reason why I am here today to testify, and why I must go on talking. I was lucky to be with my mother in Auschwitz, at least until August 23, 1944. To the rest of the world, it is the day Paris was liberated, but for me it is the day my mother was gassed and burnt. My two nephews, aged nine and eleven, were also gassed then.

"I thought I would lose my mind, but it isn't that easy to lose one's mind. I also wanted to die. But it's not that easy to die either.

"On January 19, 1945, Auschwitz was evacuated because of the Allies' approach. I'm sure you're already acquainted with the conditions in which those evacuations took place. We were twenty-five thousand when we left Auschwitz, and two thousand when we arrived at Ravensbrück. While we marched on, dying by the thousands, as had been planned, we crossed paths with other prisoners coming from different camps. I can't remember whether I have mentioned that my father was a very tall man. . . . In a group of prisoners that joined ours, I saw a head sticking out above all the others and immediately recognized him. He also saw me. With gestures, he asked me about my mother. With gestures, I tried to tell him she was somewhere behind us. I wanted him to think she was still alive. He couldn't resist the temptation of coming to kiss me. As we were about to touch, an SS officer ordered him to stop and kneel on the spot. He did, smiling, happy to be so close to me. They shot him in the head."

Simone's voice was dwindled to a whisper, which the microphones diffuse through the room. As for me, I am no longer listening. My face hidden in my arms, I am crying. I am crying for her father, for her mother, for Simone herself, for my own parents, for myself. To us, in the courtroom, Simone is not a fifty-seven-year-old woman, mother of seven and grandmother of twelve, but a thirteen-year-old child, like the one sitting next to her, now desperately sobbing in his father's arms.

During the investigation of this case in 1983, Simone Lagrange met Klaus Barbie face to face. He smiled at her. "It is always pleasant for a prisoner to see an appetizing woman," he explained.

The next witness is Ennat Léger, ninety-two years old, now confined to a wheelchair. Age has blunted her hearing (the usher repeats each question into her ear), but her blindness is a direct consequence of her deportation.

"My husband and I were arrested on March 8, 1944. I was almost fifty—no spring chicken—and knew the risk involved when, in 1942, I agreed to supervise an evacuation channel helping Jews flee to Switzerland. I saved a lot of people before I was denounced. I was interrogated every day from March 8 to March 13. Five times, all terrible. On March 10, two Germans dragged my husband before me. He had been beaten to a pulp and was dying. He cried when he saw me and with the little strength he had left, whispered, 'Poor baby, you're going to suffer, I don't know how you'll stand it.' Then they dragged him away. I still don't know whether he died that day, or later; or whether he was deported. But I don't think he was in a state to leave.

"So they kept torturing me. They stuck a bottle in my mouth

and broke all my teeth, then hit me across the face with it, splitting my lips and breaking my nose. I pissed blood for days after that.

"Barbie attended every session. I know because my torturers kept addressing a very elegant man with icy eyes as 'Herr Barbie.' It is thanks to him that I lost my sight and am in this wheelchair. When they were done torturing me, he turned to me and said, 'You asked for it. You're going to die in Germany.'"

Srul Kaplon is a distinguished sixty-eight-year-old. He was twenty-four and his brother twenty-seven when, in March 1943, they were arrested, while their mother, who refused to let them go, was slapped repeatedly.

"We were immediately brought to the Hotel Terminus, to Klaus Barbie, who showed me maps, photos, and lists of names and places. In a soothing voice, he proposed, 'If you denounce your comrades, you'll be set free.' So I put my finger on one of the photos and told him, 'I know him well, he's in the cemetery.' That infuriated him. He started kicking me in the shins, then called his dog. I hadn't noticed the dog before; he was sleeping in the corner. 'Wolf, get him. Eat the Jew, Wolf.' He kept egging him on until the dog lunged at me and left me bleeding all over.

"Afterwards, I was brought to Montluc, where I learned that my treatment was only part of a general routine. I also learned that the interrogation of Jews, resistants, and other tough cases was Barbie's specialty. Then I was transferred by train to Fresnes, where I was kept in solitary for six weeks, but it was better than being in Montluc. After this, I was transferred to Drancy, where I was reunited with my brother. We were deported together on June 23, 1943. They needed twelve hundred men to fill a train, and we were among them. We were crammed, rather piled, into cattle cars. . . . We didn't know whether we were going to Birkenau or to High Silesia. When we arrived—it turned out to be Birkenau— there was an average of ten to twelve corpses in each car. What was surprising is that anyone should have survived the stench, not to mention the hunger and thirst. As soon as we got off the train, those who couldn't walk were loaded into trucks, never to be seen again. As for the rest of us, we were immediately stripped, shaved, tattooed, and reclothed in striped pajamas.

"Birkenau was a sort of manpower station that supplied free labor to different work sites. Hundreds upon hundreds of people died on those sites every day, as planned. Those who died were immediately replaced by new recruits. We were not considered men but machines, and as machines we were already so worn out that quantity had to make up for quality. For a year, I worked in a mine, pushing wagon after wagon, until one day I slipped and one of the wagons rolled right over my legs. I couldn't get up. My comrades forced me to stand and dragged me to my barracks. The following morning, I was too sick to get up. I thought I would die within the day and felt relieved. The barracks guard brought me a bowl of good warm soup, then offered me another portion. As I looked at him questioningly, astounded at such unexpected generosity, he told me, 'You'd better eat now, since tomorrow it'll be too late—you're scheduled for the oven.'

"I was shocked by such frankness, even though I knew I was going to die anyway. And, indeed, the following morning, I was loaded into a van along with all the casualties of the previous day. We were brought to the Medical Experiments Center of Revier. A prisoner who worked there asked me what I was doing among all those corpses. I told him I was on my way to the oven. So he dragged me out and hid me in a nearby barracks. Apparently we were together in Drancy, and he wanted to help me. I remained hidden in that barracks for two weeks. Every day, my friend would bring me water, bread crusts, and potato peelings, barely enough to keep me alive. Then one evening he came to me terrified. 'They're going to search all the barracks,' he told me. 'You have to get out of here.' I was still unable to walk, and knew that one way or another I was doomed to the oven. I told him I wanted to stay where I was. But he wouldn't let me. He was sure I was safer outside than in the barracks. And he was right. Everyone there was gassed.

"Somehow or other, I found myself assigned to a disciplinary camp, over two miles away. My companions helped me walk there. Now and then people would fall on the way, as if death had stricken them between steps.

"I was in three different camps, including Auschwitz and Dachau. Auschwitz was something else, terrible and terrifying. Its crematoriums were filled round the clock, seven days a week. Once I saw a large group of Gypsies, new arrivals, immediately led to the ovens where they were all exterminated.

"There is no way I can describe Auschwitz, just as there is no way you can possibly imagine what it was like. One has to have been there to believe it. I was lucky I survived, but when I got back I weighed less than sixty pounds, and was completely alone. See this list? These twenty names were once members of my family: my parents, siblings, uncles, aunts, cousins. They were all exterminated. I have seldom been happy since my return. Klaus Barbie? As soon as I saw his photo in the papers back in 1972, I recognized him, without a doubt. Eyes don't change. A face can wrinkle, or sag, or shrink, or fill out, but the eyes remain the same."

The next witness, Michel Stourdze, has a long white beard. A surgical collar prevents him from turning his head. He speaks slowly, deliberately.

Stourdze was also denounced and arrested in 1943, and immediately brought before Barbie, "a small man, strapped up tight in a uniform that looked as if it had been sewn right on him, it fit so snugly. . . .

"I still have a physical memory of the slaps and words that welcomed me to his office: 'Jewish swine, you'll end up in the salt mines.' I believe you are already fairly well acquainted with what went on in Montluc. But I would like to add a few things which the women who have testified before me have passed over out of modesty. You have heard about the physical tortures they were submitted to, but there were other, psychological tortures as well. Young girls who had never before been in contact with a man were stripped naked and offered to everybody's eyes. The Germans would laugh, criticize, touch. I have seen women ashamed and humiliated to the point that I myself felt ashamed and humiliated for witnessing their suffering.

"I'm going to try to illustrate for you what Auschwitz was like. When I first got there, I was among a group of men assigned to a barracks inside of which were rows of cots. One of the SS who escorted us there announced that he was going to teach us a lesson in obedience, at gunpoint. He was having great fun and was probably drunk. He ordered us to stand by the cots, one prisoner per cot. At the first whistle, we were to jump on our cots, and at the second, we were to jump down. And so on, up and down. Each time we hit the floor we had to be sure to take off the caps covering our shaved skulls and stand at attention. Among us was a musician, very thin and pale, who was always the last to obey the orders. Finally, he stood stubbornly still, his head lowered. He just couldn't jump one more time. This infuriated the SS; they seized him, hurled him to the ground, kicked him all over, and finally crushed his throat under their boots. A few days later, I was also punished for being slow to remove my cap in front of an SS. He broke the handle of a shovel on my back, though it felt as if it was my back that was broken. This is why, forty years later, I am still wearing this prosthesis.

"Like most of your previous witnesses, I also went through the evacuation of Auschwitz. My back was all mangled, my legs were limp as noodles, but the fear of a bullet in my head kept me walking. First we got to Mauthausen, but there was no room there, so we proceeded to Oranienburg, and from there to Flossenburg, where I was immediately assigned to a horrible task: gathering corpses, throwing them into pits, and covering them with lime. I also experienced the agony of scalding showers followed by a session in the snow. A friend of mine, who was still able to joke, which is probably how he survived, would tell me, 'Don't complain, Michel. In Sweden they call it sauna and it's very expensive. Here we have it for free.'

"This is the hell Barbie sent us to. We weren't supposed to come back. . . . I'm not seeking revenge, too much time has gone by.

But I assure you, the man we have seen, briefly, in the defendant's box is Klaus Barbie, the same man I faced forty-four years ago at the Ecole de Santé in Lyon. I recognized his eyes, his grin, his entire face, just as it was then, taking pride in our humiliation."

The second week of the trial ends on these words. On the train that brings me back to Paris for the weekend, I wonder whether my father met Simone Kadosche's father in the Jewish barracks at Montluc. They were there at the same time, around the beginning of June 1944. I thought about approaching her during recess, but she was surrounded by people and looked very tired. Besides, I have very little to offer her now.

June 1944

On June 6, 1944, a new rail convoy is about to leave Lyon for Auschwitz. At dawn, men and women are gathered in the courtyard of Montluc prison. It is an *appel avec bagages*, a roll call with luggage, meaning that all those who are called are going to be deported. Jeanne is among them.

It is a long wait. Suddenly, the mournful rows of deportees begin to stir, imperceptibly at first, then more and more energetically, as if an electric current is passing through them. The Allies have just landed in Normandy. The news has made its way through the thick walls of Fort Montluc before reaching most French cities. Ironically, a group of prisoners about to be deported to death camps are among the first to hear.

Jeanne is also reassured by the presence of her best friend, Idette. A shy, sentimental young woman, Idette is ten years younger than Jeanne, and they couldn't be more different; yet their friendship has been a haven of peace in this hell. They've only known each other six days, but have shared the same cot and innumerable confidences. Each strengthens the other for their imminent journey. Both stagger when a new order cracks in their ears: *"Kahn, Zelle zurück!"* ("Kahn, back to your cell!") Idette's eyes follow her as Jeanne returns to the cell she has just left, wondering what could possibly be next.

After so many months of overcrowding, the emptiness of the cell is strange and disturbing. As she listens to the other prisoners slowly shuffling toward the slaughterhouse, Jeanne begins to believe she might be spared. After all, she is neither a Jew nor a resistant. While wondering why she has been reprieved, Jeanne makes herself as comfortable as possible. She piles all the pallets one on top of the other—the pile is thinner than a plump mattress—and drags them under the sunbeam falling through the skylight. Since the cell is getting really hot, she strips down to her briefs and lies down on her new cot. At last alone! She can stretch out, make faces, shake her clothes vigorously to get rid of bugs, walk around without having to step over bodies or worry about stepping on hands and feet.

Suddenly her cell door bursts open and another woman stumbles in as if kicked from behind. She collapses next to Jeanne. Two seconds of silence and then a suitcase follows the same path and lands against the wall. Jeanne welcomes the new prisoner as if she has just dropped in for tea. "Please, sit down. You'll see, we can be quite comfortable. No running water, but we do get some heat from sunlight," she jokes, not even bothering to put her clothes back on.

The newcomer, a small brunette with Oriental features, stares at her with a big smile. "You're from Paris! I'm so happy!"

Jeanne, who has just lost Idette, finds a new friend in Sacha Gottheimer. All three will survive the camps—where Idette will lose her parents and Sacha her husband—to become the best of friends after Liberation. But they will never be heard talking about Auschwitz.

On June 6, 1944, the Allies land in Normandy. On that day Marshal Pétain also happens to honor Saint-Etienne with a visit. Hundreds of children have been lined up to greet him, waving small paper flags. Avuncular, the head of the Vichy government bends to kiss a rosy cheek here, caresses a golden lock there. By his side walks Dr. Werner Knab, Barbie's boss. Not far away, at the Perrache station, a trainload of deportees is about to depart.

Meanwhile, Philippe Frecon, my father's loyal secretary at Siderexpor, is getting married. It is a modest ceremony, and Frecon can't figure out why the justice of the peace is delivering such a lengthy speech. He doesn't know that the councilor, who is also deputy mayor, keeps repeating himself so as to avoid attending the ceremony in honor of Pétain.

June 6, 1944, is also the day the Germans found out that my father was, in fact, Robert Kahn, a Jew.

A few years earlier, my mother had bought two lottery tickets out of pity for an old woman selling them on the street. She won enough money to buy an American refrigerator, a blue fox stole for herself, and a Dunhill watch for Robert. Generally the Gestapo stripped their prisoners of all their valuables—gold chains, medals, bracelets, rings, watches—but occasionally they overlooked a few things.

Robert managed to keep his watch past his first interrogation, and from then on smuggled it from cell to cell. He liked to think of it as his lucky charm, which seemed to amuse his cellmates until one decided to report it.

On the morning of June 6, the Gestapo decides to search Robert's cell and finds the watch hidden in a mattress. If the owner does not come forth, the entire cell will be punished. Renaud confesses. After all, hiding a watch is not such an egregious crime.

Suddenly, however, the Germans—who had forgotten all about him—begin to wonder who Renaud is, and why he has been there so long.

One of the SS officers has a sudden inspiration. Maybe this Renaud is a Jew. While his cellmates avert their eyes, Renaud is stripped. The Germans find the only proof they need. Without wasting any time they begin to kick the "dirty Jew," that "Jewish swine," who, crouching on the floor, desperately tries to protect his head from their boots.

Dragged into an office, my father admits that his name is Robert Kahn. There are five Kahns in Montluc at the moment. One of them is a woman, Jeanne, and about to leave on the train to Auschwitz. Is she his wife, by any chance? Robert nods, knowing anything would be better than for Jeanne to end up in Auschwitz.

Since her maiden name, Labouret, is unmistakably French, she still has a chance to survive in Montluc.

Yes, Jeanne is his wife, he confesses, but she is not Jewish. Doubled over in pain from their kicks to his belly, he tries to make his captors understand that his wife has nothing to do with anything, that she is there by mistake. This seems to amuse them. After all, their operation thrives on such errors; their prisons are filled with them. Yet why on earth did she marry a Jew? There are only two plausible explanations: She was depraved or she got knocked up. In either case, they had better get rid of her, but not until they see if she has anything interesting to tell them about her Jewish relatives. Some of them may still be around.

"Kahn, Zelle zurück." This is why my mother does not leave with Idette on June 6. Instead, she will board the last train for Auschwitz roughly two months later, on August 11.

12 A Truckload
of Earth

Barbie may appear in court tomorrow. The public prosecutor has asked that he be present to face some of the victims who have identified him in photos but not in person. Both President Cerdini and Maître Vergès seem amenable to the idea, but the president won't inform us of his decision until the end of today's session.

Meanwhile, the witnesses keep filing in. This hearing, the eleventh, is primarily devoted to the testimony of three resistants: Lucien Margaine, Mario Blardone, and André Frossard.

Lucien Margaine and Mario Blardone were members of the same Resistance group, based at Lons-le-Saunier. They were arrested at different times, and after the war neither tried to find out what had happened to the other, for fear of learning he was dead. Barbie's trial has brought them back together.

"I was arrested on May 2, 1944, and placed in the care of Barbie's men, though not of Barbie himself," Margaine recalls. "I knew names, places, plans; for seven days and seven nights they did their best to get them out of me. Barbie attended each session without, however, actively participating. But the day my blood stained the wallpaper of the room, he lost control. He pushed his men aside and came up to me with a bicycle lock in his hand, the sort one still sees around today: a bunch of steel threads, very strong but flexible, covered with a red plastic sheath. With it he quickly broke two of my vertebrae. When I came to, I was in a cell in Montluc.

"I hoped he had forgotten me, but he hadn't. Several days later, he summoned me to his office, quite kindly, but I didn't trust him. He talked to me about this and that, then he announced I would be 'N and N,' and that I would never see France again. . . . I had never heard of the *Nacht und Nebel* decree. Before I knew it, I was on my way to Dachau, in a cattle car trundling through the hellish heat. When we arrived, we had to drag all the corpses out onto the platform. Words make it sound banal, but the images that still haunt my nights are harrowing. Of the twenty-four hundred deportees who worked with me in an underground factory, only some hundred came back."

Mario Blardone was the "Combat" liaison assigned to kill Klaus Barbie and Francis André. He was arrested before he could carry out his mission. At sixty-four, he is a handsome man, with an angular face and a mischievous glint in his eye.

"At first, the Gestapo kindly offered me money and a police officer card in exchange for information. I beat around the bush for a while, but after three days they realized I was stringing them along. . . . I won't go into detail about the torture I went through. They tried everything, with lasting consequences. What marked me the most, however, was the torture I witnessed of some young women. There was nothing I could do. Once they ushered a woman into the office carrying a few-months-old baby. Barbie grabbed the infant and hurled it into the hallway. . . . He just threw it away, as if it were a used Kleenex. A few prisoners in the hallway, waiting their turn to be tortured, tried to reach the baby. I could see their arms stretching for it, but I don't know what happened to it. Most likely, it died on the spot. Barbie then forced the young mother to strip, and the more she cried the more he laughed. It was terrible.

I was young, barely twenty-one, and wanted to protect her, but after watching what they did to her for a few seconds I felt very, very old. Barbie forced the woman to run around the room on all fours while a dog chased her from behind. Then he had another woman brought in—I remember her being very beautiful—had her stripped, and forced her to have intercourse with the dog, under his men's eyes, and mine.

"After being tortured, whether singly or in a group, we had to return to our cells in the cellar. Some of us could not walk and had to be carried by those who still could. There were sixteen steps down to the cellar, and often Barbie would accompany us so he could shoot someone in the back of the neck, generally on the third step. He did this four times in eighteen days. Once he waved his gun at me, grinning: 'You were afraid, weren't you? You thought it was your turn, didn't you? Later it will be.'

"But later never came. I was transferred to Compiègne, and on July 2 I boarded the famous death train. That day was a real scorcher. We were crammed by the hundred into cattle cars that could have contained at most forty men. . . . A believer's hell couldn't possibly be worse. We had little to eat, and all we had to drink was half a barrel of water, set in a corner of the car and empty by midafternoon. People went crazy, literally. They started fighting, howling, screaming, tearing at each other's hair. It took them a long time to die. I vaguely remember myself feebly pounding against the sliding door during a stop, begging whoever was beyond it to shoot us all so that we could die quickly and with dignity. This nightmare lasted forty-eight hours.

"At Saarbrücken they opened the doors. It was such a delight to feel the fresh air caressing our faces, sweeping the stench of death away. First we had to unload the corpses. There were sixty-two in my wagon; only forty-one of us had survived. We thought that was horrible until we heard that in another car there were ninety-seven dead and only three survivors. By the time we reached Dachau, nine hundred people had died out of the two thousand and forty we had started out with. I was still young, I had never gotten close to death before, and, like most people my age, whenever I spoke of it I laughed it off, in defiance. Then all of a sudden I was getting it wholesale. I don't know how we stayed sane. The human brain is astounding. I kept mulling over my past life regretting not having taken better advantage of it. They told me I was delirious for a number of days."

Blardone describes how the Resistance operated even in Dachau, led by Edmond Michelet (later a member of General de Gaulle's cabinet) and General Charles Delestraint, the resistant arrested in Paris while waiting to meet René Hardy.

"The two of them had taken over the organization of that part of the camp where we resided. We had transformed it into a modest copy of our Resistance networks, with a hierarchy, a set of responsibilities, different tasks. We did wonders. There were all sorts of people in our group: intellectuals, workers, con men, and we all got along wonderfully, thanks to Delestraint, who was an extraordinary guy. But he despised the SS, and didn't bother to hide it. He was eventually shot in the back."

Throughout his testimony, Blardone looks at ease. He tells us he's soon going to retire, that he's glad to have had the chance to tell his story in a trial which he considers the most important event of his life since the war. Immediately after his testimony, he seems deflated, as if he has lost his reason for being. He will die just four months after the end of the trial.

André Frossard, a writer and journalist for *Le Figaro* (and "a quarter Jew," through his grandmother) is not one of the plaintiffs but a general witness. In other words, he is not here to tell of his own suffering as a war prisoner, but of the gratuitous suffering of others, the men with whom he shared his captivity in Montluc between December 10, 1943, and August 16, 1944.

"I spent eight months in the Jewish barracks, the eight worst months of my life. . . . For all practical purposes, we were already corpses. From our barracks the German police selected victims for reprisals, and since the death of one German could only be avenged with the blood of several prisoners, the turnover was practically constant. No sooner was it half empty, than it was filled again.

"In the Jewish barracks I first became aware of what a crime against humanity really is. I saw an entire family—grandfather, father, mother, a few children, and a young mother with a baby—pushed toward the cellar, where the filthiest cells were. An SS grinned and said, 'There goes all Israel.' And indeed, Mr. President, it was all Israel. . . . The people who disappeared into the cellar were not only a Jewish family from Villeurbanne or Port-Dieu, they were the people who, since the beginning of time, have been carrying all the sins of the world on their shoulders. . . .

"After seeing this, I became keenly aware of the distinction they made between Jews and non-Jews. Jews . . . were not treated as enemies, nor even as an inferior race, which would have nevertheless included them among mankind. . . . They were considered vermin, like roaches or lice. A crime against humanity occurs whenever people are killed for the simple reason that they exist. . . .

"Among us there was a shopkeeper from the suburbs of Lyon, a good Jewish guy, whom an SS had decided to turn into his own private scapegoat. One day this SS asked his whipping boy to recite the following sentence: 'Every Jew is a parasite who lives on the skin of the Aryan people.' A simple sentence if it weren't that the SS wanted our comrade to recite it in German, and he did not speak the language. Every time he made a mistake, whether in grammar or pronunciation, the SS slugged him. At last the shopkeeper managed to learn that damned sentence, but he practically lost his mind in the process. He had been so traumatized by then that every time the door opened he would start walking up and down the room like a mechanical toy, reciting his litany. The day he was dragged in front of the firing squad, his torturer ordered him to recite the sentence one last time. He died with those words on his lips.

"This is why I consider this trial of the utmost importance. Not because of Klaus Barbie, but because this is the first time that a French tribunal has been called upon to try crimes against humanity. This trial will allow us to see how Barbies are made, that is to say, how even the worst mediocrities, by selling their souls to the Party, the way others sell it to God, can acquire the power of life and death over other beings. The Party tells them what is good and what is bad, and they accept it. More than any other repressive system, Nazism attacked what is most human in us: our dignity.

". . . I wrote against torture in Algeria, but it was not the same thing. Obviously, I am opposed to torture, and believe that rather than debasing its victims it glorifies them. But I cannot see any relation between what happened in Algeria during the war and the cold-blooded actions perpetrated in the name of a specific ideology against an entire people. . . . Every nation has, at one time or another, committed some war crime. No one is innocent in that context. And I understand exactly why Maître Vergès wishes to blur the distinction between the two situations. But I blame him for forgetting what it means to fight. There were no soldiers at Izieu. There were only children whose sole sin was to be born Jewish. And that is the difference. The victims of the UGIF raid were unarmed Jewish civilians who threatened nobody, and those of the Izieu raid were children sitting before bowls of hot chocolate. And this is why I endorse the point of view of those Lyon magistrates who, in their proceedings, made a very sharp distinction between the crimes committed against the Resistance and those committed against Jews, and regret the Supreme Court's decision to blur the difference between the two."

I ask André Frossard whether he knew Robert Kahn, also known as "Renaud," in the Jewish barracks at Montluc. But he does not remember. "There was such a crowd," he explains almost apologetically.

August 1944

After the episode of the watch, the Gestapo start to put two and two together: Robert Kahn, the Jew who goes by the name of Renaud, and the escaped resistant named Renaud (who also admitted to being a Jew) are one and the same man. Klaus Barbie does not like to be made a fool of. The escape from the Saint-Etienne hospital still sticks in his throat; he hasn't had much time to dwell on it, but the file is still open. He is going to have it out with these two Renauds.

Unfortunately, Robert Kahn doesn't have much to say after almost a year in prison. He is tortured in vain. First he is sent to the *bagnoire;* then his hands are attached to the ends of a steel bar hooked to the back of his belt, so he can be knocked around by Barbie, Bartelmus, and Twisted Mug. He gladly reveals secrets of old networks which, as he knows from old comrades met in prison, no longer exist. He denounces former colleagues both by name and by code, but his only reward is a string of insults: foul Jew, shitface. What the hell does he take them for? He hid out for eleven months like a cockroach, and he thinks he's going to get off just like that? "Kurt, come here, dog. Attack."

On command, the well-trained shepherd lunges and throws Robert to the ground, where he curls into a ball, trying to protect his face. The dog becomes more excited and tears at his leg, his thigh, his buttocks, his arm.

By the time he is dragged back to his cell, his clothes are in tatters. His cellmates use the strips to bandage his wounds, and disinfect the bites with a bottle of cologne one of them received in a Red Cross package. Robert no longer feels anything; his entire body is anesthetized by pain. But this is the last time he is questioned and tortured. Barbie is done with him.

The second half of August 1944 will remain forever engraved in the historical memory of Lyon. In just a few days, its inhabitants live through a paroxysm of Nazi rage such as they have never witnessed before. Only the collaborationist press still tries to conceal the truth, that the Occupation is over. While Jeanne's train slowly pulls out of Perrache station, Brittany is being devastated, and so is Normandy.

All SS and Wehrmacht headquarters receive the order to disband. Most of their staff, however, have already deserted in a cold sweat and civilian clothes. Random cables end up in empty offices still faintly smelling of schnapps. In Lyon, however, Barbie and

Knab refuse to panic. They still have work to do before they leave
their posts.

On August 14 and 15, Lyon is bombed as the Allies try to protect
their landing on the Côte d'Azur and pave their way through the
Rhône Valley. All the major targets have been hit: oil tankers,
barracks, garages, railroad stations, airports. The Perrache station
is out of commission, the Bron airfield is in shambles. Its runways,
full of large craters rimmed with tarmac, look like lace. Most of
the aircraft have either been blown up or damaged. Yet if the
Germans leave by car, they may bump into some enterprising GI's;
and on the road they will be an easy target for Allied planes. To
leave by train would be even more conspicuous. They have no
choice but to repair the airport.

The Gestapo wastes no time in requisitioning trucks, tools, and
workers from French police stations. The prisons of the city, Montluc in particular, will provide the rest of the manpower.

On August 17, a Thursday, fifty men are assembled in the courtyard of Montluc. Since it is not an *appel avec bagages,* they assume
they will be back in the evening. Robert is among them. He is
wearing a light beige shirt and a dark blue wool suit with gray
pinstripes. It may be a little warm for the season, but it is the only
decent thing he has left. Before leaving, he slips two handsome
monogrammed cotton handkerchiefs into his pocket, presents from
Jeanne at Christmas 1939—one burgundy and the other navy
blue.

Outside, in a bright morning sun, he sees other men of all ages
pour out of the buildings, and soon realizes they are almost all Jews.
The two Catholics among them are quickly sent back to their cells
and replaced by two more Jews: Charles Schwartz, a forty-four-year-
old bank clerk with a limp, arrested by the Militia in Valence on
June 23, and Fernand Bloch, a forty-year-old cloth merchant from
Alsace, arrested in the street by mistake five days earlier. (The
Gestapo was looking for someone else, but when they checked his
papers and saw he was a Jew, they took him anyway.)

Sublieutenant Witmayer oversees the loading of the prisoners
onto three covered trucks. My father is sitting across from Jacques

Silber, a thirty-four-year-old net maker from Poland who had fled to Lyon. Silber was arrested while having lunch in a restaurant on June 25; he made the mistake of asking the man sitting at the next table with his wife and baby for a light. The man happened to be a member of the PPF, the French fascist party. In exchange for the use of his lighter, he asked to see Silber's papers, which were not a good enough fake.

Robert recognizes a few other faces: that of Colonel Pierre Bernheim, an important figure in the Lyon Resistance, and, in back, praying, that of Rabbi Chaim Dominitz, the father of four children of whom he has had no news. There are also the six people arrested four days earlier in Macon during a Militia raid: Frédéric Krieger, a toymaker of Viennese origin, two Polish refugees (a furrier and a hosier), and the three Levys. Alfred Levy, a salesman, has one arm around the shoulders of his son, Jean, who at sixteen will be the youngest of the Bron martyrs, and the other around those of his nephew, Raymond, barely one year older.

The prisoners must suspect they are going to be killed (even though it seems too ironic, with the war almost over and freedom so close at hand); why else would the SS have called only Jews? But at Bron they breathe a sigh of relief. Obviously they've been brought there to work. In groups of three, they climb into the bomb craters, and, with the help of a few tools and their bare hands, scrape the bottom to make sure there are no unexploded bombs. My father works next to Léon Eisenstein, a doctor arrested on August 9. Their third companion is Robert Nahon, a twenty-five-year-old notary clerk, arrested the previous Saturday on his way to dinner at his fiancée's. He is still all dressed up, with a silk pocket handkerchief and leather gloves, thanks to which he will be the only one to keep his nails.

Around midmorning, Brau, the warrant officer in charge, starts looking for an interpreter among the civilians busy filling cleaned-up craters with concrete; he is having trouble making the prisoners understand his German. A baker by profession and a new father, Brau is reputed to be a ruthless hater of Jews, resistants, and Frenchmen. No one volunteers.

"Will this help?" he screams, cocking his gun. Otto Huber, a theater usher from Paris, reluctantly steps forward.

Besides simultaneous translation, Otto's job is to keep track of the origin of the workers brought to Bron each morning, whether on foot or by truck. He is also in charge of gathering them into the hangar where at noon they are given a bowl of soup. Otto, who as a Frenchman feels much closer to the prisoners than to the Germans, can't stand to see them quake in front of Brau. He is particularly moved by Jean Levy's youth and the soulful look in his eyes. He approaches him with a kind word, and the boy begs him for some water. "I haven't had anything to drink since yesterday afternoon. I'm dying of thirst, could you please . . ." Otto translates his plea to the warrant officer, who, shrugging his shoulders, answers, "Let him croak." Then, not wanting to alienate Otto or the other civilian workers, Brau says quickly, "In half an hour, at noon, go get the water tank and give them one quart of water each. Just a quart, mind you."

Suddenly Otto is swamped with requests—a little tobacco here, a message for one's wife there—he can't possibly remember, let alone fulfill them all.

It is soup time. The prisoners must wait for the civilians to finish eating in order to use their bowls, unwashed of course. Otto goes to look for the water tank and in his absence Jacques Silber manages to escape. He takes advantage of a moment's inattention on the part of the guards to slip among the civilians finishing their soup. Some of his companions follow him with their eyes, some envious, others worried they will suffer a reprisal. Most think that escaping now is a useless act of bravado, since freedom is only a matter of days away. Lost among the civilians, Jacques Silber jumps into the back of a truck, but, realizing that the vehicle is not going to move for a while yet, jumps off and lets himself roll down the hillside. Once he's sure no one can see him, he starts running and keeps running for some five miles, all the way to Décines.

His absence is noticed almost immediately. He may still be hiding in the truck when the warrant officer, counting the prisoners filing by on their way to the soup, realizes there are only forty-nine. He stops the food service; the prisoners must not eat or drink until their companion is found. In the meantime, everybody must stand perfectly still, facing the wall. If the fugitive is not found by 2:00 P.M., ten prisoners will be shot. But two hours later Brau's anger seems to have subsided. After all, why bother to kill ten now when all of them are supposed to be executed later on?

The soup, now cold, is finally served at 2:00 P.M., and the prisoners return to their work. By the time they stop, around six-thirty, they are exhausted, starving, and dehydrated. The soldiers are leading them to the trucks when, suddenly, Brau orders them back to clean up two more craters. While Otto Huber leaves with the group of civilians, the prisoners drag themselves back to pits D and E. There, they are asked to drop spades and shovels and stand on the rims of the pits. They stare at each other inquisitively until they see the Germans positioning their machine guns. In minutes, the prisoners' bodies have filled the craters left by the RAF planes just four nights earlier.

I realize I have been speaking of "the prisoners." It is increasingly difficult for me to separate my father from his companions, to isolate his death from theirs. I thought his death belonged to me by right, the most precious thing he had left me. But now it seems almost sacrilege to disassociate Robert Kahn from the collective massacre. The forty-nine men fell together into the void, their eyes filled with the same image of a cloudless sky, their blood soon fused in the earth below them.

At Montluc that evening, the prisoners' cellmates wait for them in vain. On August 18, at eight o'clock in the morning, Sublieutenant Witmayer calls twenty-three new names, once again, all Jews.

That morning, Otto Huber is already back on site at the airfield. He notices the abandoned tools next to what the previous evening were two gaping holes. "You must have worked hard last night," he notes with a smile. "None of your business," Brau retorts. But a few seconds later, in a friendlier tone of voice, Brau adds, "We were here until about nine. We did a good job. The matter is closed now."

What matter? Otto wonders as he watches twenty-three new recruits climb down from the trucks. He doesn't recognize anyone from the day before except two of the guards. Perplexed, Otto approaches one of the new workers, a man in his thirties with both arms wrapped in bloody bandages who seems to be in great pain. "I was questioned yesterday," Jacques Israelovitch explains. Otto feels sorry for him and intercedes with his boss to let him rest awhile. Brau casts him a scornful look; obviously he needs things spelled out. "Don't worry. By this evening his suffering will be over. Now you know what happened to the other prisoners."

Otto cannot believe his ears. Brau must be joking.

At noon, the prisoners stop for a half-hour break and a cup of broth. At the end of the afternoon, Brau brings Otto to hangar thirteen, surrounded by the holes and scattered equipment left by the bombings. After rummaging through the rubble with the tip of his boot, Brau finds what he wants: the hose of a kerosene pump. He asks Otto to cut it into three pieces, each about a yard long, and when Otto brings the segments back to him, Brau's rosy round face lights up with a smile. He tests the flexibility of the rubber on his boots and, with a cryptic "This will do," walks back to the prisoners, Otto in tow.

It is 6:30 P.M. The twenty-three prisoners are led to the rim of another crater. Otto hears a soldier ask Brau, "Is there going to be music tonight?"

"Yes. Come with me," Brau answers. Then, noticing Otto's perplexed look, Brau dismisses him until the following morning. Before leaving the airfield, however, Otto sees the soldiers strike the prisoners with their new truncheons, the lengths of rubber hose. One prisoner is already on the ground: Gustave Dreyfus, a seventy-five-year-old grandfather of four, the eldest of those murdered at Bron.

Otto Huber doesn't sleep at all that night. Now that he knows what must have happened after his departure, he doesn't know how to report it. After all, the Germans are still in charge. Something else worries him: the fact that Brau now knows that Otto knows.

He is a dangerous witness. They may want to make sure he's not going to talk.

When Otto reports to work the next morning, he is white as chalk and has dark rings under his eyes. Then Brau arrives, but no truck from Montluc is expected. Only the civilians are there. Otto is about to go get their coffee—a luxury not allowed to prisoners—when Brau stops him.

"There is something more urgent to be done," he tells him. "I need a truckful of earth, and those jerks pretend they don't understand me." Once the truck is filled, Brau orders it driven to the pit where Otto last saw the twenty-three prisoners the night before. Brau stands on the rim and kicks some earth into the hole with the heel of his boot, then orders the truck to back up and dump its load into the crater.

That evening, in the Jewish barracks of Montluc, Vladimir Korvin-Piotrowski is alone and surrounded by silence, and it is driving him crazy. He is Russian Orthodox, and therefore a notch more respectable than a Jew, which is why he has been designated the head of the barracks. Charming, well-educated, and refined, he maintains he is the descendant of some princely family. "Blue blood runs in my White Russian veins," he likes to say.

At the beginning of the week, there were about a hundred people in his barracks. Then, on August 16, in the evening, a handful, including André Frossard, were freed for no apparent reason and suddenly found themselves on the sidewalk outside the prison. (Forty-three years later, Frossard still does not know why.) Fifty people were taken away on Thursday, and twenty-three more on Friday. Since no one has come back, the barracks is now quite empty.

Earlier in the day, Sublieutenant Witmayer had stopped by to order Vladimir to gather all his cellmates' belongings and pile them in the courtyard for the authorities to collect later that evening. Vladimir knows no more trains have left for the camps, and can't imagine where his companions have ended up. He asks an office clerk, who tells him, without looking up, "The twenty-three who left yesterday are in heaven with the fifty who left the day before."

Vladimir wants to scream and cram the words back down the German's throat.

But he knows it's no use. He clenches his fists and returns to his mournful chore, gathering everything left behind by those he now calls "my friends." He didn't know any of them very well, except for Robert, since most had been arrested only a few days before. But Robert had been there nearly two months, and so, along with Vladimir himself, was one of the old-timers. He considers keeping a few of Robert's things for his wife, who he knows was deported on August 11. The list of deportees had clandestinely reached their barracks, and Robert had tried to hide his worry as well as he could, saying that since his wife was not a Jew, she would certainly be spared. Robert has not left much behind: some underwear, two ties. Vladimir could keep the ties for Jeanne, but if the Germans find them on him they'll think he's stolen them from the dead and will make him pay. Besides, two dirty rags are not going to bring her much comfort.

Vladimir liked Robert. Together they dreamed up the most sumptuous meals, down to the least detail, from market to the presentation and subsequent consumption. Robert's descriptions were extraordinarily vivid, and his imagination so intense that he would drool over Vladimir's imaginary pirozhki, borscht, and blinis. At the end of those "feasts," they always promised each other that as soon as they were out they would stuff themselves with all the delicacies in the world. Now Robert will never be out, and Vladimir can't help but wonder—as he gathers his friends' clothes into the courtyard—whether he ever will be either.

On August 21, early in the morning, a hundred and ten men and women in chains are escorted from Montluc by thirty-five Militia men to the unused Fort de Côte-Lorette, in the town of Saint-Genis-Laval. There, they are led into a first-floor room where, ten by ten, they are felled by a firing squad. The last groups have to climb on top of the still warm corpses of their predecessors before they themselves are shot. Few will be identified, since, after the last group is eliminated, the SS douses the pile of corpses with gasoline and sets it on fire. Then they blow up the building. The explosion is heard throughout the city. It is 9:30 A.M., and, frozen in place, the inhabitants of Lyon quietly wonder what's going on. The martyrs of Saint-Genis-Laval will thus be honored with a few seconds of silence.

Three days later, Cardinal Pierre Gerlier learns what happened in the Fort and immediately hurries over to Werner Knab's office. The cardinal does not know about the massacres of Bron, but what he has just learned is enough to horrify him. Banging his fist on Knab's desk, he warns him that unless the SS put an end to their murders they will be sorry.

That very evening, the few prisoners left in Montluc sense a change. The noises of the prison are different. No heavy footsteps are heard in the hallways, no German voices echo through the courtyards. The calm and quiet are in themselves so unbelievable that it takes the prisoners a long time to realize they are free. At nine-fifty that night, the French national anthem rings out to welcome the resistants who have come to open the prison.

What the resistants find in Montluc and at Saint-Genis-Laval greatly dampens their spirits. But by the time Cardinal Gerlier bursts into Knab's office, Klaus Barbie (who left immediately after the operation at Saint-Genis-Laval) is already far from Lyon. Some believe that, before returning to Germany near the end of the month, he came back to Lyon incognito to eliminate the most eloquent traces of his crimes, that is to say, the twenty-odd French Militia men and collaborators who had openly supported him. In any event, by the time the Americans enter Lyon, on September 3, the SS is gone.

But on the heights of Bron, 109 corpses are rotting in their makeshift graves. After the seventy-two Jews murdered on August 17 and 18, thirty-seven partisans, among them seven women, filled two more pits. The morning after the liberation of the city, some of the civilians who worked on the runways return to the airport to confirm their suspicions before informing the police and the public prosecutor of Lyon. First, they check the crater behind hangar 69, where, on August 21, a few workers saw the Germans shoot at least eighteen people point-blank. What they discover makes them shudder with horror. Under a thin crust of earth they uncover a head, a leg, a shoulder, a shoe.

All the dead of Bron are quickly exhumed and autopsied. Each is assigned a numbered file containing whatever information it has been possible to gather: foot size, dental work, physical peculiarities. Other clues that might help relatives identify the bodies are placed in plastic envelopes: belt buckles, rings, dental prostheses, ties. The 109 envelopes and files are then placed on as many chairs lined up in a special room at police headquarters, where relatives can examine their contents. After each identification, a chair disappears. This morbid procedure takes place two steps away from the room where couples are married.

13 "JUDE, JUDE"

As the police sirens slash the air, a crowd gathers at the foot of the Palais de Justice. When the police try to force the on-lookers back behind the barriers, there are catcalls: "Fascists! SS!"

When Barbie first appeared in court, we were all curious to see how cruelty, hatred, and violence had branded him. We were disappointed in the gray banality of his face, and the fragility of his seventy-year-old body. It seemed impossible that someone so weak could be responsible for so much horror. Some of us almost felt sorry for him. But then we saw the witnesses and heard their stories, and almost imperceptibly, while Barbie was reading Virgil in his cell, our impression of him began to change. When he reappears in his bulletproof box later in the afternoon, we will all see him as the incarnation of Satan.

First we will hear from Fortune Lanfranchi, a resistant who re-members being "led into an office of the Ecole de Santé, where I met a very well-dressed young man who held a whip in his hand. The walls of the room were streaked with blood from ceiling to floor. I was methodically whipped all over and then dragged to the cellar, where I was confronted with a human being who had been mutilated beyond recognition. After this, they took me to Montluc, where I was told that the young man I had met at the Ecole de Santé was Klaus Barbie, a monster. . . .

"There were one hundred and ten of us squeezed in a train car [on the way to Dachau]. Some fainted. Fortunately, a sudden storm cooled the air that had become unbreathable. It saved our lives, even though we fought with one another like wild animals to get to the cracks in the walls of the wagon. By the time we got to Dachau, our clothes were in shreds. As we crossed the town on our way to the camp, the population greeted us with stones and insults as if we were the worst kind of criminals. . . .

"When I saw Barbie on TV in 1972, his face immediately rang a bell. He had not changed much; he has changed more since."

The next witness, Robert Clor, a painter and interior decorator, is a little deaf and very emotional. He looks tired and apologizes for sitting down. The usher, even more solicitous than with the other witnesses, immediately brings a chair and sits next to him in case he needs help.

"I was arrested on May 17, 1944, and spent six weeks at the Gestapo's disposal. One day, as I was being treated to the *bagnoire,* I saw a very young girl hanging by the wrists, which they had bound above her head, from a hook stuck in the wall. She was entirely naked and looked very frail. Klaus Barbie ordered the Germans who were in the room to penetrate her with their truncheons, and when they hesitated, he showed them how to do it with an obscene grimace on his face. She screamed and screamed, and I could do nothing to help her. This is the last time I saw Barbie. I can't remember all the torture I went through, but that, what they did to that girl, caused me more pain than I can say. When I came back from deportation, in 1945, I saw a picture of Barbie in the paper. They already called him the 'Butcher of Lyon'—it was the first time I had heard the expression. I wouldn't mind facing him again."

. . .

Raymonde Belot, a retired doctor, is one of the women whose extraordinary courage has been for me the most significant revelation of this trial. "I was twelve the evening my father darkly announced that Hitler had been elected and that there would be a war," her testimony begins.

"By the time I was sixteen, I had read *Mein Kampf*. The war did not take me by surprise. I immediately joined the Resistance. I started by distributing clandestine papers with my fiancé, Fernand Belot. When we heard that the Resistance was looking for people with connections in the country and the local towns to organize escape channels, we applied and, before we knew it, found ourselves buried under an avalanche of forged and lost documents supplied by sympathizing policemen. We used them to help entire families cross the Swiss border. We also worked for Témoignage Chrétien [Christian Witness]. We got married at the beginning of 1943. We didn't know we had so little time ahead of us. Our network was betrayed by one of its members. . . .

"I was questioned three times in one week. My cellmates told me that the man in charge of the interrogation was a certain Barbie or Barbier. During the third interrogation Barbie did not hit me. I had been playing it dumb all the while, and he was beginning to believe me. 'Fine,' he told me. 'Either you don't know anything or you don't want to talk. Your husband doesn't want to talk either. So I'm going to offer you a deal. I am going to leave you alone together for a while and you are going to convince your husband to talk. Otherwise I'll get your parents.'

"They placed me in a cellar with Fernand. He told me he had already suffered a great deal and told me to tell them he would only answer their questions after the war. When I told Barbie, he flew into a rage and immediately threatened to shoot my husband. I told him he couldn't, since we were neither Jews, nor communists, nor terrorists.

" 'You are worse than all of them, since what you write arms them against us.'

"That was the last time I saw or heard of my husband. [True to his word, Barbie had Fernand Belot shot with eighteen other Montluc prisoners on June 9.] On July 1, I left for Ravens-brück. . . . I was in a group of seventy French women, all under twenty-five years old. They asked us whether we wanted to become the whores of the German soldiers on the Russian front. We all refused, and for some strange reason, they did not insist.

"Until August, we spent most of our time responding to inter-minable roll calls that went on from four in the morning until six in the evening. We were left in the courtyard for hours, in the rain or under scorching sun. We looked like herons, since to rest our legs we would often stand on one at a time. Then we were assigned to the salt mines, two miles away from our camp. We worked from seven in the morning until seven at night, but we had to get up at four, since we went there on foot. We dragged our famished bodies along a road that passed by the homes of German engineers. On our way over to the mines everyone was asleep, but on our way back we were always met by groups of children who threw stones at us. I wonder what they thought we were, what they had been told.

"We were literally devoured by hunger, a ravenous void that kept gnawing at our entrails. They went out of their way to make us suffer. The only water we had was kept in pails where, early in the morning, the SS officers came to vomit the excesses of the night. And then they forced us to wash in it. Then again, we were forced to live in the worst filth. Do you know what it's like not to wash one's hair for a year? To wear clothes that are stiff with excrement and swarming with lice?

"After the salt mines, I was sent to a tool factory. One day, our boss discovered that some two thousand pieces were defective. He sent for us and very calmly told us, 'Don't ever forget that we don't care what you do on this job; we just want you to die in it.'

"When in April they decided to evacuate Ravensbrück, we were loaded into a train going north. There were a hundred and forty of us in each car, and no food or water for several days. Some of the women in my car ended up drinking their urine. Others went crazy, others died. We had to throw their bodies onto the station platforms. I'll never forget the thud they made on landing.

"This went on for twelve days. One day, at a stop, I was given a pail and ordered to go fill it at a nearby faucet. I stared at the fresh running water but could not drink it; I could only wet my lips. Still, that pail of water made our life easier for some forty-eight hours. Then they gave us some bread, but we could not swallow it because we had no saliva. It was awful to be as hungry as we were, with something to eat in our hands, and to be unable to swallow.

"When we arrived at Hamburg, they immediately ordered us to dig a ditch. Our shovels were heavier than we thought. We managed to dig the ditches and to bury the bodies of our dead companions. Some were still warm, some might have been alive when we threw them into the pit and trampled on them to pack in as many as possible.

"By the time we left Hamburg, there were only fifty of us in each car. At last, our train stopped at a station on the Danish border. The Germans had disappeared and there were Red Cross people on the other side. We were so weak that they had to pick us up in their arms to lift us out of the train. It was the first humane gesture we had experienced in months and months of atrocities."

Andrée Majerowicz, like Raymonde, was only twenty-three when the Germans burst into her office on June 15, 1944. But while Raymonde was arrested as a resistant, Andrée was arrested as a Jew.

"I had forged documents stating that my name was Geneviève Roger and that I was Catholic. I showed them to the Gestapo, but they sneered at me and said nothing. A few months later, other Germans brought my younger brother and sister in. Clearly, we had been denounced. One of the SS walked up to me, put out his cigarette on my cheek, and hissed, 'Jude, Jude.' . . . On June 30, we left for Drancy, and on July 31 for Auschwitz. Since there were still a few places on the train, the Germans filled them with five hundred and fifty children between six months and seventeen years of age. They cried and looked at us with wide, terrified eyes. For the three days and nights that our trip lasted, we took care of them as best we could. . . .

"Toward mid-October we were transferred to the Sudetes, where there was a little camp next to an arms factory. It was worse than Auschwitz. It was very cold and they gave us only a cup of broth now and then and a piece of bread. One day Mengele paid us a visit and told six women who had just given birth in the infirmary that if they would poison their own babies he would spare their lives. Four complied; the other two chose to go to the gas chamber holding their babies in their arms. I have never dared mention this before for fear of discrediting the four women who chose to poison their babies with their own hands, but I should say, to their credit, that had they refused, their babies would have died anyway, whether from lack of nourishment, or of dehydration, or in the gas chamber.

"One reason I never spoke much of my deportation before has to do with people's reactions. Some were so horrified by what they heard that they would question its truth, to the point that at times I wondered myself whether I hadn't dreamed it all, even though I knew better. Others would be so pained by what I told them they would beg me to stop. So I stopped. But I had to speak at this trial, if not for myself, then for my companions, who were also tortured and deported by Barbie, but, less fortunate than I, did not come back."

All eyes are turned to the defendant's box when Barbie is finally led in by two guards; he takes his place in his bulletproof stand. Suddenly his presence seems intrusive, almost as if we had forgotten that this is his trial, that he has any right to be here. Everything has gone so well without him that we can hardly wait for him to leave. First, however, some ten witnesses must file by, one by one, and officially identify him. Barbie returns their gazes condescendingly, the slightest grin stretching his thin lips.

Mario Blardone speaks for all when he addresses him: "Those eyes, that smirk have not changed in these forty years. Look at me, Barbie. We have something to tell each other! Look! He closes his eyes, turns his head away, doesn't dare look at me. He is a coward. I want you all to see this: Without his uniform and his whip, this SS is merely a coward."

GERMANY, 1944–51

Back in Germany after his brutal farewell to Lyon, Klaus Barbie is reassigned to a fighting unit, and is once again promoted, from SS *Haupsturmführer*—captain to *Sturmbannführer*—major. High ranks go a dime a dozen in the Wehrmacht now, as victories are replaced by stripes and Himmler's compliments.

On April 17, Barbie's unit is surrounded in the vicinity of Wuppertal. Barbie and four of his companions quickly bury their arms, put on civilian clothes, and take off on bicycles they have stolen in advance. Barbie, the deserter, hides by day and walks by night to reach his family in Trier. Stopped at a road block, he has no trouble convincing the American soldiers that he is a mere private "on his way to Kassel," where he is supposed to report back to his unit after a short leave.

In Marburg, Barbie hides in the apartment of an old Nazi colleague and registers at the law school as an auditor, under the name of Heinz Mertens. His registration means little but provides him with an ID card. At the law school, he joins a group of ex-SS who dream of founding the Fourth Reich. For the time being, however, their role is limited to helping other SS elude the court at Nuremberg.

Barbie's job, in this underground organization consisting of some sixty members, is to forge false Wehrmacht demobilization papers for ex-SS, and help them obtain ID cards under false names. By a strange twist of fate, he becomes an artist at the same trade that earned False-Papers Pierre a trip to Dachau.

Barbie is number 239 on the list of wanted war criminals compiled in December 1944 by a United Nations commission in London. There is an international warrant out for his arrest, issued by the Lyon military magistrate. Three years later, he appears on the CROWCASS list, compiled by the Central Registry of War Criminals and Security Suspects. Better researched than the 1944 list, this one gives not only Barbie's real name but some of his pseudonyms: Barbier, Barby, von Barbier, Klein, Kreitz, and Mayer.

But by then Barbie is already under the protection of American intelligence. At the beginning of 1947, he had managed to elude the operation "Selection Board," which had resulted in the simultaneous arrest of more than sixty escaped Nazis throughout the American zone of Germany. When the Americans came knocking on the door of the apartment where Barbie was hiding in Kassel he jumped out the bathroom window and disappeared. His friend and host, Fridolin Becker, whose reflexes proved a little slower than Barbie's, was arrested.

On the run, Barbie contacted a friend from his days at the Abwehr in Dijon: Joseph Merk, (a.k.a. Kurt Merk). For several months now, Kurt had been working in the CIC—the Counter Intelligence Corps of the American army—whose mission was the denazification of Germany. With seven hundred men and large funds at its disposal, the CIC was meant to arrest the leaders of the Nazi Party, prevent the formation of new paramilitary organizations with Nazi tendencies, and hunt down Nazi sympathizers. However, the escalating Cold War soon distracted the CIC from its initial goals to involve it primarily in anti-communist intelligence.

Barbie's employers choose to close their eyes to their new informer's past service record. "His value as an informer is more important to us than his past as an SS," says Robert Taylor, his CIC boss in 1947.

Barbie is not the only one to serve his former enemies; most former Nazis, terrified at the thought of what may happen to them if they are caught, readily accept any compromise. Nevertheless, some of Barbie's superiors at the CIC are not very supportive of his presence on their staff. Major Earl Browning, for instance, tries to have him handed over to the French authorities. But Barbie is protected by petty bureaucrats who maintain that he is providing the corps with valuable information. When Barbie is wanted by the German criminal police for jewelry theft and assault, only his two accomplices are arrested and tried. On his comfortable income from his work as a secret agent and from the black market, he begets and supports a second child with Regine: Klaus George.

In 1948, the CIC installs him and Merk, with their respective families, in a lovely house in Augsburg. They have an office, a secretary, a large team of informers, and a considerable budget from which they draw a generous salary. The documents they often request, and receive, in payment for services rendered, are used to help former SS officers flee Germany. Barbie may manage to penetrate the KPD—the West German Communist Party—but for the most part the information he gathers consists of barroom gossip and data from specialized technical and political magazines.

By the end of the year, the expensive and inefficient Merk-Barbie network is roundly criticized. Their investigative team is a joke. And Barbie's past and current troubles with France are no mystery to anyone. His boss, the last of the many who have succeeded Robert Taylor, points this out in a memo: "Barbie is afraid of France and keeps an informed eye on the evolution of the French mentality. He knows that if he falls into their hands, he is going to face the firing squad."

The Americans, however, don't consider Barbie's troubles with France any of their business. In 1949, when the service is restructured, Merk is dismissed but Barbie stays. His name and reputation open doors at German government services, including the police and many a provincial city hall, whose major posts are now filled by ex-SS.

In the meantime, France has twice tried René Hardy, the man suspected of betraying the Caluire meeting, for treason. The first time, in January 1947, Hardy was acquitted. But new evidence causes the case to be reopened. As before, however, the main witness—Klaus Barbie—is missing.

It is not easy for the French police to locate Barbie, what with his false identities and the smokescreen set up by the CIC. When he is at last discovered, the Americans refuse to let him testify in France. "He's more useful to us free here than imprisoned in France," they say. Nonetheless, representatives of France's Ministry of Justice are allowed to come to Germany to question him. During the summer of 1948, there are three sessions, held in secret. Barbie contradicts himself and is very vague; the French go back empty-handed. However, Barbie's name has resurfaced, and the Ministry of Justice begins to gather charges and testimony against him. The people of Lyon demand that he be handed over to them. The Americans hide Barbie from a French group searching for him in Augsburg, and throw his pursuers off the track with false leads.

Shortly before René Hardy's second trial, in April 1950, the French multiply their requests, but their letters go unanswered. In the absence of the critical witness, René Hardy is again acquitted.

The French don't give up, but the more insistent they are, the more the Americans seem to shrug their shoulders. Two requests for Klaus Barbie's extradition are denied without being officially turned down; things are allowed to become mired in red tape. First, regulations require the precise address of the wanted person; as soon as that information is provided, the exact dates of Barbie's presumed crimes are necessary, and so on, while deadlines go by and files are lost in office drawers. When, at the end of the summer of 1950, the French think they are getting somewhere, their last extradition request is returned stamped "Impossible to Locate." This is at a time when hundreds of people know exactly what bell to ring to see Klaus Barbie open the door.

In retrospect, the CIC's behavior was unconscionable. But at the time Americans were obsessed with the communist witch hunt. The CIC—which by then was being absorbed into the brand-new CIA—saw France as sympathetic to Moscow, and imagined that the French were not interested in Barbie because of his conduct in Lyon, but because they wanted to pump him for information about the American infiltration of the KPD.

In 1951, the CIA helped Barbie escape to Bolivia, which explains why, for the three months before, his entire family was taking Spanish lessons.

14 THE RAT LINE

There was once a children's home in Izieu, where forty-four Jewish children lived in hiding but also in relative peace. Most of their parents were already ashes, but the children did not know it, and still had faith in the future.

The founder and soul of this home was Sabina Zlatin, who managed it with the help of her husband, Miron. Now eighty years old, she seems younger, despite her white hair and uncertain step. Her mind is quick, her voice clear as she testifies:

"First I must go back a few years to tell you how Izieu started. I was working in the military hospital of Montpellier when, suddenly, in 1941, I was fired, without explanation. Not that I needed one. Anti-Jewish laws were just beginning to be implemented. So I went to the prefecture and requested authorization, as a social worker, to visit the camps for Jewish and political refugees coming from other countries. Nobody has yet told you what the Agde camp was like. It consisted of a few wooden barracks with straw scattered over the ground, no beds. There was no hygiene; people had to stand in line to get a glass of water. The first time I visited the camp, I was greeted by total silence, because of my uniform. Then there was a scream, followed by a heartrending appeal. A mother held out her baby to me, begging me to take him away. I had permission to take five children, but there were dozens who needed help. I had to choose which ones to take. I was allowed to visit the camp three times a week. Each time I took away as many children as possible, hiding the smaller ones under my cape. Then I would hand them over to the OSE—Oeuvre de Secours aux Enfants, the Children's Aid Commission—which took care of placing them while waiting to reunite them with their families. I don't know how many of those children found their families after the war, but I know that by taking them out of those camps the OSE saved their lives. When the Agde camp was evacuated and relocated at Rivesalte, I followed it there.

"I had seen stables and cowsheds before, but I had never seen human beings living in such conditions. Never. So I went on visiting the camp and sneaking out children until the Germans took over and I was no longer let in. That's when I met some extraordinary priests. Abbé Prévost was one of them. He placed five children for me. He took them to the mother superior of a convent and told her, 'My sister, take these children. They are Jewish, therefore they do not have to attend mass.' Then he placed a few more, but he advised me to leave the region as quickly as possible. . . .

"Eventually a friend of ours found us a home in Izieu. . . . Pretty soon our group had quadrupled. We had to transform the barn into a dormitory. . . . We were too many not to run a big risk.

"I returned to Abbé Prévost for advice, and he introduced me to Reverend Father Chaillet, an extraordinary man who managed to place some forty children throughout the region, leaving us with only forty-four, which was as many as we could handle. But when the Jewish doctor who lived in the village was arrested, we had to start thinking about an alternative to Izieu.

"On April 5, I paid one more visit to Abbé Prévost, who helped me make plans to leave Izieu. He could not place forty-four children, but he would take care of fifteen, whom I was supposed to bring to him the following Monday, April 12, after Easter. The next morning I received the cable: 'Family sick. Fear contagion.' I immediately knew what had happened. I hurried to Vichy without even bothering to remove my nurse's uniform. I had an ID that did not specify I was a Jew. I managed to see a top civil servant and told him all I could about Izieu. He listened to me with a very bored expression on his face. I insisted, 'If there is anything you can do for those children, you must do it.' He looked at me with surprise, then answered, 'Why in the world did you get involved with those dirty Jews? Go see Joseph Darnand, he will tell you what to do.'

"Darnand was in charge of the Ministry of the Interior, and his office was right across the street. So I went to see him. He said the same thing and added, 'If you don't get out of my office right now, I'll have you arrested.' But I was too desperate to give up. I went to Paris, where I told my story to the woman in charge of the Red Cross and others. Finally, a few powerful people pulled strings to get the children out of Drancy, but by then they had already left for Auschwitz. The only people left were my husband and two older boys. A few days later they were deported to Lithuania. I later heard that Miron worked in a mill to get enough flour to feed his companions; good habits die hard. Then, on July 13, 1944, he and the two boys were sent to gather wood. It was a pretext. Once in the woods, they were shot. It was our wedding anniversary. . . .

"Barbie maintains he only dealt with *maquisards* and other resistants, that is to say, with the enemies of the German army. But then why did he deport the Izieu children? Were they dangerous? Were they terrorists? No. They were just children, and children are children, whether they are white or black, Jews or Protestants. The world can neither forget nor forgive such a crime."

Sabina, like many other people who lived near the home, is convinced they were betrayed by a neighboring peasant, Lucien Bourdon. In 1945, Bourdon was tried in absentia, found guilty, and deprived of his civic rights for ten years for having been too nice to the Germans. Did he denounce Izieu for a reward, or to buy himself an "indulgence" that would allow him to go on trafficking

on the black market? Only he and Barbie can answer these questions. But Barbie will never answer, and Bourdon will never be
asked, since he never answered his subpoena, and nobody knows
where he is.

The actual witnesses of the raid are three: Léon Reifman, the
medical student who jumped out the window; Lea Feldblum, who
was so shaken by the event her mind has never been the same; and
Julien Favet, a local farmhand who, for forty-three years, has been
saying that he saw Klaus Barbie in the children's home that
morning.

"Because of the racial laws, I had to drop out of medical school,"
Léon Reifman explains. "When Sabina Zlatin opened Izieu, she
took me on as a nurse, and my older sister, Sarah, as a doctor.
Sarah lived there with Claude, her eleven-year-old son. I left in
September 1943 because I was wanted by the STO and didn't want
my presence there to put the children at risk.

"Claude had been staying with my parents for a few days. They
were going to bring him back to Izieu for Easter, and I decided to
go along, since we hadn't been all together for a while. . . .

"When I entered the house, the breakfast bell was ringing. I
immediately rushed upstairs to hug my sister. We were coming
downstairs when we saw the dining-hall door open and three men
in civilian clothes step into the hallway. The smallest of the three
saw us and, in French, ordered us to come down. But Sarah signaled
me to run away. So I hurried back up, ran to the other end of the
house, and jumped out the window. One of the soldiers stationed
outside saw me drop into the bushes but did not fire. He gave me
time to hide, and when he and the other soldiers began searching
the bushes, they all pretended not to see me.

"From where I lay hidden, I could follow everything that went
on: the screaming and crying of the children, the pleading of the
adults, the shouting of the Germans. Then I heard the roars of
several engines, the crunch of wheels on the gravel, and the voices
of the children singing '*Vous n'aurez pas L'Alsace et la Lorraine*'
[You shall not have Alsace and Lorraine], maybe to give themselves
courage. By and by, all these noises faded away and I was left in

deathly silence, outside as well as inside the house, which usually echoed with the daily activities of forty to fifty children. Gone, it was all gone. All the children were gone, along with my sister, my nephew, and my parents. I sobbed all day long. In the evening, some neighbors gathered around the house in anger and dismay. They knew those children who had often stopped by their homes looking for milk or fruit. I came out of my hiding place, and they helped me escape during the night. . . .

"I don't know whether Barbie was among the three men I saw at the foot of the staircase that morning. All I know is that the shorter of the three seemed to be in charge. When I first saw Barbie here, something clicked within me, and I again saw the short man ordering us downstairs. But I could not swear he was Barbie, though he certainly looked like him.

"So what if Barbie refuses to attend these hearings, since he refuses to express any regret for the atrocities he committed. But I do hope that through him you will condemn an ideology that sullied and dishonored all humankind."

"I loved them, loved them all, and my little Emile, clinging to my skirt, refusing to let me go!" Lea Feldblum's memories pour out in confusion. She is sixty-nine, and has been living in Haifa, Israel, since her release from Auschwitz. It is difficult to follow her. She seldom finishes her sentences, as if she were unable to fully draw them out of the past. But a terrible story emerges from those fragments.

"I was twenty-four. I was both a teacher and a supervisor. My parents died in Montpellier in a refugee camp. My sister and brother were deported to Auschwitz in September 1942 and died there. I had false documents in the name of Marie Louise Decoste, and it is as such that I was arrested with the children. We were brought to Fort Montluc for questioning. Naturally, the children told the truth, they were much too young to be able to lie to the Gestapo. In any case, their foreign accents and the fact that the boys were circumcised were eloquent enough. We spent the night in Montluc, and the following morning, April 7, we were transferred to Drancy.

By then I knew we were going to be deported, and so, to be sure I would go with the children, I revealed my true identity. I couldn't stand the idea of watching them leave.

"We left on April 13, and arrived two days later in the middle of the night. It was cold. I lined the children up on the platform at Birkenau and placed myself at the head of the line. A German officer unkindly asked me whether they were all my children—as if at my age I could have had that many children, and some in their teens. I told him they came from a children's home, and that I was their teacher. He grabbed my arm and pushed me to the side. Emile Zuckerberg was five years old, and I was everything he had. They pulled him away from me. Then they loaded all the children into the trucks and drove them off. They refused to let me go with them. They refused to let me die holding Emile's hand."

Lea can't go on. Her voice breaks, and she leaves the witness stand.

When he takes her place, Julien Favet keeps turning and twisting his cap with the gnarled fingers of a man who has spent his entire life working on a farm. He is sixty-eight, but his weatherbeaten face looks much older. He is here to repeat one more time, as he has for the last forty-some years, that on April 6, he saw Barbie at Izieu.

"Generally, when I worked in the fields, someone would bring me a snack around eight in the morning. By eight-thirty nobody had come. So I decided to go up to the boss's farm. The road I took went right by the children's home. In the village, we called it 'the colony.' As I rounded the corner, I saw the trucks and three men leaning against the coping of the well in the courtyard. They were talking. As I came a little closer, I recognized Lucien Bourdon. It surprised me. I couldn't figure out what he was doing there. Then the children started coming out of the house. Some of them climbed into the trucks by themselves, but the others, the smaller ones, were thrown in like sacks of potatoes. A soldier blocked my way. One of the three civilians, a small, thin man, approached and, looking me over, asked me whether I had jumped. I couldn't figure out what he meant, but later I realized he thought I was young Reifman. Finally, he realized I was only a farmhand and told the soldier to let me go. The short civilian was Barbie. I know it as I know I am looking at you, Mr. President. I have no doubt about it.

"So they left me there and went back to their trucks filled with children. You see, I am not a racist, I am not a Jew, I am nothing in particular, I'm not smart enough to talk politics. But when I see a bunch of men taking it out on children, I'm disgusted. The oldest children tried to jump over the sides of the trucks, but the Germans pushed them back with the butts of their guns. It was awful. I went on up to my boss's farm and there I threw a fit. I waited for everything to be over. There was nothing we could do. All the village people looked out their windows, trembling with fear and disgust. The trucks passed by the farm. We could hear the children singing. It was so beautiful it made me shiver. Then it was all over.

"As soon as I faced Barbie I recognized him. He is the man who asked me, 'Did you jump?' and who told the soldier to let me go. I know it for a fact. Just as I know that one of the men standing by the well was Bourdon. Barbie's lawyer laughs at me, and reproaches me for not having testified at Bourdon's trial in 1947. He wants people to think my memory woke up only after Barbie's arrest. But in fact, the only reason I did not testify at Bourdon's trial is because no one asked me to. I didn't get any papers. I cannot be held responsible for that."

The hearings are going to be suspended for four days. Tomorrow, Thursday, is Ascension Day, and all France is taking a long weekend. But the memory of the Izieu children will follow all of us who have heard their story wherever we go.

BOLIVIA, 1951–83

The Rat Line is a channel through which political criminals can flee Europe for Latin America. Originally meant for Russian refugees, its new clientele are former Nazis headed for Peru, Argentina,

Colombia, and Bolivia. The most difficult part of the route is reaching the Italian ports in Naples or Genoa, and hiding there while waiting to board a ship. But once the anchor is pulled up, all ties with the past can be cast off, and one is free to begin a new life.

Ironically, it is a German Jew who handles Barbie's escape. On March 2, 1951, Klaus, Regina, Ute, and Klaus Jr. leave Augsburg and their homeland with new luggage and new clothes. Everything they have is new. They have no letters or photos. A travel document for stateless people describes Klaus Altmann as a mechanic two years younger than he actually is.

In Genoa, the fugitives are welcomed by Father Krunoslav Draganovic, a Croatian priest who helps people for profit. What he does for Barbie he has already done for many other SS. He takes care of the Altmanns' stay in Italy, their transit papers, their new residence permits. Barbie would like to go to Argentina, but at the moment Bolivia is easier, and what matters most is to put the Atlantic between himself and France. While waiting to board ship, the Altmanns settle in a small hotel, one room above Adolf Eichmann's. On March 23, they board the *Corrientes*, and by April 23 they are in Bolivia.

It is a new life for Barbie. Despite his CIC earnings and black market profits, he no longer has a penny to his name and bitterly regrets not having profited more from the Jewish raids. Other SS left the occupied countries with small fortunes. It's not that he refrained from looting Jewish homes; while his men took care of the arrests, he stuffed his pockets with jewels and money. But while other SS sent the booty home, Barbie spent it all on Lyon whores.

It's not easy to start a new life without money or skills. Unless, of course, you have connections, and La Paz swarms with former SS eager to lend each other a hand. Barbie has been given a few addresses and soon finds himself the foreman of a sawmill connected to a large forest estate. The owner is a German Jew, Ludwig Kapauner, who emigrated to Bolivia at the beginning of the 1930s. He has only a vague idea of what has happened in Europe and none of Herr Altmann's past. He doesn't even hear about the 1952 and

1954 Lyon trials which condemn his foreman to death in absentia.

After three years with Kapauner, Barbie has learned enough about wood to start his own business: a sawmill specializing in the production of wood crates. By 1957, he and his family qualify for, and are granted, Bolivian citizenship.

In 1965, Barbie begins exporting cinchona, the basic ingredient in quinine, and he becomes the main supplier of a German chemical laboratory in Mannheim. But soon demand for quinine diminishes and Barbie makes a deal with the Bolivian government for 51 percent of the capital and a low-interest state loan to fund a new enterprise: the Transmaritima Boliviana Limitada. Officially, the company is in charge of all Bolivian shipping; in reality it is a cover for arms and drug trafficking, which help to finance frequent coups d'état. Barbie's Transmaritima always sides with the winner, and so survives. He even obtains a diplomatic passport that allows him to travel anywhere he pleases in order to make contacts for Transmaritima. He travels to Europe and the United States. Later he will provoke the French by claiming that he even went to France, incognito, to place flowers on Jean Moulin's grave.

Meanwhile, however, Transmaritima is accumulating debts. Barbie relies on credit, and uses administrative and legal bureaucracy to gain time. But in early 1971, Transmaritima shows enormous liabilities, and Barbie's tenure as Klaus Altmann is coming to an end. His background is again being seriously investigated, without his knowledge, both in Germany and France, because his children's invented pasts have aroused suspicion. In June 1968, Klaus Jr. married Françoise Craxier-Roux, a French woman. The French embassy, charged with comparing the entries in the marriage certificate with the civil status of both parties, found the young groom's name, birthplace, and date of birth definitely suspect. Similarly, in 1969, Ute requested a long-term residence permit from the German consulate in La Paz; her origins, too, seemed questionable.

In September 1969, the Ministry of Foreign Affairs in Bonn sends a confidential note to its office in La Paz requesting a "discreet investigation of Klaus Altmann, since it appears that he is in close contact with influential members of President Salinas's circle, as well as with a number of former Nazis who are currently occupying important posts throughout Latin America." To avoid jeopardizing its relationship with Bolivia, Bonn advises its representative to exercise "great caution." Barbie will go on living in tranquillity while behind his back France and Germany seek a legal basis for his arrest. Treaties, conventions, agreements between France and Germany all forbid the arrest of a German national (Barbie's Bolivian citizenship, acquired under a false name, is considered invalid) for the purpose of trying him in a French court. Germany also maintains that the 1952 and 1954 trials have already settled all disputes, while France argues that there is at least one unresolved file that can be easily reopened—the file on the raid on the Jewish children's home in Izieu. Germany wants definitive proof that Barbie knew he was sending the children to their deaths. France is unable to provide it, and the matter is closed.

In 1971, Colonel Hugo Banzer seizes power after a typically Bolivian coup d'état, in which he is supported by the German expatriate community. He appoints Barbie counselor of the secret police and head of the paramilitary units which constitute Banzer's "Praetorian Guard." When Transmaritima goes bankrupt because of its owner's greed and mismanagement, Barbie is not even reprimanded. He moves his household northwest, to Lima, Peru, where his new home looks like a Hollywood version of a Tyrolean chalet. His neighbor is an old friend, Friedrich Schwend, a self-styled former SS colonel who escaped to Peru laden with money. It will be a very pleasant summer of peaceful days in La Paz, peaceful nights in Lima, until a very small woman gives it all a big kick.

Beate Klarsfeld is a Nazi hunter. Born in Berlin in 1939 of a Protestant family, she has been a French citizen since 1963, when she married Serge Klarsfeld, a young Jew who lost his father and several other relatives in the Holocaust. A convert, Beate perhaps needs to feel more Jewish than she might if she were born to Judaism; and as a German she wants "to atone for her country's sins." In her idealism she cannot understand how her country can refuse to judge its criminals, and itself. She wants to force it to do so.

Throughout 1971, Beate and Serge work simultaneously on two different fronts: trying to prosecute Kurt Lischka, Herbert Hagen, and Ernst Heinrichson, former Gestapo officers in Paris involved in the deportation of Jews, and trying to find Klaus Barbie. At one point, Beate is arrested, accused of having tried to kidnap Kurt Lischka. But undaunted, and revolted by Germany's decision to bury the Izieu story for lack of evidence, she is determined to find evidence. To support the charge that Barbie knew full well what the Izieu children were headed for, she has collected the testimony of two mothers: Itta Rose Halaunbrenner, who lost two daughters in the raid, and Fortunée Benguigui, who lost three sons. She also produces a declaration by one of the survivors of the UGIF raid who heard Klaus Barbie announce, "Shot or deported, for a kike it's the same thing." Armed with this new evidence, France can now request Barbie's extradition from Bolivia. Meanwhile, the French press has published a photo of Klaus Altmann, startling readers who recognize him and identify him in letters to the editor, as "the man who tortured me in Lyon," "the SS officer who had me deported," or "the butcher who tortured and deported me."

It will take eleven more years to bring Barbie to France. In the meantime, his identity is revealed in the Latin American press, and Barbie, realizing he is not safe in Peru, quickly returns to La Paz. He hides at a friend's, guarded by soldiers; after President Banzer, Barbie is the best-protected man in Bolivia.

Beate Klarsfeld, however, is expelled from Bolivia three days after her highly publicized arrival. She couldn't have wished for anything better; her misadventure makes some front pages of the international press. Meanwhile Altmann agrees to be interviewed by a French television reporter, thinking he can handle him. But his interviewer knows Barbie's service record backward and forward, and forces him to admit that he was an SS, and that he was posted in Lyon. To protect him, Hugo Banzer has Barbie jailed for tax evasion.

As soon as the excitement subsides, Barbie is released. Beate Klarsfeld returns to La Paz, but her second visit, though it ends less dramatically, is also unsuccessful.

Nevertheless, Barbie is in trouble. In May 1973, he is forced to admit to a Bolivian court that in Lyon he went by the name of Klaus Barbie. He is sent to prison, where he spends seven months in relative comfort. His family can visit him at leisure, his meals are prepared outside the jail. When Peru adds its extradition request to those from France stubbornly piling up on President Banzer's desk—Peru wants to try Barbie for fraud, including extortion and phony exchange transactions—Banzer brushes off the entire question and his law courts follow suit.

Barbie is not sent to Lima, nor is he sent back to France; instead he retires to Cochabamba, a city southeast of the capital, where he bides his time working for a construction business. Once the storm has blown over, he is called back home and given the honorary post of adviser to President Banzer. He is invited everywhere, and now that he no longer has to hide his past (which no one in his social circle seems to hold against him), he can brag about his exploits as a Nazi and his role in the German occupation of France. Yet he lives in fear of being kidnapped by the French, as Eichmann was by the Israelis.

In July 1978, after seven years of dictatorship, Banzer is ousted. His fall is followed by a series of coups. When the country leans to the left, Barbie will be in danger, but in the meantime the Department of the Interior uses him to gather information for the police—a job much like his old one in Amsterdam. He also becomes more and more involved in the enormously profitable cocaine trade. Barbie's illegal income helps him to engineer the downfall of Lidia Gueler's civilian government and the ascent of a new military man, General Luis Garcia Meza, in 1980. Meza nominates Colonel Luis Arce Gómez, also known as "Mr. Cocaine," as Secretary of the Interior. The production of Bolivian cocaine triples under Gómez, but the Meza administration doesn't last long; Meza and Gómez abscond with their profits after a year.

In October 1982, the left re-enters the political scene with President Siles Zuazo, who, in his earlier tenure as President in the late 1950s, signed Barbie's citizenship papers on the basis of his false identity. President Zuazo does not like to be deceived. He also wants to prove his democratic intentions by handing the old Nazi criminal over to those who want him. Barbie can be sold as easily as a bag of cocaine to people willing to pay for him.

Zuazo has files full of letters from potential buyers. The most recent extradition request is from Germany, dated May 1982. It incriminates Barbie in the murder of Joseph Kemmler, an Alsatian partisan who was beaten to death on April 9, 1944, at the Hotel de France in Saint-Claude, Jura, with a leather strap and metal snap hook. With the charges is the testimony of several Wehrmacht soldiers outraged by the cruelty of the man who ordered that torture session: "Barbie . . . smug, spiteful, sloppy." The document also points out that since his naturalization is fraudulent, Barbie remains a German citizen, responsible before German law, and therefore can be extradited back to Germany.

On the other hand, the Federal Republic of Germany did not seem to have any intention of trying Barbie. But Germany was eager to demonstrate its good intentions, and didn't expect Bolivia to respond.

President Zuazo, however, digs the paperwork out again, and considers the request favorably. Barbie is now sixty-nine. A few months earlier he had watched his son hang glide to his death; and his wife, Regine, had died of cancer over Christmas. He is a lonely, useless old man, but he can still be sold. In January, the procedures leading to his extradition-expulsion begin.

An Elysée emissary, acting as intermediary for Germany, arrives at La Paz. Officially, he is there to discuss France's financial aid to Bolivia. Unofficially, he must find the best way to transfer Barbie to France.

On January 25, much to his surprise, Barbie finds himself arrested and charged with the embezzlement of $10,000 from a state-owned mining corporation back in 1968.

As soon as Barbie is in prison, Germany renews its extradition request, as agreed. Lufthansa has a biweekly flight between La Paz and Frankfurt, and on January 29 Barbie is about to be escorted to the airport—before the Supreme Court has had the chance to deliberate on his case. If the verdict is not guilty and Barbie is still in Bolivia, the scheme might fall apart, but if he is already out of the country, the government will only have to express its regret for "excessive haste." Suddenly, the Germans reiterate an earlier refusal to let Barbie land on German soil, because then they will not be able to extradite him to France. Like most countries, Germany does not extradite its own citizens.

Zuazo is beginning to tire of the whole matter. Moreover, Barbie's Bolivian lawyer, Carrion Constantino, wants to know why they don't release his client, who pays his debt in full on January 31. He is told it will take a few days to clear Barbie's record. Meanwhile, Aeroperu and Lufthansa have both been forbidden by their respective governments to transport Barbie; and Germany has made it clear that despite its request, it doesn't really want him.

At 9:00 P.M. on February 4, a French army plane disguised as a private Bolivian aircraft—to prevent Barbie from balking when he is asked to board—lands on one of the military runways at El Alto airport. Barbie is surprised when he hears a key turn in the lock of his cell door in San Pedro prison, as it is relatively late and he is already in bed. Rueda Pena, the Minister of Information himself, appears in the doorway and informs him that, since his debt has been paid, he is free; but since he fraudulently obtained Bolivian citizenship, he will be expelled from the country and returned to Germany. Barbie is escorted to the airport in an armored car.

Barbie is not exactly pleased, but he knows things could be worse. He still has a few friends and relatives in Germany. He does not know what to expect from the German authorities, but he is not too concerned. Too many people in Germany have skeletons in their closets to want to rattle them. On the other hand, it is odd that he should have to leave so suddenly, without being allowed to pull together a few personal belongings.

It is cold at the airport. Somebody puts a blanket around him, maybe to keep him warm, maybe to hide him from the gathered officials, soldiers, Bolivian policemen, and the small group of quiet men in civilian clothes. They are not German, as Barbie may think, but a team of French agents sent to supervise the operation from beginning to end.

At ten-thirty Barbie's plane takes off. The passengers include a Bolivian television journalist and cameraman. Barbie's return is scrupulously filmed. It is a long trip. Barbie eats, drinks, naps, daydreams, talks, talks, talks. "It must be cold back home. I hope somebody has thought of getting me some warm clothes. In a way I am glad I am going back. I will be a little closer to Ute, my daughter. She lives in Austria with her husband. . . . Is life expensive in Germany? . . . There are wonderful forests, you know, particularly in Bavaria and along the French border. You should stay awhile. It's really worth it. . . ."

Suddenly at daybreak all the lights of the plane go out in preparation for landing. Barbie suddenly worries. The plane is not a Concorde, so they cannot possibly have reached Europe. "Technical problems," he is told.

The plane lands at the Rochambeau airport in Cayenne, on French territory, and suddenly tongues loosen—they are speaking French.

Barbie begins to panic. Once again a door opens and a government official stands before him. A representative of the French Ministry of Justice informs the little man shivering under his woolen blanket that he is charged with crimes against humanity and is under arrest. Behind him, the outlines of a dozen French soldiers with guns slung over their shoulders stand out against the brightening sky. Barbie cannot figure out their nationality; uniforms have changed in forty years.

The prisoner is transferred to a DC-8 belonging to the French army. By the time he disembarks at the Orange military airfield, just south of Lyon, he seems to have lost the little haughtiness he had left. It is Saturday evening, February 5. Not one journalist is present—the secret has been well kept. Barbie will travel the last few miles to Lyon by helicopter. At 10 P.M., the helicopter will set him down at the end of the Bron airfield runway, where the five mass graves were discovered after Liberation.

It is unlikely that, on this very cold night almost forty years later, Barbie will remember what happened there on the sweltering evening of August 17, 1944. To him it was a day like any other.

15 MOTHER'S MILK

This is the fourteenth day of Barbie's trial. All of today's witnesses are indirectly connected with the Izieu raid. Henri Borgel, the son of the manager of a candy store near Izieu, was standing in the doorway of the store when the trucks came to a stop right in front of him.

"At first, I thought they'd come to raid my father's store. There were three civilians at the head of the convoy. From their talk, I gathered they were hauling wood. But when I walked up to the trucks, I realized it was something else. There were children in those trucks. One of our employees told me they all came from the home in Izieu. I jumped onto my bicycle and rushed to André Favre, the head of the Maquis in Glandieu. I hoped he would be able to stop them. But Favre couldn't do a thing, since his men were scattered through the woods. It would have been impossible to bring them together in time."

· · ·

Edith Klebinder, seventy-three, is, together with Lea Feldblum, one of the last people who saw the Izieu children alive. She was arrested on March 20, 1944, and spent some ten days in Montluc, the word *Jude* scrawled on her cell door. Toward the end of March, she was transferred to Drancy.

"We had been told we were going to a work camp, and, to prove it, we had all been given a five-zlotis banknote. On April 13, fifteen hundred prisoners left Drancy. . . . It was nightmarish. A woman went crazy and started pawing all the other prisoners, frantically searching for a purse she claimed she had lost. Another woman, from Morocco, kept singing lullabies to her daughter to keep her quiet, while a very old couple held hands in silence. At last we reached our destination without knowing it was Auschwitz. The Germans needed someone who spoke their language. I volunteered. They wanted to know everyone's age, and I soon realized that all those who fell below fifteen and above fifty-one were allowed to ride in trucks. I thought it was a surprising mark of civilization after such an uncomfortable trip. I can't believe how naive I was.

"Finally, a large group of children led by a young woman approached from the last car. Three or four adults walked alongside them. The SS asked them whether they wanted to stay with the children. 'Of course,' a woman answered. Then, with a very courteous gesture, one of the SS officers showed them to an empty truck and invited them to climb in. 'It's faster this way,' he said. But he pulled the young woman who was leading the group away and pushed her aside. She protested. She wanted to go with the children, but they wouldn't hear of it.

"When I was left alone on the platform, I was told to join the group of those who were walking. There was a pregnant woman among them, whose state, however, was only visible to the knowing eye. I told her she should have taken advantage of the trucks, but she told me she preferred to walk. A wise choice, as it turned out. . . .

"In my group there were five or six other pregnant women, besides the one who didn't show. They were taken away during a second selection and we never saw them again. We were asked whether we could sing or dance. They needed people to form an orchestra and a theater group to enliven the SS's evenings. They even filmed those performances to show the entire world what fun Nazi prisoners had in their concentration camps. A girl in her teens sang a Schubert Lied for them, with a clear, lovely voice that brought tears to our eyes.

"I realized that the children who had arrived on my convoy came from Izieu only when I reported to the Hotel Lutetia. Their families had asked the people in charge to post notices detailing their number, their names, and the date of their deportation. There was no doubt that those were the children I had watched file into the trucks, bound for the gas chambers. I even heard some of their relatives asking questions about them, but I didn't have the courage to tell them what I knew.

"For a while, I was put in charge of sorting out the clothes of the people who had been gassed. My co-worker was a Hungarian woman. One day we heard that a train had just arrived from Hungary. She kept watching the flow of people pouring into the camp. Suddenly I heard her groan: she had just recognized her mother and her two daughters in a line of prisoners slowly making their way toward the gas chamber. She threw herself at the feet of an SS officer and begged him to spare them. But he pushed her away with his foot, telling her, 'By now, they have already been gassed.' She started screaming like an animal, then she collapsed on the floor, by the wall, and did not move, speak, drink, or eat for several days. Then one morning she was no longer there, but her image still haunts me.

"The Polish woman had her baby in February. We had been able to hide her pregnancy for such a long time, we thought we could also hide the baby. But the barracks head, afraid that her complicity might cost her her life, betrayed us. In no time the SS guard was at the young mother's bedside with a syringe. Three shots and the baby stopped crying. She took it away in a cardboard box; then she came back to bring the mother a glass of milk. Such was Nazi humanity."

June 2, 1987

Itta Rose Halaunbrenner and Fortunée Benguigui, both eighty-three, fought at Beate Klarsfeld's side to reveal the true identity of "Klaus Altmann" and bring him to trial. A very small, frail old lady, Itta Rose walks to the stand supported by Monique, "the only daughter left me."

"What's dearer to a mother than her children? I had five, and my profession was to be their mother. Barbie is still alive: he eats, drinks, sleeps. But I still suffer. When they took away my husband and oldest son, I was left without money, without a job, family, or friends. I had to do my best to feed the four children still with me, but I couldn't make ends meet. We were poorer than beggars, absolute wretches. It broke my heart to see Mina and Claudine leave with a stranger, but I knew that [at Izieu] at least they would be fed and would not be cold."

Fortunée Benguigui then testifies "to honor the memory of my three sons: Jacques, Richard, and Jean-Claude.

"I was deported on June 6, 1943, and was immediately locked up in building 1C, the one where they carried out their medical experiments. Among other things, they inoculated me with typhus to see how I would react. If it hadn't been for my companions, who did everything they could to help me, I would have died of a hemorrhage. I survived these tests because I was sure my children were safe. In our building there was a woman doctor with a fourteen-year-old son. One morning I noticed he was wearing the sweater I myself knitted for my oldest boy. I couldn't believe my eyes; I pulled the child closer and started feeling the wool. There was no doubt this was the sweater I had knitted. I realized something had happened and started crying. The others kept telling me not to get strange ideas, that I was certainly wrong. But when back in France, at the Hotel Lutetia, I saw their names, it didn't come as a surprise."

These two women have one small consolation: They still have photos, drawings, letters from their children, which they can look at, read, and reread. But Isidore Friedler has nothing. At seventy-two, he has only a few memories of a beloved only daughter.

"Her name was Lucienne. She would be forty-eight now, as of last February 18. The last time I saw her, when the French gendarmes came to get me near Grenoble, where I was hiding after having left Belgium, she was three. I was sent to what they called a 'work camp,' that cesspool in Agde. The following year, I was deported to Auschwitz. Before leaving, I heard that my wife, Mina, had joined the staff of a Jewish childen's home in Izieu, and that Lucienne was with her. So I tried not to worry and kept telling myself that every day I survived brought me closer to them. My certainty of their existence kept me warm when I was cold, fed me when I starved, and quenched my thirst when I was dying of it. My desire to be reunited with them kept me alive. But among the first things I saw, on my return to France, at the Hotel Lutetia, were notes and bulletins concerning the raid on Izieu. That's how I learned that my wife and daughter were gone, hand in hand, leaving nothing behind except, of course, my memories of them. Lucienne's face has faded in time, but it is still vivid enough to remind me that I once had a little daughter."

August 1987

When my brother and I were younger, my mother told us very little about Auschwitz. But I now believe we were partly, and more or less consciously, responsible for her silence. When she had returned from her captivity, we were too young to understand what had happened. Then, as we grew up, we kept her busy—too busy to indulge in remembrances. She was all alone, and we were difficult children, very possessive of her and absolutely intolerant of any male intrusion into our little universe.

As adolescents, we were not very curious. Neither Poumi nor I ever felt the need to ask her about her past. We were not indifferent; we knew our parents had gone beyond the limits of mere suffering, and we were afraid of following them there, even in imagination. Partial ignorance is often necessary in order to maintain some psychological balance, peace of mind, and confidence in the future.

My brother, who as a rule avoids introspection, agrees with me:

"It takes courage to admit it, but this is probably the way most survivors' children behave." It surprises me that he should feel the need to justify himself. Yes, there was some cowardice in our refusal to confront reality, but it made it easier for us to go on. One must be very strong to share the suffering of one's parents. Our childhood and adolescence as war orphans and half-Jews did not give us the necessary strength.

As for my mother, no doubt she didn't make a point of telling us because she was afraid of causing all three of us pain. Poumi and I clearly preferred to have a vague—and therefore tamer—idea of our parents' experience in the Holocaust. What if we were to greet her tale with boredom, or indifference, or, more simply, incredulity?

I remember my mother's reluctance to share her memories when I first approached her, three months after the end of the Barbie trial, in her lovely garden in Normandy. The garden was full of currants, raspberries, and the heady scent of roses and nasturtiums. "You're forcing me to recall things that belong only to me, things I'm not terribly eager to share," my mother said. "Memories can be cruel. Sometimes images I thought I'd forgotten come to mind unexpectedly, and I have to try not to look at them. Besides, I'm not sure any longer that I can trust my memory. What I went through is all mixed up with other people's experiences. There's always the risk of overstating, or understating, what actually happened. Not everyone received the same treatment in the same camp, stories often differ, and when they do, people become suspicious. . . . I know that during the trial some of the survivors said that Auschwitz was a hell created by men for other men. . . . I really don't see what I could add to that."

Still, I want to know everything, not just for this book but for myself, for my children, and for all those who will follow them. I am determined to make her speak even if it means reopening old wounds. But suddenly I feel as if I am becoming my mother's torturer; as if I am treating this seventy-five-year-old woman, sitting peacefully under her red parasol, just as the Gestapo did so many years ago. Ashamed, I mutter an apology and begin to leave. My mother holds me back.

"Your father had good reason to write me, 'I think we'll get out of it.' We all felt that way in Montluc. We knew the Americans were approaching, we mentally followed their progress, sure that soon they would come to free us. Your father and I felt that we had reached the end of the tunnel. But on August 11, they brought me to Perrache station.

"They must have run out of cattle cars, because they stuffed us into third-class compartments with wooden benches. I was in the last car with Sacha. We clung to each other for fear of being separated. It was awfully crowded. I kept looking for Robert. Somehow I was sure he was also on the train. Sacha's husband, Elie, a big man, was with us, in our compartment. They took him away as soon as we arrived, and Sacha never saw him again. There was also a Jean Kahn, but he was not related to our family. He lived on Quai de Jemmapes, in Paris. As soon as I got back, I went to see his wife, to bring her some news. She didn't even know that he had been in prison in Lyon, let alone that he had been deported on August 11. He has never come back either. And sitting by the door there was Vladimir Wolinetz, an antique dealer on Avenue de Suffren. He too must have gone up in smoke. There were three more men. Two were dropped off at Schirmeck, and the third at Rotau. Non-Jews were not meant for the extermination camps.

"Our convoy was headed by an Oberstleutnant we all knew because he had been at Montluc. He was as beautiful as an angel and as mean as a devil. Our car was guarded by two young Wehrmacht soldiers who clearly disliked what they were forced to do. I asked one of them if he could find out whether there was a Robert Kahn on the train. He brought me an answer three days later. He had found no Robert Kahn, but there was a Salvator Kahn with whom I was able to speak for a few moments when we arrived. He could not figure out what was happening to him, since at first they had indeed called a Roberet Kahn. He had been forced to replace him at the last moment. Shortly thereafter, I heard that Salvator Kahn had been gassed. Had he been your father, the news would have killed me. If I made it through Auschwitz it was simply because I thought your father was still alive and free. . . .

"We were bound for Drancy, the usual destination of all the trains carrying deportees. This is where they were sorted out, like dirty laundry: the rags on one side, the towels on the other. Later, when I came back, I heard that your paternal grandmother had managed to obtain a certificate stating that I was not a Jew, and that she was in daily contact with someone at Drancy, trying to find out whether her son or I had arrived there, so that she could try to get me released. She didn't do it for me, but for the mother of Robert's children. She may have been a terrible mother-in-law, but as a grandmother she was irreproachable.

"At Dijon we had to stop; a partisan attack had blown up the tracks. We had no choice but to go east. And so we proceeded toward Germany, by fits and starts, as if we were traveling a dotted line. We stopped everywhere even remotely resembling a station. It was terribly hot. Sacha and I slept in the luggage racks and the men on the seats and the floor. Near Strasbourg, a German walked along the train screaming, 'All those who are not Jewish must get down.' I saw lots of people leave the train. Sacha tried to convince me to get down too. But I hesitated. Not out of bravery, mind you, since I did not know where we were going. Had I known, I would have left the train without waiting to hear more, and I would have ended up in Schirmeck, where I would have been worked to death."

I no longer see the blue of my mother's eyes. She has closed them.

"Of all the people on that train I am sure very few women came back, and no men that I know of. We went through fields spotted with brown and white cows being milked by old peasant women. We envied the people who lived on those farms. We crossed lush forests where it would have been so pleasant to walk. During the stops prisoners could try to escape; it seems some did, successfully. Sacha and I thought about it. One of the soldiers in charge of our compartment, a certain Bruno Kiljan, was very kind. He felt sorry for us. Whenever we stopped at a station, the moment the other guards turned around to go have a bite, he let us get out to use the bathrooms. He kept an eye on us, but we could have easily eluded his surveillance. We didn't do it, because we didn't want him or the other prisoners to be punished in our place. Everybody would have paid for it; it was too much of a responsibility. Besides, as I said, we still did not know what awaited us at the end of the trip. And anyway, Sacha could not have taken off without her husband.

"We finally arrived at our destination. The train went through that heavy iron gate and stopped alongside the ramp. We were many fewer than when we had started, since, besides the non-Jews, we had also left people at Dachau and at Ravensbrück.

"I'll never forget what we saw as soon as we looked around us. To our right there was the Gypsy camp. There were a lot of Gypsies, and they kept running from one side of the camp to the other, confined by barbed wire in what could have been a pasture, except there wasn't a single blade of grass. In my memory, they are as naked as my hand, dark-skinned and hairy, and they swarmed about like ants. We stared at them, transfixed with horror. It suddenly dawned on us that we had reached the kingdom of death, and that we had come such a long way only to die. Slowly, one by one, we got out of the train. And, believe me, that place smelled like death. Everyone was quiet, some of us wept in silence. There were some children among us. They didn't cry, but they looked very old and resigned, as if they knew better than anyone else what was going to happen. The eyes of those children! You don't know how they broke my heart. I kept thinking about the two of you, telling myself I'd rather you were killed brutally, at once, by a bomb, than go through anything like that. Kiljan and Kinsholz, our guards, were standing by us, deathly pale. Obviously they too had had no idea. . . . I can still hear Kiljan tell the other. 'I didn't know what was going on here. I thought Auschwitz was a prisoner camp, like the stalags. The world will never forgive what is going on here.'

"During the trip, Kiljan and Kinsholz had often given us their own food rations, and we had shared them equally, almost down to the gram, with the other people in our compartment. At Vittel, we received a few Red Cross packages. It was crazy. They gave us chocolate but they let the train go on. I want to believe that, like us, the Red Cross did not know what we were heading for. In any case, we didn't starve on that train, nor did we die of thirst. Quite the contrary, by the time we arrived in Auschwitz, Sacha and I felt quite feisty.

"Since our train arrived unexpectedly, it was received in total chaos. They were not ready for us. We weren't even sorted out. Not really, since we were all shoved into a huge hangar—men, women, and children—except that a few guards picked out those who looked either too old or too sick to last. They were immediately dispatched to the gas chamber, and from there to the ovens."

Suddenly I feel I have heard all I can stand. I have to stop my mother from going on. Stunned, I look at her. She is calmly telling me the most horrifying story I have ever heard. And she has lived through it. Now that, for the first time, she has made the effort to speak about it, she can't stop.

At the Barbie trial, I was astounded, like everyone else present, by the clarity of the witnesses' memories, the vividness of their details. At first, I had a hard time maintaining a journalistic distance; on occasion, I even had to leave the room. But eventually I managed to get hold of myself. After all, I was there as a professional observer, chronicling a particular period in history. That it was related to my own history was of no consequence.

The voices that rang through the Lyon courtroom were not my mother's. It was not her life, or mine, that was being relived for the magistrates, lawyers, and journalists. It was not our hearts that were being laid bare.

I have heard all I can hear for this evening. Paradoxically, my mother now calms and reassures me, something I have never been able to do for her.

The following morning, I don't have to beg her to continue her story. She has discovered so many years later that it feels good to talk.

"I feel as if I'm unburdening myself on you. But you're strong, you can bear it; it might help me to sleep. Do you know, since I came back I've never been able to sleep through the night without a sleeping pill?"

I know. I have often been the impatient witness of difficult awakenings and weary mornings. Besides, other survivors said the same thing at the trial.

"We spent our first night in that hangar without either food or water. That's when I met Henri Silbermann, Idette's brother. I didn't know he was on my train. That night we all took advantage of being in the same place to find out as much as we could about the people we cared for. Voices rose in the darkness: 'Does anyone know my parents, Mr. and Mrs. So and So?' 'Does anyone here have any news about my son, Maurice X?' When I heard Henri Silbermann's voice inquiring about his sister Idette, my heart skipped a beat. He hadn't had any news of her for over a year. That night I also spoke to Salvator Kahn, but nobody could tell me anything about Robert. . . .

"We still had our bags with us, since the Germans hadn't had time to confiscate them. Before we were locked up in the hangar, we had seen a row of women with shaved heads. It shocked us. Rather than suffering the humiliation of having our heads shaved by the Germans, we decided to take care of it ourselves. And so we did, with the help of a pair of sewing scissors, a nail clipper, and a razor. We ended up looking like scrubbing brushes. It made us laugh and laugh. But it did not relieve my anger. Quite the contrary.

"When they came to open the doors of the hangar the following morning, as if we were animals they were letting out of a cowshed, I immediately started screaming, 'What the hell am I doing here? I'm not Jewish! You've made a mistake.' Of course, they wouldn't believe me. 'That's what everybody says,' they said. But I didn't give up. I kept yelling and hollering. You know how I can yell when I'm not happy?"

Indeed I do. When we were children the entire building knew when Poumi and I had done something wrong.

"So I kept on ranting and raving until they couldn't take it any longer and were forced to pay attention to me. It was about time; I had hardly any voice left. Eventually they realized I looked like a perfect Aryan. Then I told them that my last name was my husband's. This really threw them. They couldn't believe any Aryan would want to marry a Jew. Obviously, I told them, I did not know he was a Jew until it was too late. In France, people don't pay attention to those things."

(Some don't, at least not my mother, who, upon learning that my father was Jewish some two weeks after their first encounter, had nothing to say except "So what?")

"They started treating me better right off," my mother continues. "They pulled me out of that hangar and brought me to a place where there were lots of other women. There, they took off all our clothes and tattooed us, as if we were cows. See this blue number on the inside of my forearm? I was, and still am, Number 87.158. Then they left us, hundreds and hundreds of us still entirely naked, in a sort of concrete courtyard. The following day we were divided into groups of forty. It seemed everyone spoke a different language. There were Poles, Russians, Italians, Hungarians, Austrians, but not many French.

"I wasn't in Auschwitz long enough to know all that went on. However, I remember one thing very clearly: All the women in my barracks, 12A, mostly non-Jews, were forbidden to look at the flames spouting out of the chimneys all day and night. Like the other barracks, ours also had some openings—it would be ridiculous to call them windows—that had been boarded up, but loosely enough to leave a few cracks. We were formally forbidden to peek through them unless we wanted to go up in flames ourselves. But that threat wasn't enough to deter us, or to quell our fascination for the mystery and horror of those orange flames as they dissolved into black smoke. We spent most of our time with our eyes glued to those cracks, quiet and still, mesmerized. One afternoon we did not hear them coming. Two or three women were peeking through the cracks when the barracks guard walked in with two SS officers. They were immediately taken away, and we never saw them again.

"I spent one more month there doing nothing. I chased fleas, spread my clothes out in the sun, learned some Polish and some

Russian. When Osram, a light-bulb factory, requested some manpower, I was sent to Plauen, in Saxony, with two hundred other prisoners.

"We arrived around October 25. We were given clean lodgings with running water, soap, new blankets. We were fed real soup and plenty of bread. Our work uniforms were a little rough on the skin but no bugs. For us, it was like heaven. We lived in dread of the day we would have to go back to Auschwitz.

"Around March 20, the factory was bombed. We were crammed into the cellars. Above us the building was burning. It was terrifying. We could see the flames through the air vents. Soon smoke started pouring in, and people panicked. Some of us went crazy, screaming, 'We are going to broil like chickens! At least in Auschwitz they gas us first!' At last the fire went out. The factory was burnt down to a skeleton of metal rods. The following morning I found a way out of the cave. It led into a sort of alley flanked by walls. I ran until I found myself trapped in the middle of what looked like workers' gardens enclosed by a tall iron fence. Between me and freedom there was that seven-foot barrier and a bolted gate, and nowhere to hide. It was early morning. A guard saw me. I must have looked like a parrot in a canary cage. I was brought back to the cellar, where I was promptly stripped in front of everybody else. Then my head was shaved and I was slapped for such a long time I thought it would never end. Then I was left alone in the cellar, without food or water, for two days.

"There was a great commotion outside. I could hear German voices nervously giving orders, which they would immediately call off. It had to do with the evacuation of Plauen. I hoped they would forget me. I prayed they would. It was the first time since those few hours I had spent alone in Montluc, between my canceled departure and Sacha's arrival, that I had the luxury of being alone. You have no idea what it means, the rush of bliss running up and down your spine. At last alone, I abandoned myself to thinking of you and my husband. I hadn't let myself before, I'd refused to be weakened by tenderness. . . . The moment the Germans realize you are giving in to tears and despair, they get rid of you. First because you yourself are of no use, and secondly because they know your feelings are contagious. So whenever I found you creeping into my thoughts, I chased you away, telling myself, 'They're fine. Robert's certainly free by now. It's I who am bearing the brunt of it.' I convinced myself I was the victim of an awful injustice, a martyr. But then, as I relished my solitude in that cellar, I longed to be with you. . . . I felt wretched. I even started thinking I might never see you again. . . .

"The guard came back. She threw a few rags at me and a pair of wooden clogs, much too small for my feet. Wearing them was just another form of torture. The other women were waiting in front of the factory ruins. They made us climb into a few trucks. We didn't know where they were taking us. The wildest rumors started circulating: They were taking us to Flossenburg, where they were going to exterminate us with a flame thrower. Soon enough we were all convinced we were going to die in a way our minds refused to imagine. . . . There's a French movie, made by Bernard Tavernier, with Romy Schneider and Philippe Noiret, called *The Old Gun*, in which the heroine and her daughter are killed in precisely such a way. I've never seen the movie, I couldn't, but somebody told me about it. I wonder what it feels like to be incinerated by a flame thrower.

"By the end of the day, we had run out of trucks. They had all broken down on the road, one after the other. We had to continue on foot. It was very cold, and all we had to cover ourselves was a blanket. I walked in those tight clogs for three days. You used to wonder why I had such trouble putting my shoes on, why I was always afraid of someone stepping on my feet. . . . Since then, I have always bought shoes that are a touch too large.

"We stopped at a factory, in Johann-Georgenstadt to pick up a squad of men to escort us. We walked during the day and stopped only in the evening to eat and sleep in the ditches. . . . In the morning, the SS woke us up with insults and kicks in the side. Those who gave in to exhaustion, hunger, and other kinds of suffering, and did not respond, were killed on the spot. We would hear only the gunshots, behind us, and never a single cry. They died quietly, fully resigned. I began to think it might be a relief to go that way, rather than having to feel one's life slip away at every painful step. Those who fell along the way were killed like those who couldn't get up in the morning. Their bodies have remained anonymous. We had no papers, nothing that could identify us. . . .

"In the evening of the third day I was sure I would never make it through one more day. My feet were bleeding. Every step sent pain shooting through my body. I couldn't think or care any longer. I wanted to die. I couldn't stand another hour. . . . At least I could choose which way to go, and I knew I didn't want to go up in flames."

My mother notices that I am shivering, my face turned away. I stopped taking notes a while ago, while my mother has gone on talking as if all these things had happened to someone else. But she assures me it's easier to talk about her own experience than that of others: "Since, after all, I'm still here, forty-two years later, talking about it in words that evoke only images and no pain. . . . I'm sure it's much more painful for you to hear it than for me to talk about it. You asked for it, however."

I can read my mother's thoughts as if they were written on her smooth face: "You never asked any questions, never showed any interest in your parents' past. I could have doled it out to you drop by drop to make it easier for you to take. Now suddenly you want to know everything, you are starved for the whole truth. Well, here it is."

As we lunch under a stormy sky, my mother tells me of her escape.

16 Long Columns of Ghosts

It is appropriate that Elie Wiesel, who was awarded the Nobel Prize for Peace, should testify as a representative of the children of Izieu. At fifteen, he too was deported to Auschwitz.

"I will try to speak about some of the nameless absent," Wiesel begins, "but not for them. No one has a right to speak in their name. If the dead have something to say, they will say it in their own way. Perhaps they are already saying it. Are we capable, are we worthy, of hearing them?

"May I say immediately that I feel no hatred toward the accused? I have never met him; our paths have never crossed. But I have met killers who, like him, along with him, chose to be enemies of my people and of humanity. I may have known one or another of his victims. I resembled them, just as they resembled me. Within the kingdom of malediction created by the accused and his comrades, all Jewish prisoners, all Jews, had the same face, the same eyes; all shared the same fate. Sometimes one has the impression

the same Jew was being killed by the enemy everywhere six million
times over.

"No, there is no hatred in me: there never was any. There is no
question of hatred here—only justice. And memory. We are trying
to do justice to our memory.

"Here is one memory: the spring of 1944. A few days before the
Jewish Pentecostal holiday—*Shavuot.* This was forty-three years
ago, almost to the day. I was fifteen and a half years old—my own
son will turn fifteen in three days. A profoundly religious child, I
was moved by messianic dreams and prayers. Far from Jerusalem, I
lived for Jerusalem, and Jerusalem lived in me.

"Though subjected to a fascist regime, the Jews of Hungary did
not suffer too much. My parents ran a business, my three sisters
went to school, the Sabbath enveloped us in its peace. . . . The
war? It was nearing its end. The Allies were going to land in a day,
in a week. The Red Army was twenty or thirty kilometers away.
But then . . .

"The Germans invaded Hungary on March 19, 1944. Starting
then, events moved at a headlong pace that gave us no respite. A
succession of anti-Semitic decrees and measures were passed: the
prohibition of travel, confiscation of goods, wearing of yellow stars,
ghettos, transports.

"We watched as our world was systematically narrowed. For Jews,
the country was limited to one town, the town to one neighborhood,
the neighborhood to one street, the street to one room, the room
to a sealed boxcar crossing the Polish countryside at night.

"Like the forty-four Jewish children of Izieu (shipped to Auschwitz in 1944), the Jewish adolescents from my town arrived at the
Auschwitz station one afternoon. What is this? we wondered. No
one knew. The name did not evoke any memory in us. Shortly
before midnight, the train began to move. A woman in our car
began shouting, "I see a fire, I see a fire!" They made her be quiet.
I remember the silence in the car. As I remember the rest. The
barbed-wire fences stretching away to infinity. The shouts of the
prisoners whose duty it was to 'welcome' us, the gunshots fired by
the SS, the barking of their dogs. And up above us all, above the

planet itself, immense flames rising toward the sky as though to consume it.

"Since that night, I often look at the sky and see it in flames. . . . But that night, I could not look at the sky for long. I was too busy clinging to my family. An order rang out: 'Line up by family.' That's good, I thought, we will stay together. Only for a few minutes, however. 'Men to the right, women to the left.' The blows rained down on all sides. I was not able to say goodbye to my mother. Nor to my grandmother. I could not kiss my little sister. With my two older sisters, she was moving away, borne by the crazed, black tide. . . .

"This was a separation that cut my life in half. I rarely speak of it, almost never. I cannot recall my mother or my little sister. With my eyes, I still look for them, I will always look for them. And yet I know . . . I know everything. No, not everything . . . one cannot know everything. I could imagine it, but I do not allow myself to. One must know when to stop. . . . My gaze stops at the threshold of the gas chambers. Even in thought, I refuse to violate the privacy of the victims at the moment of their death.

"What I saw is enough for me. In a small wood somewhere in Birkenau I saw children being thrown into the flames alive by the SS. Sometimes I curse my ability to see. It should have left me without ever returning. I should have remained with those little charred bodies. . . . Since that night, I have felt a profound, immense love for old people and children. Every old person recalls my grandfather, my grandmother, every child brings me close to my little sister, the sister of the dead Jewish children of Izieu. . . .

"Night after night, I kept asking myself, What does all this mean? What is the sense of this murderous enterprise? It functioned perfectly. The killers killed, the victims died, the fire burned, and an entire people thirsting for eternity turned to ash, annihilated by a nation which, until then, was considered to be the best educated, the most cultivated in the world. Graduates from the great universities, lovers of music and painting, doctors, lawyers, and philosophers participated in the 'final solution' and became accomplices of death. Scholars and engineers invented more efficient methods

for exterminating denser and denser masses in record time. . . .
How was this possible?

"I do not know the answer. In its scope, its ontological aspect,
and its eschatological ambitions, this tragedy defies and exceeds all
answers. If anyone claims to have found an answer, it can only be
a false one. So much mourning, so much agony, so many deaths
on one side, and a single answer on the other? One cannot understand Auschwitz either without God or with God. One cannot
conceive of it in terms of man or of heaven. Why was there so
much hatred in the enemy toward Jewish children and old people?
Why this relentlessness against a people whose memory of suffering
is the oldest in the world?

"At the time, it seemed to me that the enemy's aim was to attack
God Himself in order to drive Him from His celestial throne. Thus,
the enemy was creating a society parallel to our society, a world
opposed to ours, with its own madmen and princes, laws and customs, prophets and judges.

"Yes, an accursed world where another language was spoken,
where a new religion was proclaimed: one of cruelty, dominated by
the inhuman; a society that had evolved from the other side of
society, from the other side of life, from the other side of death,
perhaps; a world where one small piece of bread was worth all ideas,
where an adolescent in uniform had absolute power over thousands
of prisoners, where human beings seemed to belong to a different
species, trembling before death, which had all the attributes of
God. . . .

"As a Jew, it is impossible for me not to stress the affliction of
my people during their torment. Do not see this as an attempt to
deny or minimize the sufferings of the populations of the occupied
countries or the torture undergone by our comrades, our Christian
or nonreligious friends whom the common enemy punished with
unpardonable brutality. We feel affection and admiration for them.
As though they were our brothers? They are our brothers.

"It is impossible for me, as a Jew, not to stress that for the first
time, an entire people—from the smallest to the largest, from the
richest to the poorest—were condemned to annihilation. To uproot

it, to extract it from history, to kill it in memory by killing all memory of it. Such was the enemy's plan.

"Marked, isolated, humiliated, beaten, starved, tortured, the Jew was handed over to the executioner, not for having proclaimed some truth, nor for having possessed envied riches and treasures, nor for having adopted a certain forbidden behavior. The Jew was condemned to death because he was born Jewish, because he carried in him a Jewish memory.

"Declared to be less than a man, and therefore deserving neither compassion nor pity, the Jew was born only to die—just as the killer was born only to kill. Consequently, the killer did not feel in any way guilty. One American investigator formulated it this way: The killer had not lost his sense of morality, but his sense of reality. He thought he was doing good by ridding the earth of its Jewish 'parasites.'

"Is this the reason Klaus Barbie, like Adolf Eichmann before him, does not feel guilty? Except for Höss, the commander of Auschwitz, condemned and hanged in Poland, no killer has repented. Their logic? There had to be executioners to eliminate a million and a half Jewish children; killers were *needed* to annihilate four and a half million Jewish adults.

"Auschwitz and Treblinka, Maidanek and Ponar, Belzec and Mathausen, and so many others, so many other names. The apocalypse was everywhere. Everywhere, mute processions headed toward pits filled with dead bodies. Very few tears, very little crying. From their appearance, resigned, thoughtful, the victims seemed to be leaving the world without regret. It was as though these men and women were choosing not to live in a society disfigured, denatured by hatred and violence.

"After the war, the survivor tried to tell about it, bear witness . . . but who could find words to speak of the unspeakable?

"The contemplative silence of old people who knew, of children who were afraid of knowing . . . the horror of mothers who had gone mad, the terrifying lucidity of mad people in a delirious world . . . the grave chant of a rabbi reciting the Kaddish, the murmur of his followers going after him to the very end, to heaven . . . the good little girl undressing her younger brother . . . telling him not to be afraid; no, one must not be afraid of death . . . perhaps she said, One must not be afraid of dead people. . . .

"And in the city, the grand, ancient city of Kiev, that mother and her two children in front of some German soldiers who are laughing . . . they take one child from her and kill it before her eyes . . . then, they seize the second and kill it too. . . . She wants to die; the killers prefer her to remain alive but inhabited by death. . . . Then, she takes the two little bodies, hugs them against her chest and begins to dance . . . how can one describe that mother? How can one tell of her dance? In this tragedy, there is something that hurts beyond hurting—and I do not know what it is.

"I know we must speak. I do not know how. Since this crime is absolute, all language is imperfect. Which is why there is such a feeling of powerlessness in the survivor. It was easier for him to imagine himself free in Auschwitz than it would be for a free man to imagine himself a prisoner in Auschwitz. That is the problem: No one who has not experienced the event will ever be able to understand it. And yet, the survivor is conscious of his duty to bear witness. To tell the tale. To protest every time any 'revisionist,' morally perverse as he may be, dares to deny the death of those who died. And the truthfulness of the memory transmitted by the survivors.

"For the survivors, however, it is getting late. Their number is diminishing. They meet one another more and more often at funerals. Can one die more than once? Yes, one can. The survivor dies every time he rejoins, in his thoughts, the nightly procession he has never really left. How can he detach himself from them without betraying them? For a long time he talked to them, as I talk to my mother and my little sister. I still see them moving away under the fiery sky. . . . I ask them to forgive me for not following them. . . .

"It is for the dead, but also for the survivors, and even more for their children—and yours—that this trial is important; it will weigh on the future. In the name of justice? In the name of memory.

Justice without memory is an incomplete justice, false and unjust. To forget would be an absolute injustice in the same way that Auschwitz was the absolute crime. To forget would be the enemy's final triumph.

"The fact is that the enemy kills twice—the second time in trying to obliterate the traces of his crime. That is why he pushed his outrageous, terrifying plan to the limits of language, and well beyond: to situate it out of reach, out of our range of perception. 'Even if you survive, even if you tell, no one will believe you,' an SS told a young Jew somewhere in Galicia.

"This trial has already contradicted that killer. The witnesses have spoken; their truth has entered the awareness of humanity. Thanks to them, the Jewish children of Izieu will never be forgotten.

"As guardians of their invisible graves, graves of ash encrusted in a sky of eternal night and fog, we must remain faithful to them. We must try. To refuse to speak, when speech is awaited, would be to acknowledge the ultimate triumph of despair.

" 'Do you seek fire?' said a great Hasidic rabbi. 'Seek it in the ash.' This is what you have been doing here since the beginning of this trial, this is what we have attempted to do since the Liberation. We have sought, in the ash, a truth to affirm—despite everything—man's dignity; it exists only in memory.

Thanks to this trial, the survivors have a justification for their survival. Their testimony counts, their memories will be part of the collective memory. Of course, nothing can bring the dead back to life. But because of the meetings that have taken place within these precincts, because of the words spoken, the accused will not be able to kill the dead again. If he had succeeded it would not have been his fault, but ours.

Though it takes place under the sign of justice, this trial must also honor memory.

These intense two hours spent with Elie Wiesel have left the courtroom in a state of emotional exhaustion. Whatever follows can't but be anticlimactic. Two mayors take the stand, one after the other: Henri Pierret, the current mayor of Izieu, to express his deepest regret, and that of his fellow citizens, for what happened on April 6, 1944; and the mayor of a nearby village, Bugey Cordon, to propose turning the Izieu home, which is up for sale, into a museum to the memory of the young martyrs.

June 3 and 4, 1987

We have two days to summarize the twelve days during which train number 14.166, carrying Jews, resistants, children, and old people, wound its way through France and Germany from Lyon to Auschwitz-Birkenau. It stopped at Struthof, to drop off male resistants; then at Ravensbrück, to deposit female resistants; then it made innumerable other stops while its passengers sweltered in the infernal heat without food or water.

As mentioned, there are no formal documents implicating Barbie in this deportation. The voices of the witnesses are the only testimony.

"I am here on a mission," says Alice Vansteenberghe, a seventy-eight-year-old retired doctor, once a resistant. Her back is crippled; she leans on crutches that have supported her every step for forty-three years. Still, she exudes strength and determination. "Women I have never met have begged me to come and tell you what I know. I am not a historian, or a novelist, or a philosopher, but I was arrested at the beginning of August 1944, by seven men: six civilians, among them two French fascists and a uniformed man with a machine gun.

"I was taken to Gestapo headquarters on Place Bellecour and escorted to a handsome drawing room on the fifth floor, where I was surprised to find a large fire burning in a monumental fireplace. In the middle of the summer. A giant blond by the name of Schmitt, one of Barbie's assistants, came in to question me. Fifteen minutes later I had no nails left, but I had kept my mouth shut. Schmitt left me in a chair at a long table. Then Barbie walked in, slowly, calmly, and came to sit at the table, right across from me, all the while staring at me with his piercing eyes. He did not address me directly, but he ordered the others about. I observed him very carefully, so that I would never forget him. I noticed his left ear, and the affectations of his little finger. . . .

"So he shouted orders and Schmitt's men stripped me and laid me down on my belly on that long table. Then Schmitt proceeded to bust my spine with a knout, I think, though I couldn't tell you with any certainty what kind of instrument he used. Suffice it to say I have not walked straight since.

"Then I was brought to Fort Montluc and locked up in a tiny cell with several other women, and no air or light. Our only toilet was a washbowl. This deliberate degradation of one's humanity is the worst possible torture. We were forced to gulp down our food on all fours.

"I was tortured again on August 7, 1944, the day they brought me face to face with the leader of my group, Colonel Pierre Bernheim. There were pokers in the fireplace, and this time I understood why they lit fires in the middle of the summer. They burned Bernheim's feet and left cheek with a poker. But he did not talk, nor did I.

"That evening I was brought back to my cell. Among my cellmates were a ninety-year-old woman and a few fifteen-year-old girls. On August 11 we were woken up at dawn. All my companions were summoned into the courtyard. I was the only one left, since I was not Jewish.

"My cell overlooked the courtyard. Through the peephole I could see what went on out there. I saw Barbie and his men gathering prisoners from all over the prison, dividing them in groups, counting and recounting them. Hundreds and hundreds of them.

"After they left, the prison was very quiet. Then, six days later, on August 17, a Thursday, they gathered some more people into the courtyard, and again I followed the whole thing from my peephole. This time they had assembled only men, some fifty of them. Among them was Colonel Bernheim. They were all Jews, and they would all be murdered at Bron that same evening. The following day, they gathered a few more men for the same destination, and finally on August 21 they gathered a hundred and ten more people, some of whom had just been arrested and hadn't even been ques-

tioned, and took them away. They were going to be shot and then
burnt at Saint-Genis-Laval. I recognized some of them: Abbé Bour-
sier, Robine Bernheim (Colonel Bernheim's wife), and little
Thomas, the son of a Draguignan lawyer.

"Three days later, something extraordinary happened. The
Americans entered Lyon. It was like a resurrection. . . . Recently,
a journalist wrote, 'What's left of all that?' Everything. Because if
we are here now, enjoying our breakfast in the morning and falling
asleep without too many worries, free to bring up our children the
way we want, it is only because then we defeated the Barbies of
this world."

Alice Zohar was among those gathered in the Montluc courtyard
on August 11. She had been arrested less than two weeks before.

"I was betrayed by a neighbor who received five thousand francs,
no doubt stolen from the Jews, in exchange for a 'Jewish head.' He
was an Alsatian by the name of Charles Goetzmann. . . . He denounced several people. His mistress, Jeanne Hermann, was involved in the sale of Jewish children; she sold twenty-two, at five
hundred francs each."

Charlotte Wardy, a professor of literature at the University of Haifa,
was fifteen when she was deported, on August 11, along with her
mother and invalid uncle.

"I was in cell number ten, with the largest roaches in Montluc.
They crawled all over the ceiling, back and forth, back and forth,
relentlessly, and now and then they dropped on us. One night while
we were sleeping, the door opened and a body was thrown onto
ours. It was Doctor Alice Vansteenberghe, whose nom de guerre
was Yvonne Maurier. She groaned and asked for water, but we had
none. So we gave her the stone of a prune to suck on. The following
day she took off her clothes. Her back was as black as ink. But
with her courage, dynamism, and strength, she transformed the
mood of the cell; she brought back some hope in the future.

"When we were gathered in the courtyard before our departure,

I found my mother and my uncle, supported by two companions without whom he could not move. Our journey was surreal. We stopped at the Stuttgart station, where a loudspeaker announced our arrival: 'Jewish train, everybody clear the platforms." But a large group of children stayed behind and spat on us when we got out of the train to use the toilets and wash. At Vittel, while the Red Cross tried to stop the train for good, I was ordered to clean the first-class car occupied by the SS. One of them told me, 'Where you're going it will be like family.' And they all roared with laughter.

"When we arrived, I received the worst shock of my life. A train of cattle cars stopped right across from ours. The doors opened and masses and masses of barely human beings, walking skeletons, poured out, prodded by cudgel blows. To avoid the blows, they scurried all over the place. After a long time, Dr. Mengele himself came to sort us out. People over forty-five or fifty, children, and all those who showed signs of weakness were pushed to one side. My mother was among them. That's when I last saw her. In our group, there was a twelve-year-old girl with blond hair and blue eyes. Mengele did not notice her at first, but the following day he paid us a visit and took her away. One hour later he was back with her clothes, which he threw in her mother's face.

"I was transferred to a work camp where, with ten other women, I was chained to an assembly line sorting ammunition. When the camp was liberated, I weighed sixty pounds, but at least I was alive."

"I would like to tell you about my friend Pfeiffer," says Isaac Latherman, a tall, soft-spoken man. "When he came back from his interrogation, he didn't have an inch of sound skin on his body. His ears had been pulverized. He died shortly thereafter, while he was being beaten up by Barbie and his henchmen. Klaus Barbie . . . I will never forget the arrogance of that man. He was a tyrant. But I can't remember whether he was at the station on August 11. Two of his sidekicks were there, 'Medor' and 'Danube'—those were the nicknames we had given them.

"When we got to Auschwitz, there was another train on the

tracks. We could hear the screams and moans of those inside. Then we saw wave after wave of living skeletons pour out onto the platform, dragging corpses after them.

"People died every day. We went to work at dawn, and when we returned in the evening we had to carry all the bodies of those who had died back with us to match the morning's body count. The evacuation of the camp was a nightmare. Unbelievable. We were all on our last legs when we arrived at Bergen-Belsen, but we were still thirty-two thousand. By the time the Allies freed us, however, thirty thousand had died, and the two thousand who were left lay dying on the ground. Half of us died in the next few months.

"My brother was arrested because his name was David. He never came back. My brother-in-law, Charles Levy, was on my train, but unlike me, he did not come back. I have never spoken of all this before."

Anatole Lilienstein, a TV producer, is still surprised he managed to keep his sanity after Auschwitz. "The barracks where we were sorted out reminded me of Dante's Inferno: sheer madness. The veterans of the camp were unable to tell us clearly what was going on, to explain those long naked processions of people staggering to their deaths. At the end of August, the camp was invaded by huge waves of Hungarian Jews who were immediately sent to the oven, without even passing through the gas chamber. They were burnt alive, to speed up the process. Entire families were burnt alive.

"Then they evacuated the camp because the Russians were approaching. I don't know how many thousands of us walked day and night, without ever stopping. Those who did were shot on the spot. I lost several comrades that way. The SS had fun scaring us by firing in our midst when we least expected it. The shots would scatter us in all directions, and then the SS took aim and shot as many of us as they could, as if we were pigeons. . . .

"I was arrested with eight other members of my family, including my mother. But other relatives had been arrested before us, and yet more after. We were a very large family, but by the end of the war I was the only survivor."

. . .

A Jewish tailor and a resistant, Benjamin Kaminsky, was in his shop when, on August 1, 1943, he was visited by four Militia men. Handcuffed with his father and mother, he was thrown into the cellar at Montluc by a sneering SS. "Don't complain. Tomorrow you are going to face Barbie, and that's something else, I can assure you."

"Indeed the following morning I found myself in front of a short, thin man with rattlesnake eyes who started questioning me Nazi-style: He hit me with whatever he could lay his hands on. Then I was taken to the *bagnoire*, three times. They wanted me to give them at least ten names of either Jews or resistants. The last sentence I heard them utter was, 'If he's a resistant we'll shoot him; if he's a Jew we'll deport him.'

"They must have decided I was more of a Jew than a resistant, since they took me to Birkenau. I won't tell you what it was like, since you've already heard it from others. I weighed sixty-five pounds when the Americans freed the camp. The doctor who took care of me fed me one spoon of milk a day. Two would have killed me. Then, by and by, I was able to swallow a whole cup. My brother and my father died just a few days before Liberation. They couldn't take it any longer. Out of the seven members of my family who were deported, I am the only survivor. It isn't easy. I can't swear to you that Barbie was on that platform when my train left. But the man who tortured me *was* there, and I was told that that man's name was Klaus Barbie."

Fernand Hahn, a sixty-four-year-old retired customs officer, is quite firm. He saw Klaus Barbie on the platform of Perrache station, "just as I see you, Mr. President.

"They took us to the station and lined us up against the train. While I was there, waiting to climb into my car, I noticed a short man laughing and hamming it up as if he were on stage. At one point he walked up to me and told me, 'I can promise you not one of you will come back alive.' He spoke very good French, with the kind of accent one hears in dubbed movies. Then he added, 'I'm the head of the Lyon SIPO-SD, but I'm not crazy. I don't believe Germany will win, but I've taken precautions. I have plenty of money stashed away, and I'm in cahoots with the Americans. There's a plane ready to fly me to South America.' At first, this sort of talk startled me, but then, on second thought, I realized it was perfectly consistent with the way most Nazis behaved. He wanted to humiliate his victims to the hilt, to put them down by showing them how much smarter and cleverer he was, getting out of the whole mess without a scratch and with money stolen from the Jews. The Allies had landed in Normandy two months earlier. The Germans knew they had lost, but before leaving they wanted to annihilate as many Jews as they could.

"I cannot swear that the man who uttered those horrible words was Barbie. All I know is that he introduced himself as the head of the SD. Our train stopped innumerable times. In Strasbourg I came very close to running away. I could have, easily, but I was afraid they would shoot the rest of my car in retaliation. In Munich, women and children were let onto the train to spit on us and call us swine. They had been told we were Bolsheviks.

"In Dachau, I worked as an interpreter. Some of my companions had worked in the armory of Saint-Etienne, but I said they were all farmers because I didn't want them to be forced to make arms that would later be used against France. I never saw them again, and am often gnawed by remorse."

Rolande Clair did not see Barbie at the station, but in the courtyard at Montluc. "The friend who left with me knew him, and pointed him out to me in the courtyard as 'Klaus Barbie, the man who tortured me.' She made me swear that if she died and I survived, I would denounce him. But I didn't know how. Until today, nobody had ever asked me whether I had seen Klaus Barbie on the morning of August 11."

Seen from the back, Francine Gudefin has a proud bearing. Tall, thin, and elegantly dressed, she wears her eighty years very well. Then she turns; and we realize that the entire left side of her face is a huge scar, her mouth is a grimace; her cheek a shapeless hollow. "I don't know where to start my terrible story. My restaurant was a front for the Lyon Resistance. I was aware of the risks I was running, but as long as they remained abstract it was difficult to really believe in them. Then one day as I was standing behind the cash register, a few civilians I had never seen before walked in. . . . They led me into a Gestapo office to face Twisted Mug—if I look like him, it is thanks to him—and Klaus Barbie, whom I saw practically every day for the next three months. And so the interrogation got under way. Barbie slapped me and beat me with his fists. Then they took me to a bathroom where my brother was sitting naked in a bathtub. They were slowly drowning him. One SS pulled him out of the water by the hair and another pulled him back under by the feet, and so on and so forth for an eternity. Pierrot, my brother, was green, already comatose. It scared me so much I started urinating, and that really maddened them. They beat me again. My ear bled profusely. I thought I was going to die, but I was determined never to denounce any of my colleagues.

"Not only did their daily tortures disfigure me, they also left me deaf. My head was as hard and swollen as a soccer ball. But I did not speak. My brother and sister probably paid for my silence. I don't know, but the mere possibility still pains me. Nevertheless, I'm proud I didn't talk, proud of having done all I could for the resistants. I had fed them, hidden them, given them money. . . .

"We were deported on August 11. I wasn't surprised, since Barbie kept telling me, 'Your brother is going to be shot against the prison wall and you will be deported. You'll die in Germany.' He was in the courtyard during roll call, and at the station to watch us leave.

"I almost died in Ravensbrück. My head was still swollen and hard, but it no longer hurt. In the spring of 1945, the camp was evacuated and we were transferred to Königsberg in the usual manner. The Russians freed us on June 25. As soon as they saw us, they knew they had to do something quickly. They killed chickens, rabbits, anything they could lay their hands on and brought them to us, still warm and bleeding, and we ate them raw, like animals. I weighed some fifty-eight pounds, had a huge belly, and typhus.

My ear was a big abscess. The Russians took me to a hospital where I underwent several operations. I had a few more later, in France. To no avail. The damage was too severe.

"For forty-three years I kept silent. I never forgot, but I couldn't speak. I didn't know that my butcher's name was Barbie. I found out when, on November 25, 1984, I saw the accused face to face, and immediately recognized him. And so, for the first time, I told my story to the examining judge. When I was finished, Barbie responded in his thin, calm voice barely altered by age, 'Madame has seen too many horror movies.' "

March 1945

In the dewy twilight, long columns of ghosts—five abreast and a hundred to a group—slowly advance along a paved road through a pine forest. They are as gray as the armed SS who walk alongside them. New growth at the tips of the fir branches already hints at the approaching spring, as do the daisies growing in the ditches, but the ghosts do not see them. Nor do they hear the birds, deafened as they are by the heavy, monotonous scraping of their clogs on the pavement. Jeanne is in the last row, to the right. The road—the road which she believes leads to Flossenburg and the flame thrower—curves right. The next column is not yet in sight, and the SS escorting her group are looking straight ahead. Jeanne acts on impulse, prodded by despair. She jumps into the ditch and hardly dares to breathe, her face hidden in the damp earth.

She hears the groups of prisoners march on right above her: one, two, then the last column. The scraping of the clogs recedes until it becomes practically inaudible. The echo of a gunshot breaks the silence. Then nothing.

Jeanne is free, though still in danger. But she is thirty-three and desperately wants to live. It is night, and the underbrush greets her with dozens of pleasant noises: the scurrying of chipmunks, the rustling of an owl's wings, the creaking of branches, a breeze. A lump forms in her throat, but she swallows her tears. She cannot let herself fall apart, not yet. Wrapped in her blanket, she falls asleep on the cold earth, shivering, but no more so than on previous nights.

The following morning she wraps a rag around her shaved head, gathers a bunch of sticks to carry under her arm, and trudges through the forest toward one of the villages they passed the day before. She looks like a withered old woman. A Wehrmacht patrol walks by her without even seeing her.

After a third night spent in the forest, eating nothing but sorrel, Jeanne comes upon a small village: a few houses, scattered here and there, a church. She is starving, her head is spinning, she feels empty and very light. If my mother had spent one more day in the forest, she probably would have died there. Months later, someone would have found another anonymous skeleton propped against a tree.

There are a few old women in the church. Jeanne kneels in a pew and pretends to pray. She feels dizzy, her ears buzz; she hallucinates being surrounded by food and radiant children. She clings desperately to the pew in front of her. Intrigued by this strange new parishioner, the priest approaches Jeanne and speaks to her, and without the slightest hesitation she tells him her story. Torn between patriotism and Christian charity, the German priest decides not to offer her his roof. Nor does he volunteer to find her a place with any of his parishioners. They are all scared and could easily give her away. But he brings her some bread and four marks, and lets her rest awhile in the confessional. She cannot stay long; soon children will come for catechism, then a few villagers will sweep the nave and change the water in the vases of flowers before the evening vespers. She must be gone by noon.

Back in the woods, Jeanne lingers near the edge of the village, and at dusk she breaks a barn window and slips in. She curls up in the hay and finishes the bread she has been saving since morning. For the first time in months, she won't be freezing in her sleep.

She is in Tachau, a village they had passed the day before she escaped. The villagers, outraged at the spectacle filing before their eyes, had blocked the column and with pleas and insults forced the SS to let them distribute hot potatoes among the prisoners. The

SS had protested on the grounds that, after all, their prisoners were only Jews. "Jews or not," the villagers had answered, "and wherever you're taking them, you have no right to treat them worse than animals."

Jeanne is hiding in a barn which belongs to the Boschs, a family of farmers. Their house is close to the barn, and she falls asleep lulled by the noises of family life.

Jeanne sleeps all that night and the following day. Once again, she is putting herself in danger, but the warm hay is so much more comfortable than the cold shade of fir trees. Suddenly the barn door bursts open and a voice shouts, "Who's there? Come out with your hands on top of your head. Quick." Brandishing his pitchfork, the farmer advances, followed by some villagers and the local Hitler Youth, guns cocked. The broken barn window has given Jeanne away, but no one expects this human wreck, shriveled like an apple in winter and covered with a dirty rag, to emerge from the hay. With a voice so feeble it is only a whisper, my mother cries, "Don't shoot! I am a woman. I am not dangerous." She tries to cover her face with her arms, but they are too thin to give her any protection. Her assailants are ashamed of their fear and of the weapons in their hands.

A woman approaches my mother and asks her whether she is one of the prisoners who passed their village four days earlier. "Yes," my mother admits, sure that this time it is all over, that she will be shot. Instead, the woman helps her up from her bed of hay and, taking her by the hand, leads her out of the barn. In the house, the woman immediately prepares a tub of warm water and, hiding her revulsion, helps Jeanne remove her dirty rags and throws them into the fire. Then, with the help of three or four other women, she eases Jeanne into the bath. Under their gentle touch, Jeanne begins to revive. They dress her with clean clothes: underwear— how long it has been since she last wore any!—a woolen skirt, a sweater, socks, and clogs, her size. Then they sit her down at the kitchen table, close to the stove, and serve her some ersatz coffee with milk, eggs, and toast. Jeanne throws herself on the food with a voracity she did not know herself capable of. She eats everything on her plate, then vomits it all. Obviously, her benefactors do not know that people who have been starving must be reintroduced to food little by little. They give her some more milk, one slice of toast, an apple. Then they hitch up a cart and bring her to the police to register her, but by now Jeanne knows the Boschs won't let anything bad happen to her. They have not saved her for nothing; they feel responsible for her and are going to make sure she is dealt with fairly. They are all there, waiting to hear what the Wehrmacht lieutenant decides to do with her. But he doesn't decide anything.

"Can you work?" he asks her. "I can help in the fields," Jeanne answers, ready to do anything to stay where she is.

"The Boschs are willing to keep you until we find a better solution," he tells her. Then he adds darkly, "It won't be long now. The war is over and we have lost."

This is how my mother learns that the tide has turned, and that she has been rescued by the losers. On the other hand, as a near-skeleton with a shaven head, shaking hands, skin as yellow and dry as parchment, and her belly aching from the little food she has eaten that morning, she is far from feeling like a victor.

That night, Jeanne sleeps in a wonderful bed that had once been the family's grandmother's. It looks like a trunk. At night the lid is raised to reveal a plump goosedown puff, and in the morning the puff is shaken, the lid is lowered, and the bed once again becomes a trunk or bench. Jeanne lets herself sink into the soft warmth of a real country eiderdown. It is a balm to a skeletal, aching body which for months has only known rough straw pallets, bare floors, and hard earth.

News travels fast. The following morning, a man in a khaki uniform shows up at the Bosch farm. He is a French prisoner of war from a nearby camp. The life of prisoners of war is not so bad; they must reside in an assigned place, but otherwise they are free to come and go as they please. If they want to escape back to France, they can try at their own risk, but if they behave, they are left alone. To them, their camp, like an embassy, is French territory in a foreign land. As soon as they get wind of Jeanne's situation, the POW's decide that her place is with them.

"In fact," as their emissary explains to Jeanne, "the Wehrmacht lieutenant told us about you. He suggested we come and get you because he was afraid those farmers were going to feed you to death, which would have been a real pity, since you'd already come this far. Besides, he didn't like the idea of abandoning you among Germans now that Germany's been unofficially defeated. The Boschs are good people, but he can't vouch for the rest of the village." Outside, a horse-drawn carriage is waiting. A Tachau forester has lent it to the French to go fetch Jeanne.

Régis Dégremont installs Jeanne in the carriage as if she were a princess. On the way, he tells her he is a blacksmith from Hirson, in the Aisne, and that his seven companions have cleaned up their barracks and prepared a room just for her, with a stove and a washstand.

The POW's have spiffed themselves up in her honor. Their uniforms look freshly ironed, their hair is slicked back, their boots are polished. They have put flowers in her room, hung curtains on the window, and hung fresh clothes on the back of an armchair. Jeanne can't believe her eyes.

At forty-five, Dégremont is the oldest of the POW's. The group as a whole provides a perfect sampling of French manhood: there is Victor, with his sunny accent, from the Midi; Jean-Jacques, a red-headed electrician who can fix anything; Bernard, a cook from Le Havre; Colin, a cheese expert from the Brie region who teaches my mother never to eat the crust of a cheese; Roger, a teacher from Saintes; Blaise, a high-strung, taciturn chemistry student; and Denis, a wine merchant from Alsace. Jeanne feels reborn. They all bend over backwards to take care of her, at least when they're home. Except Dégremont, they all have girlfriends in the nearby villages. "Which is how we got the clothes, the armchair, and the curtains," he confides.

Two weeks later, when the Americans arrive, Jeanne is on her way back to health. Since she speaks English, she acts as interpreter when the Americans are invited to have lunch at the barracks. In their honor, the cook prepares a succulent wild rabbit stew. "It doesn't take magic," Bernard modestly explains. "To get good game in our neck of the woods, all one has to do is lean over and grab it." On the spot, they organize a hunting expedition for the following morning. Meanwhile, Jeanne has told her story to the GI's, who, moved, offer her a car so that she can tour the area before going back to France. And since she is not yet strong enough to drive, they also lend her a driver.

Jeanne has gained some weight, and though she still bears little resemblance to the attractive young woman she was before Montluc, she at least looks like a woman again. She has even learned to wrap a scarf around her shaved head to her advantage. She has told her friends about her children and her husband, and now she misses them more than ever.

The war is practically over, but the political confrontation over the East-West division of conquered territory may yet create problems for the French prisoners. The Russians' approach from the east hastens their departure; they have two hours to get ready to leave on a convoy of American trucks. Among the ex-prisoners already aboard, my mother recognizes some from the evacuation of Plauen. They hug with great joy.

"We were so scared at the end of the evening, when we realized you were no longer with us," one of these women tells Jeanne. "We thought you'd collapsed on the way and the SS had killed you. We asked the people in the group behind ours if they knew anything, but no one did."

"We went on walking, but even the SS were exhausted," says another. "Soon, maybe the day after your escape, they started letting us go in small groups every time we passed a village. But we had to fend for ourselves. We were put up in a school. The peasants couldn't do anything for us, but they brought us something to eat every day. We didn't know when we could go back home, but we could write letters, and some of us even got an answer. Then, last week, three jeeps arrived loaded with these handsome blond guys bursting with health, and chewing gum. We threw our arms around their necks, and they let us do it, even though we looked about as sexy as a bag of bones."

"Perfect products of a successful crash diet."

Everybody talks at the same time, everybody laughs. The trucks drop their loads off at Strasbourg, where trains wait to bring the survivors to Paris. Ironically, most are made up of cattle cars, since there are few passenger cars left. But the cattle cars have been made as comfortable as possible. The doors are left open, and each has a tub of fresh water.

There are frequent stops at the stations along the way so the passengers can use the bathrooms, and at every stop a crowd welcomes them back. But joy turns to consternation the moment the crowds see the cargo of skeletons in striped pajamas whose eyes still betray the pain of recent loss: parents who have lost their children, children who have seen their parents and siblings die and who will see them die for the rest of their lives. The people gathered at the stations feel powerless, out of place, ashamed. Their health is an insult to the others' suffering.

Nancy, Bar-le-Duc, Châlons-sur-Marne, Château-Thierry, La Ferté-sous-Jouarre. The last miles are always the longest. Meaux, Lagny. At last, Paris, with its gray outskirts, its dark buildings, its streets full of cars, carriages, and people, people everywhere. The train slows as it approaches the Gare de l'Est. For a moment, Jeanne believes she will find her husband and children waiting on the platform.

The station is chaos. But the voices coming over the loudspeakers speak French, and Red Cross women direct the passengers toward the exits, where buses wait to take them to the Hotel Lutetia. Everybody must report there. That's where their families have left messages or are waiting for them. That's also where the government has set up offices in charge of survivor and refugee files. As Jeanne follows the movement of the crowd, she realizes she has come through all right. Some survivors are carried in on stretchers, few are wearing decent clothes. They all have shaved heads, and their eyes look huge and haggard in their hollow faces.

In the bus, Jeanne is mesmerized by the spectacle of the streets.

Passersby glance at the buses absentmindedly, unaware of what they are carrying. But the welcome is warm at the Hotel Lutetia. Now that aliases are unnecessary, Jeanne gives her real name. Similarly, the message she is handed is signed not Madame Mahé but Angèle Kahn. It says, "When Madame Jeanne Kahn arrives, she should call her mother-in-law at once."

17 A Sensitive Person

A few more voices, a few more stories, and this oral history of the Holocaust will end, leaving the world with the memory of all the courageous old men and women who have come to Lyon on an impossible pilgrimage. They will soon die. But their memory will remain, and their voices will echo from generation to generation, repeating their terrible tales.

Barbie is again going to grace us with his presence, if only for five minutes. But first, still more victims.

Josephine Ambré worked as a secretary in the garage where the Gestapo parked their black Citroens. Day after day, she faced the SS with the calm, indifferent face of one who could care less, but at home she hid some Jewish friends, the Levis. She was arrested by two members of the Militia, "irreproachable" Frenchmen shot after the Liberation without trial.

"The Levis were arrested, deported, and gassed in Auschwitz, and their oldest son was shot at Portes-les-Valence with twenty other people, in retaliation for something or other. . . . It was my turn on August 11. Was Barbie in the courtyard or on the platform of the Perrache station watching us leave? I don't know, but what difference does it make? He knew that we were going to be deliberately and systematically killed. It was all planned. The sort of work we were going to do in Ravensbrück, where I was deported, had been scientifically calculated to finish us off in a certain amount of time. . . . We were not supposed to last more than six months. . . . Barbie was certainly aware of this, whether he was at the station to see us off or not."

Two more witnesses speak. One tells of the execution of a Polish pole-vaulting champion after an aborted escape; another of his first impression of Auschwitz: "I thought I had ended up in some industrial town in the Ruhr. I wasn't that far from the truth. Auschwitz was an industrial town, specialized in the mass production of death. The soap I used there was made with the little fat they had squeezed out of my murdered companions."

Finally Barbie is brought back in to face Julie Fanceschini, a seventy-eight-year-old woman in a wheelchair. His presence is disturbing. Nor does he seem happy to be back; now and then he casts a bored, scornful look at the witness.

"In February 1944, my fiancé and I came to Lyon to get married, but before we could, we were denounced by an employee of the hotel where we were staying, and arrested. My fiancé was shot at Villeneuve-sur-Ain; I was brought to the Ecole de Santé. I have never recovered from the torture I received there: they left me in agony. But before I got to that point, I witnessed the most gratuitous cruelties. A very sweet, pretty young girl, Marie Martin, was handed over to two SS who used her the way they pleased. Women were not only beaten up but also raped. When they brought her back to the cell, she was bleeding from head to foot. She had no clothes, so I gave her a skirt of mine. She was wearing it when they took her to Saint-Genis-Laval to massacre her. They must have thought she was me. She had been arrested for having helped two American parachutists.

"But the worst memory of my detention has to do with a little Jewish boy. He must have been ten. On Easter Eve, the Red Cross sent us two hard-boiled eggs each. When the guard brought them to our cell, he told us not to give any to the child. Of course, I gave him one of mine. He was so happy, he threw himself in my arms and asked me, 'Does this mean you love Jews?' I told him I loved everybody, and particularly children. Later that night, they came to fetch him while he was asleep, and kicked him to death right in front of our cell door.

"Yes. That old man is the very same one who tortured me then. I recognize his eyes, eyes like those are hard to forget."

"Small, cruel eyes in a jackal's head" is how André Courvoisier describes them. An octogenarian Lyon industrialist, once an escaped prisoner of war tortured and deported by Barbie, Courvoisier is the last witness to speak. With his words, this tragic oral history of Barbie's activities in Lyon between November 1942 and August 1944 is finished, as complete as it can be without the testimony of the thousands who can never testify.

Not even as talented a defense attorney as Jacques Vergès can exonerate Barbie now. The only real question is whether he will summon the courage to plead guilty.

Pierre Truche, the public prosecutor, urges him to confess:

"The Klaus Barbie of 1933 was a twenty-year-old youth who, though enthralled by the ideals of National Socialism, was still capable of devoting himself to others and doing some good. How could such a normal youth, with often generous impulses, become a committed SS? What happened to you between 1933 and 1937? At the beginning of this trial, you were able to speak movingly of your father and the death of your brother. You did so to show us that you are capable of feeling, that you are a sensitive person. This is why your silence has been so puzzling. You know as well as I do that you will never go back to Bolivia. This trial will reach its end, and in a few years the films made in the course of it will fall into the public domain. Those who will see them will wonder. Your own descendants will wonder why you had nothing to say. For the last time, you have the opportunity to explain yourself, to tell us what turned you into the man described by all the witnesses we have heard. There lies the key to your life, to your trial, to you."

Barbie's response is, "Nein. I am juridically absent, since I was kidnapped."

More witnesses will take the stand in the course of the next week, the so-called historical witnesses: Geneviève de Gaulle, Jacques Chaban-Delmas, the historians Laurant Schwartz and Jacques Delarue, and Yves Jouffa, president of the League for Human Rights. They will testify because the lawyers of the civil parties have asked them to add some finishing touches to the large canvas others have painted. Barbie's trial will broaden to become the trial of Nazism. It will be nearly a month before we hear the verdict.

JULY 1945

It is two months before my mother finally agrees to visit Lyon police headquarters. She has avoided this ceremony as long as she could, but has finally given in to the arguments of a few well-meaning friends who offer to accompany her: "Jeanne, you cannot live with this uncertainty, nor can you doom Robert to anonymity. Robert must be buried under his name. You won't be able to face reality as long as you haven't identified him. You've been back for two months now. You're stronger: you can and must do it."

Everyone knows that Robert Kahn was among the prisoners massacred at Bron, but he hasn't yet been formally identified. Jeanne must do it for him and for herself, but also for us, his children. She is crying, but she is already at the door. A staircase, a hallway, another door. There are still some thirty chairs in the room, numbers scribbled on their backs, envelopes resting on their seats. They are the sole memorials of those who will probably remain forever unidentified: refugees passing through Lyon whose relatives still do not know they were arrested, or survivors of previous raids in which their families were caught and deported.

My mother reads through the files. There is always something that does not fit: too tall, too short, too hairy, dentures, bald. She is quickly nearing the end. The last chair bears the number 106. My mother is beginning to hope again until she reads these cruel lines: "X, male, five foot seven, brown hair, light beige shirt, gray-green cotton socks, white briefs, two handkerchiefs with the initial R, dark blue suit, brown belt with a metal buckle, brown shoes." She doesn't have the courage to look through the envelope. Her friends, who were also my father's friends, pick it up and pour the contents onto a desk. Jeanne recognizes the two handkerchiefs, and the swatch of material cut from the elegant suit she and Robert had bought together.

My father was hit by a single bullet in the back of the neck. I hope he died on the spot, without pain other than the fear felt in anticipation. I know that his last thoughts before plunging into nothingness were for us.

18 THE VERDICT

The Saône shines like liquid silver in the moonlight; the sky is black satin. It is a hot summer evening, but a light breeze cools the crowd gathered at the foot of the Palais de Justice: babies sleeping in their carriages, old men fanning themselves on park benches, young men in T-shirts strolling up and down the square. It seems as if the entire city has come to hear the verdict. Sidewalk café tables spill into the streets.

Everybody knows what the verdict is going to be, yet the air is tense when, shortly after midnight, an usher appears at the top of the stairs and announces to the people of Lyon that after six and a half hours of deliberation the jury has reached a verdict.

Barbie has been convicted of crimes against humanity. The sentence is life imprisonment.

Far from soothing the crowd, however, the announcement seems to generate more tension. The buzz of voices grows louder, more threatening. The police call for reinforcements. The crowd's anger, however, focuses on Jacques Vergès. When he appears on the top step a ripe tomato misses him and splatters on the shirt of one of his bodyguards.

Vergès has insisted on leaving from the main entrance, even though he was strongly advised to leave quietly through the back door. Over and over again he has greeted the witnesses' testimony with skepticism and outright sarcasm, implicitly accusing them of bolstering their failing memories with ready-made images culled from cheap horror movies. This has not been appreciated by the people of Lyon, who hurl insults and accusations at him from all sides.

From the trial's outset, Vergès claimed that a vengeful lynch-mob atmosphere has surrounded the Palais de Justice and informed the hearings. In fact, there have been no violent incidents during the trial, either inside or outside the courtroom. The dominating mood has been one of extraordinary dignity.

This afternoon, at the very moment when, after the usual midday recess, Vergès was about to conclude Barbie's defense, the bells of Saint Jean's cathedral began to toll. One by one, their slow, gloomy accents fell like tears. To all of us gathered there in silence, there was no doubt that they were tolling for Barbie's victims.

EPILOGUE

Three years have gone by and Klaus Barbie has been almost forgotten. From his cell, he sees the sun rise and set, day after day. For him months and seasons are all alike, all colorless. They bring no surprises, no hope. This is his most severe punishment. His victims, at least, could conceivably hope for the war to end, for freedom, for the chance to be reunited with their families. Barbie lives with the certainty that he will die within the gray walls of his cell, in solitude and indifference.

Those who came to testify against him recovered at least some of the peace they sought for almost half a century. They have borne witness both for themselves and for their loved ones, and their testimony will endure. As Elie Wiesel pointed out at the end of his testimony, soon there will be no survivors left. Since the last words of this book were put on paper, four witnesses have joined the shadows in whose behalf they had taken the stand. Oddly enough, they were all related, in various ways, to the children of Izieu. Paulette Paillares, a young teacher who was away from the school during the raid, died at the end of 1988. Fortunée Benguigui and Itta Rose Halaunbrenner, the two courageous mothers who helped Beate Klarsfeld in her pursuit of Barbie, died, respectively,

in December 1988 and May 1989. Lea Feldblum, who accompanied
the children all the way to Auschwitz, died on April 9, 1989.

As for me, I have come out of the Barbie trial a different person.
Thanks to the trial, and to this book, I have finally gotten to know
my father. I have taken the faint memory of a man, a mere fistful
of dust, and lent him substance.

I paid a second visit to his grave in November 1989, for a still
more moving ritual: the dedication of a street named after Robert
Kahn in a new district of Saint-Etienne, a whole block of small
homes with gardens, exclusively occupied by young couples with
small children. For years, an old comrade of Robert's, Pierre
Poughon, a decorated hero of the Resistance, had done his best to
have the city honor the memory of the man who had been at the
head of the local chapter of the MUR.

On a sunny cold Saturday morning, at eleven sharp, the mayor
of Saint-Etienne uncovered a small blue street sign which read "Rue
Robert Kahn." We were all there: Robert's wife, his children with
their spouses, his grandchildren, and his two-year-old great-grand-
daughter, Camille. False-Papers Pierre, his brother, was also there,
as well as Lucie Aubrac, who could not help sighing: "What a pity
he didn't flee the area after his first escape." Pierre Poughon was
also there, along with other former resistants, journalists, and a
great number of locals, come to pay homage to a man they had
never known but thanks to whom they were born in a free France.

And then, of course, there were people who lived on the new
street and who, because they were there, learned something about
the man to whom they owed their address. But what about their
children, and other future residents, will they ever wonder who
Robert Kahn was? Will they ask if he was a writer, a politician, an
explorer, a scientist?

He was a Jewish resistant.

ABOUT THE AUTHOR

Annette Kahn was born in Saint-Etienne, near Lyon, in 1941. She became a contributor to the national daily newspaper *L'Aurore* in 1960, and soon was known as "the youngest journalist in France." She specialized in court cases and has covered the most important French trials of the last thirty years. In 1984, she joined the weekly newsmagazine *Le Point*, where she is head of the political desk. *Why My Father Died* is her first book.